The

EYEWITNESS
HISTORY
of the CHURCH

Volume Three
JOURNEY TO ZION'S HILL
1845–1869

COMPILED BY

JENNIFER JOHNSON, CLAIRE KOLTKO,
BRITTANY MCEWEN, NATALIE ROSS

CFI
Springville, Utah

ISBN: 1-55517-963-0
v.1

Published by CFI,
an imprint of Cedar Fort, Inc.
925 N. Main Springville, Utah, 84663
www.cedarfort.com

Distributed by:

Cover design by Nicole Williams
Cover design © 2006 by Lyle Mortimer

Printed in the United States of America
10 9 8 7 6 5 4 3 2 1

Printed on acid-free paper

✐ CONTENTS ✐

ꙮ Acknowledgments ꙮ

We feel blessed to have had the opportunity to have read and collected these firsthand accounts of early Saints in order to produce the third volume of *The Eyewitness History of the Church*. We feel as though we have truly connected with the pioneers by pondering the words of those who sacrificed and endured struggles of every kind while making their way across the plains. Their first-person accounts enable us to watch Church history unfold just as they experienced it. You will be awestruck after reading all they had to forgo in order to establish The Church of Jesus Christ of Latter-day Saints in the tops of the Rocky Mountains. We stand gratefully on the shoulders of their sacrifices and recognize that we owe them an eternal debt of gratitude for their faith and endurance.

We would like to thank our mentor, Dr. W. Jeffrey Marsh, for his tireless efforts and editorial skills in helping us to complete this student mentored research project here at Brigham Young University. His guidance and research have made this book possible and have also inspired us more than he will ever know.

Collecting these wonderful first-person narratives has taken us to the archives at Brigham Young University, the University of Utah, the Daughters of the Utah Pioneers Museum, the LDS Archives in Salt Lake City, the RLDS Archives in Independence, Missouri, and Church History sites in New York, Ohio, Illinois, Nebraska, Iowa, and Utah. Thank you to all the archivists and historians who helped to preserve these treasured records and who made them available to us.

We gratefully acknowledge the contributions of Cedar Fort, Inc., for their willingness to publish this third volume of *The Eyewitness History of the Church*. A special thanks to Michael Morris, Heather Holm, and Adam Riggs. Thanks also to Nikki Williams for her beautiful work on the cover and aesthetics of the book.

We would also like to offer a special thanks to William W. Slaughter and those at the LDS Church Archives for their help in securing permission for us to use the photographs seen throughout this book.

Most especially, dear reader, thank you for your willingness to join us on this exciting journey through the eyewitness history of the Church.

⤙ INTRODUCTION ⤚

In 1947, at the centennial celebration of the Mormon pioneers' 1847 entrance into the Great Salt Lake Valley, poetess Vilate C. Raile penned a moving tribute to the marvelous heritage the Mormon migration bequeathed to their posterity and to all members of The Church of Jesus Christ of Latter-day Saints:

> They cut desire into short lengths
> And fed it to the hungry fires of courage.
> Long after when the fires had died,
> Molten gold gleamed in the ashes.
> They gathered it in bruised palms
> And handed it to their children
> and their children's children forever.
> (Asahel D. Woodruff, *Parent and Youth* [Salt Lake City:
> Deseret Sunday School Union Board, 1971], 124)

We are inspired by such a rich heritage. Learning more about the pioneers' sacrifices will help us appreciate the living legacy of faith they left us, understand better their devotion to God, and appreciate more fully their desires to follow the living prophet. Knowing this will bless our lives. Their deeds are not ours, but their inspiring examples of undaunted faith and courage can inspire us during our own times of trial. We can learn much about journeying through life well, from the "molten gold" they have passed to us.

One example will illustrate. Sister Ellen Neibaur walked to Utah in bare feet because she was so poor she could not afford shoes. For years she worked and saved to buy a pair of high-top, button shoes from the East. In 1856, she finally bought the shoes she had worked so hard to obtain. They brought her much happiness. She wore them to the October 1856 general conference where she heard Brigham Young announce that there were handcart pioneers stranded in the Wyoming snows. They needed help. They needed flour, clothing, and shoes. Sister Neibaur, after eight years of sacrifice to get her own shoes, took them off and gave them to the relief teams. "Interestingly, when the handcart companies finally came in, all the Saints went out to meet them. Typically, when meeting incoming companies, the Saints searched faces to find someone they knew. What do you think Ellen Neibaur was looking at? She was looking at feet. She wanted to see who had gotten her shoes. When she finally saw them, she was utterly astonished. It was a childhood friend from England who had not yet joined the Church at the time Ellen left but since had joined and had come across the plains with the Martin and Willie handcart companies." ("Ellen Breakell Neibaur, Wife of Alexander Neibaur," unpublished manuscript compiled by Jolene Smith Davis, copy in Gerald N. Lund's possession; as cited in "Personal Revelation and the Process of Conversion," Gerald N. Lund, *The Religious Educator*, Vol. 3, No. 1 [Provo: Brigham Young University, 2002], 26–27).

Unselfish sacrifices like this one are legion among the Mormon pioneers. Elder Dieter F. Uchtdorf commented: "I have felt a close kinship to those early pioneers who crossed the plains. They are [a] spiritual ancestry . . . for each and every member of the Church, regardless of nationality, language, or culture. They have established . . . a spiritual foundation for the building of the kingdom of God in all the nations of the world" ("The Global Church Blessed by the Voice of the Prophets," *Ensign*, November 2002, 10).

> Their example of faith will play a critical role in our future salvation. We will need to develop the same traits of character and courage in order to secure for our own posterity the same blessings they bequeathed to us. In one of the most moving descriptions of what learning about the pioneers can do for us, Elder M. Russell Ballard observed: Life isn't always easy. At some point in our journey we may feel much as the pioneers did as they crossed Iowa—up to our knees in mud, forced to bury some of our dreams along the way. We all face rocky ridges, with the wind in our face and winter coming on too soon. Sometimes it seems as though there is no end to the dust that stings our eyes and clouds our vision. Sharp edges of despair and discouragement jut out of the terrain to slow our passage. Always, there is a Devil's Gate, which will swing wide open to lure

us in. Those who are wise and faithful will steer a course as far from such temptation as possible, while others—sometimes those who are nearest and dearest to us—succumb to the attraction of ease, comfort, convenience, and rest. Occasionally we reach the top of one summit in life, as the pioneers did, only to see more mountain peaks ahead, higher and more challenging than the one we have just traversed. Tapping unseen reservoirs of faith and endurance, we, as did our forebears, inch ever forward toward that day when our voices can join with those of all pioneers who have endured in faith, singing, "All is well! All is well!" (*Hymns*, no. 30)

And how will we feel then, as we stand shoulder to shoulder with the great pioneers of Church history? How will they feel about us? Will they see faith in our footsteps? I believe they will, particularly as they view our lives and experiences from the expanded perspective of eternity. Although our journeys today are less demanding physically than the trek of our pioneers 150 years ago, they are no less challenging. Certainly it was hard to walk across a continent to establish a new home in a dry western desert. But who can say if that was any more difficult than is the task of living faithful, righteous lives in today's confusingly sinful world, where the trail is constantly shifting and where divine markers of right and wrong are being replaced by political expediency and diminishing morality. The road we travel today is treacherous, and the scriptures tell us it will continue to be so until the very end. But our reward will be the same as that which awaits worthy pioneers of all ages who live faithfully the teachings of the Lord Jesus Christ, make right choices, and give their all to build the kingdom of God on earth.

We are the inheritors of a tremendous heritage. Now it is our privilege and responsibility to be part of the Restoration's continuing drama, and there are great and heroic stories of faith to be written in our day. It will require every bit of our strength, wisdom, and energy to overcome the obstacles that will confront us. But even that will not be enough. We will learn, as did our pioneer ancestors, that it is only in faith—real faith, whole-souled, tested and tried—that we will find safety and confidence as we walk our own perilous pathways through life.

This third volume of *The Eyewitness History of the Church* comprises pioneer stories of faith beginning in Nauvoo after the death of the Prophet Joseph Smith and ending with the pioneer's arrival in the Salt Lake Valley. This compilation will not only inspire you but will also imbue you with the desire to do good. It is no small thing to create a Zion society in the world in which we live, yet, the promise is sure that there would be a generation sent to this earth in the latter days to do precisely that. Elder Neal A. Maxwell noted how those who have been reserved to live in these challenging times, and who overcome will have done no small thing:

> These really are our days, and we can prevail and overcome, even in the midst of trends that are very disturbing. If we are faithful the day will come when those deserving pioneers and ancestors, whom we rightly praise for having overcome the adversities in their wilderness trek, will praise today's faithful for having made their way successfully through a desert of despair and for having passed through a cultural wilderness, while still keeping the faith.
>
> We can make of these days ahead "days never to be forgotten" in the history of the Church. Ours can be "a voice of gladness" even amid the stern but foreseen days of "gloominess," while being "alive in Christ" in the living Church. (See Joseph Smith–History 1, footnote to verse 71; D&C 128:19; 2 Nephi 25:25.). (*If Thou Endure It Well* [Salt Lake City: Bookcraft, 1996], 28–29)

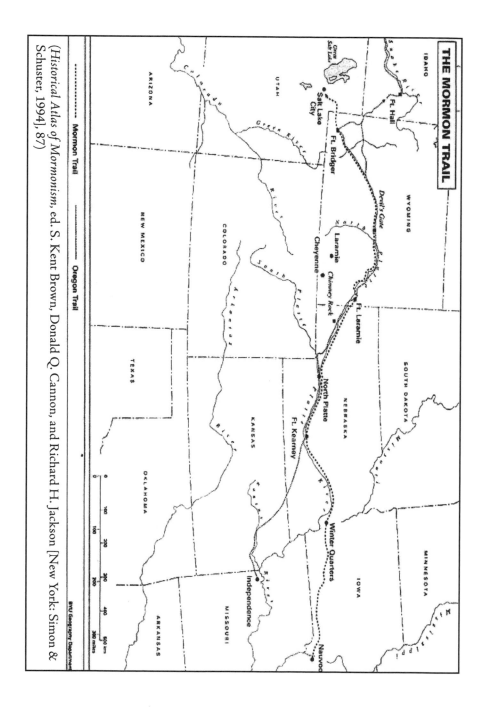

(*Historical Atlas of Mormonism*, ed. S. Kent Brown, Donald Q. Cannon, and Richard H. Jackson [New York: Simon & Schuster, 1994], 87)

~ 1 ~

A JOURNEY FORETOLD

As the Saints in Nauvoo mourned the death of the Prophet Joseph, their enemies anxiously watched to see if the bullets that mortally wounded Joseph Smith would deal a fatal blow to The Church of Jesus Christ of Latter-day Saints. As it became increasingly apparent that the Church was not falling into ruin, angry and frustrated mobs continued their work of violence and destruction in an effort to drive the Saints from the state. Hoping to stem the destruction, Brigham Young promised the citizens of Illinois that the Saints would leave the state as soon as the winter weather subsided. Although their exact destination remained uncertain, members of the Church knew they would go where the Prophet Joseph had foretold—the only place left for them far away in the West.

Doctrine and Covenants 49:25
(A revelation recorded in 1831 foreshadowed the Saints' removal to the mountains in the West.)

Zion shall flourish upon the hills and rejoice upon the mountains, and shall be assembled together unto the place which I have appointed.

Joseph Smith
(Wilford Woodruff recorded a prophecy of Joseph Smith's to the priesthood brethren in Kirtland, on August 6, 1842.)

I want to say to you before the Lord that you know no more concerning the destinies of this Church and Kingdom than a babe upon its mother's lap. You don't comprehend it. It is only a little handful of Priesthood you see here tonight, but this Church will fill North and

South America—it will fill the world. It will fill the Rocky Mountains. There will be tens of thousands of Latter-day Saints who will be gathered in the Rocky Mountains, and there they will open the door for the establishing of the gospel among the Lamanites . . . this people will go into the Rocky Mountains; they will there build temples to the Most high. They will raise up a posterity there, and the Latter-day Saints who dwell in these mountains will stand in the flesh until the coming of the Son of Man. The Son of Man will come to them while in the Rocky Mountains (Wilford Woodruff, in Conference Reports of The Church of Jesus Christ of Latter-day Saints [Salt Lake City: The Church of Jesus Christ of Latter-day Saints, 1898 to present], April 1898, 57).

Oliver B. Huntington

When we first went to Nauvoo the old Patriarch Joseph [Sr.] came into our house one day and in a very confidential way, giving us to understand that it was not to be made public, asked a question as to how long we thought the church would stay in Nauvoo, and went on to say that the Lord had told Joseph (his son the Prophet) that we would stay there just seven years, and that when we left there, we would go right into the midst of the Indians, in the Rocky Mountains, as this country, Utah, was then called. That, we have seen fulfilled (*Oliver Boardman Huntington Diary, Written By Himself, 1878–1900* [L. Tom Perry Special Collections, Harold B. Lee Library, Brigham Young University, Provo, Utah], 210).

Joseph Smith

(While the Saints were residing in Nauvoo and suffering persecution from Illinois mobs, Joseph received the following revelation on August 6, 1842.)

I prophesied that the Saints would continue to suffer much affliction and would be driven to the Rocky Mountains, many would apostatize, others would be put to death by our persecutors or lose their lives in consequence of exposure or disease, and some of you will live to go and assist in making settlements and build cities and see the Saints become a mighty people in the midst of the Rocky Mountains (Joseph Smith, *History of The Church of Jesus Christ of Latter-day Saints*, ed. B. H. Roberts, 7 vols. [Salt Lake City: Deseret Book, 1964], 5:85).

Anson Call

(Anson Call described hearing Joseph Smith prophesy that the Saints would eventually settle in the Rocky Mountains.)

I had before seen him [Joseph] in a vision and now saw while he was talking his countenance change to white; not the deadly white of a bloodless face, but a living, brilliant white. He seemed absorbed in gazing at something at a great distance, and said: "I am gazing upon the valleys of those mountains. . . . Oh the beauty of those snow-capped mountains! The cool refreshing streams that are running down through those mountain gorges!" Then, gazing in another direction, as if there was a change in locality [Joseph said], "Oh the scenes that this people will pass through! The dead that will lay between here and there!" (*History of the Church*, 5:86).

Paulina Eliza Phelps

I was a little girl when the Prophet Joseph came to Jackson County. [I] distinctly remember attending a meeting at the house of Lyman Wight, at which [Joseph] was present. At this meeting, the Prophet Joseph blessed the children who were present, and I was one of them. In blessing me, he said that I should live to go to the Rocky Mountains. I did not know at the time what the term "Rocky Mountains" meant, but I supposed it to be something connected with the Indians (photocopy of a signed affidavit by Paulina Eliza Phelps Lyman, witnesses on July 31, 1903, by James Jack, notary [L. Tom Perry Special Collections, Harold B. Lee Library, Brigham Young University, Provo, Utah], n.p.).

Brigham Young

(Brigham Young knew long before the Saints started the trek west that they must eventually relocate. The Saints, having been driven west from New York and Ohio, did not believe that they could return to the East. However, Brigham Young foretold that the Saints would first be driven east from Missouri, to Nauvoo, and then to the West.)

I will give you one revelation which I had in Far West. . . . It was in the spring of 1838, before there was any disturbance in Far West, or in Davis County.

This people, thought I, are obnoxious to these Missourians, our religion they hate, our Prophet they despise and would like to kill him;

Brigham Young
(Public Domain, Courtesy of BYU Online Collection)

they are ignorant of the things of God. . . . Therefore I saw, upon natural principles, that we would be driven from there, but when, I did not know; but still it was plain to me that we would have to leave the State, and that when we *did* leave it we would not go south, north or west, but east, back to the other States. . . . I then saw that we would go north, as a Church and a people, *then* to the west, and that when they [the Saints] went to Jackson County, they would go from the west to the east. Mark my words, write them down, this people, as a Church and kingdom, will go from the west to the east" (*Journal of Discourses*, 26 vols. [London: Latter-day Saints' Book Depot, 1854–86], 3:209; emphasis added).

Joseph Smith Jr.
(February 1844)

I instructed the Twelve Apostles to send out a delegation and investigate the location of California and Oregon [Utah was then part of Upper California], and hunt out a good location, where we can be removed to after the temple is completed, and where we can build a city in a day, and have a government of our own, get up into the mountains, where the devil cannot dig us out, and live in a healthful climate, where we can live as old as we have a mind to (*Joseph Smith Diary*, entry for February 20, 1844, in *History of the Church*, 6:222).

MOB VIOLENCE

Despite the countless sacrifices the Saints made to turn a mosquito-infested swamp into the beautiful and thriving city of Nauvoo, it became increasingly apparent that they could not stay. The mobs grew so violent that the Saints eventually had no choice but to leave their homes or be exterminated.

Jacob B. Backenstos

(Jacob B. Backenstos, sheriff of Hancock County, witnessed a mob burning an entire settlement.)

The rioters spare not the widow nor the orphan, and while I am writing this proclamation the smoke is rising to the clouds and the flames are devouring four buildings, which have just been set on fire by the rioters—thousands of dollars worth of property has already been consumed; an entire settlement of about sixty or seventy families laid waste, the inhabitants thereof are fired upon, narrowly escaping with their lives, and forced to flee before the ravages of the Mob (Jacob B. Backenstos, "Proclamation," *Nauvoo Neighbor* [September 10, 1845]: 496).

S. M. Bartlett

(Bartlett worked as the editor of the Quincy Whig.*)*

It is feared that this rising against the Mormons is not confined to the Morley Settlement, but that there is an understanding among the "anties" [anti-Mormons] in the northern part of this (Adams) and Hancock counties to make a general sweep, burning and destroying the property of the Mormons wherever it can be found. If this is the case, there will be employment for the executive of the state, and that soon. . . . The flouring mill, carding machine, etc., of Norman Buel, a Mormon, one mile and a half west of Lima is now a heap of ashes. Colonel Levi Williams, of Green Plains, has ordered out his brigade, it is said, to aid the anti-Mormons. The anti-Mormons from Schuyler [County] and the adjoining counties are flocking in and great distress of life and property may be expected. Heaven only knows where these

proceedings will end (B. H. Roberts, *A Comprehensive History of The Church of Jesus Christ of Latter-day Saints*, 7 vols. [Salt Lake City: Deseret News Press, 1930], 2:475).

Brigham Young

I received a letter from Sheriff J. B. Backenstos announcing the death of General Miner R. Deming, who died at half past ten o'clock yesterday of congestive fever; during his illness his life was repeatedly threatened by the mob, he was prevented from sleeping at night by their yells and hideous screams, as they kept up a continual row in the streets of Carthage near the general's residence which greatly aggravated his fever, and doubtless caused his death (*History of the Church*, 7:439).

Jacob B. Backenstos

The Mormon community had acted with more than ordinary forbearance, remaining perfectly quiet, and offering no resistance when their dwellings, their buildings, stacks of grain, etc., were set on fire in their presence. They had forborne until forbearance was no longer a virtue (*Comprehensive History of the Church*, 2:477).

John Taylor

A number of the brethren were rendered houseless and homeless by a few reckless desperadoes in consequence of their adherence to the gospel. What rendered it more trying for them was that they had it in their power to destroy their persecutors, and yet in consequence of our counsel endured it patiently, and looked tamely on to see their houses and property destroyed for the gospel and the kingdom of heaven's sake; they are good and faithful men or they would not have done it (John Taylor's Journal, Ms., Sept 13, 1845, 123; as cited in *Comprehensive History of the Church*, 2:478).

WHISTLING AND WHITTLING BRIGADE

When the Nauvoo Charter was repealed and the city's militia disbanded, the Saints were left with no way to defend themselves from their hostile neighbors. In an effort to protect the city's inhabitants from their enemies, a group of men and boys kept watch over the city. When strangers were suspected of harmful intentions, a small band of young people would follow them, whistling and whittling, until the suspect was too intimidated to stay in town.

Almon W. Babbitt

(In a speech given in January 1845 to the Illinois House of Representatives, Babbitt argued against the repeal of the Nauvoo Charter.)

Repeal the Charter of Nauvoo, prescribe her citizens by your public acts, and [you will] tolerate and encourage the demon of mob violence that surrounds this people, and is waiting to feast upon their destruction (Wandle Mace, *Journal, 1809–1890* [L. Tom Perry Special Collections, Harold B. Lee Library, Brigham Young University, Provo, Utah], 170).

William B. Pace

The mob element exercised such an influence on the Governor and Legislature that they repealed the city Charter of Nauvoo, and left us without any city Government, or any means of controlling the rougher element, hence the town was soon over-run with all manner of ruffians from the mob camp around about (William B. Pace, *Autobiography*, in *Writings of Early Latter-day Saints and Their Contemporaries, A Database Collection*, comp. Milton V. Backman [Provo, Utah: BYU Religious Studies Center, 1996], 7).

Mosiah Hancock

I joined the whistling and whittling band. . . . We kept a good watch, and were directed to keep an eye on the "Black Ducks." We really tried to do our duty and we succeeded in bagging some game. I was about to give some instances, but forbear by saying, "In no case did I ever help to engage in whittling any one down to make them cross the great river unless they were known to be lurking around the Prophet's premises quite late or to be seeking that which was none of their business (Mosiah Lyman Hancock, *The Life Story of Mosiah Lyman Hancock* [n.p., n.d.], 18).

Wandle Mace

Our families were exposed to the rascals who on finding them unprotected by husbands and fathers would insult and abuse them, in consequence of such things the old police formed themselves into "Whittling" companies, and guarded the city from the rascals in this wise. When a stranger came into the city they would learn if they were there upon legitimate business, if so they did not interfere with them, but if they had no legitimate business, they were then under the surveillance of the Whittlers who would follow wherever they went, whittling and whistling, they did not molest them in any way, not even by talking to them but simply follow them, whittling and whistling as they went (Mace, *Journal, 1809–1890*, 186–87).

William B. Pace

Every boy generally could whistle and most of them had knives from ten to fourteen inches long, in scabbards, "a-la-bouy," and when any of these fellows became boisterous, or showed any sign of meddling the boy discovered would draw his knife and commenced whittling and whistling. Soon a crowd of his pals gathered, then they would surround the obnoxious element, be he large or small, many or few, and whistle and whittle in his direction and stick by him until he was out of town. . . .

This was rather an amusing process. Not a word was said but an unearthly whistle (and generally everyone had his own favorite tune) and an incessant whittling with those large knives was enough to strike terror to the hearts of the victims and he got out of town as quick as his legs could carry him (Pace, *Autobiography*, in *Writings of Early Latter-day Saints*, 7–8).

∽ 2 ∼

A CHANGE IN CHURCH LEADERSHIP

At the time of the Martyrdom, most of the Twelve Apostles were away serving missions, including the president of the Twelve, Brigham Young. When news of the tragedy reached the Twelve, they returned to Nauvoo as quickly as possible, only to find the city in disarray. Sidney Rigdon, who had moved to Pittsburg, had returned to Nauvoo and claimed that because of an alleged vision, he should be appointed as the Church's "guardian." On August 8, 1844, in a historic meeting arranged specifically to consider Sidney's guardianship claims, Brigham Young was transfigured before the congregation, and Joseph Smith appeared in his place. The Twelve were sustained as the Church's presiding quorum.

THE SUCCESSION MEETING

Joseph Fielding Smith

Not long after the death of these men [Joseph and Hyrum], Elder Sidney Rigdon who had long been one of Joseph's counselors came here from Pittsburg and informed the Saints that he had an important vision after long and earnest inquiry of the Lord, in which it was shown him that Joseph had died holding the key of this kingdom, that he still held it, and would continue to do in eternity. That we as a people must build up the kingdom to Joseph. If we did not, we should be damned and that he

Joseph Fielding Smith
(Courtesy of the Church Archives, The Church of Jesus Christ of Latter-day Saints)

himself stood next in authority and he was in haste to get the assent of
the Saints in this matter. As he said he must be in Pittsburgh in a short
time, this all seemed right to some, but many felt as though it was not
the voice of the Spirit. I felt doubtful about it partly because I considered he had not been faithful in his office a long time and partly because
the Spirit did not bear witness to it. But there was a general desire that
the Twelve might come home first, i.e. before they gave a decision on the
subject and so it came to pass which soon gave a new face to things.

A meeting was called and Rigdon again addressed us, but seemed
to have no liberty or power, after which Elder Brigham Young spoke
to the people. He said he saw here a hurrying spirit, showed the true
organization of the Church and called a meeting again when all the
quorums of the Church should be placed in proper order. He said that
if the people wished Elder Rigdon to be their guardian and leader, they
were quite at liberty to take him, but it must be passed in a regular and
legal manner, by the separate quorums.

He had much liberty and the power of the Spirit in speaking and
at the said meeting, he showed that Rigdon, if he were to take his
place as counselor to Joseph, he must go beyond the veil where he was
gone, and the Saints soon began to see how things were and that the
Twelve must now hold the keys of power and authority according to the
revelation which says the Twelve are equal with the first presidency.
[See D&C 107.] Before this he asked the Church if they wished to
choose themselves a guardian, but they did not raise their hands, and
it was now no hard thing determining who should lead the Church.
It was also shown that Joseph had told the Twelve after he had
instructed them in all things that on them would rest the responsibility and the care of the Church in case he should be taken away. They
invited Rigdon to their council but he did not attend and he soon
began to use threatening language against the Twelve, Joseph, etc. to
say that he had known for some years that Joseph had not been led by
the spirit of God [and gave this] as the reason why he did not attend
with him as his counselor, he soon so far committed himself that his
license was demanded by the Twelve, but he refused to give it up. He
seemed in no haste now to get to Pittsburgh, but labored hard to raise
a party to himself and succeeded in some degree. Some few cleaved
to him, and were in a short time cut off from the Church along with
him. Among the [party] were Samuel Bennett, Leonard Soby, Samuel

James, William Cottier, etc. (Joseph Fielding, *Diary*, in *Writings of Early Latter-day Saints and Their Contemporaries, A Database Collection*, comp. Milton V. Backman [Provo, Utah: BYU Religious Studies Center, 1996], 154–55).

William Adams

Joseph had sent letters to the Twelve to hurry home to Nauvoo . . . Sidney Rigdon [a former counselor in the First Presidency] . . . hurried home from Pittsburg [before the Twelve] and laid claim to be guardian of young Joseph, the eldest son of the Prophet, and was using his influence to get the Saints to sustain him. He began to organize the Church. Ordaining apostles, and preached to the Saints sustaining his claims as young Joseph's guardian, and appointed a day for a general meeting for the Saints to sustain him, his object was to [be] sustained before the brethren of the Twelve would arrive in Nauvoo. Brother Parley P. Pratt was among the first to arrive, and he and Brother Willard Richards, two of the Twelve, labored with Sidney not to be in a hurry until the Twelve would arrive, but he was determined to have the vote taken according to his appointment. Brigham Young and Heber C. Kimball arrived one day before the meeting, and others had arrived previously so that nearly all the Twelve were in Nauvoo. William Marks, president of the stake, called the meeting to order, and took charge of the meeting. After the opening exercises Rigdon spoke of his claim as guardian to young Joseph showing the necessity of the office, which took between one half to one hour (*Autobiography of William Adams*, 1822–1845 typescript [L. Tom Perry Special Collections, Harold B. Lee Library, Brigham Young University, Provo, Utah], 14–15).

Sidney Rigdon

The object of my mission is to visit the saints and offer myself to them as a guardian. I had a vision at Pittsburg, June 27th [the day of the Martyrdom]. This was presented to my mind not as an open vision, but rather a continuation of the vision mentioned in the Book of Doctrine and Covenants [referring to the vision he and Joseph Smith had experienced that is recorded in D&C 76] (Joseph Smith, *History of The Church of Jesus Christ of Latter-day Saints*, ed. B. H. Roberts, 7 vols. [Salt Lake City: Deseret Book, 1964], 7:229).

He [Sidney Rigdon] related a vision which he said the Lord had shown him concerning the situation of the church, and said there must be a guardian appointed to build the church up to Joseph, as he had begun it.

He said he was the identical man that the ancient prophets had sung about, wrote and rejoiced over, and that he was sent to do the identical work that had been the theme of all the prophets in every preceding generation (*History of the Church*, 7:224).

Benjamin Ashby

I was present when he [Sidney Rigdon] made his silly and boastful, speech about leading the Church back to Pittsburg. . . [It was] too foolish to be worth remembering. I did not know Rigdon when he was in the spirit of his calling and cannot say what manner of man he was, but when I knew him he had lost the favor of God and he was as dry as sticks in his preaching (Benjamin Ashby, *Autobiography*, in *Writings of Early Latter-day Saints*, 10).

William Hyde

On Thursday, August the 8th [1844], I attended a special conference in Nauvoo. Elder Rigdon addressed the assembly in the forenoon. Elder Rigdon sought, as he expressed it, the guardianship of the Church, but it was plainly manifest that the Spirit of the Lord had withdrawn from him, and that he sought that which did not belong to him. From the time the saints were driven from Missouri he had evidently been on the background, and had not walked up to his station, and on one occasion I heard Joseph Smith say that he had carried Elder Rigdon on his back long enough, and then turning to the Twelve said that if they did not help him at that time in shaking him off, the time would come when they would have it to do, and that without his, Joseph's assistance. And on Thursday, the 8th of August, was this saying of the Prophet brought home with weight to my mind.

In the afternoon President Brigham Young came upon the stand and addressed the vast multitude of anxious listeners as follows: "For the first time the Twelve walk up to the stand in their place, we have walked by sight and not by faith. The Church had had the privilege of coming to Joseph and of receiving, but now he has stepped to the other side of the veil. He loved the Church even unto death, and laid down his life for it." President Young then asked the following questions: "Do you want to choose a person to lead you into the Kingdom, if so manifest it." All were silent. "If there is any person present that wishes to draw away party after them let them rise." But no one rose. "I have wanted," said President Young, "to fast thirty days, and to clothe my house in mourning, but it seems that the saints are determined to drive business. They are not willing to wait and let everything come in its place, but business must be driven, and as it falls to my lot to speak, I shall speak in plainness. Do you want President Rigdon to take Joseph's place, if so take him. Here are the Twelve. Have my knees ever faltered, have these hands ever slackened?" "No," and "No," said voices from all directions. "The Twelve hold the keys and are in authority equal with the First President when the first is absent. Do you want to choose a trustee in trust to take Joseph's place, if so the Twelve must ordain him, for the power rests in them, and in them alone, the Church cannot do it."

"The Almighty with all his train are working in cooperation with us. Then," said he, "Let us pursue a proper course. Joseph has laid an almighty foundation, and we will rear thereupon an almighty building." The President remarked that the Devil had to work faster than he ever had done to kill Saints faster than we would make them. He then showed the propriety of having a bishop to stand in his place as he never had done, and take charge of all the financial concerns, while the Apostles and Elders attend to ministering the word, etc. And then [Brigham Young] said that if Elder Rigdon wanted to be a spokesman for Joseph, let him go to the other side of the veil. "Who" said he, "ever heard of such a thing as a person on one side of the veil acting as a spokesman for a person on the other side." The President further stated that no person could stand between Joseph and the Twelve. And then turning to the people, said it was their place to rise up and help roll on the Kingdom. "But let us not undertake anything new, let us follow the law and not undertake to divide the priesthood one hair."

Elders [Parley] P. Pratt and Amasa Lyman made some very appropriate remarks, confirming what President Young had said. Elder Lyman said that he had as good a right to lay claim to Joseph's place as had Elder Rigdon but that the thought had never entered his heart. His desires and determinations were to stand by the Twelve. Elder [William] W. Phelps also made some very comforting remarks. Said that Joseph was not in a situation that he could not visit the Saints. He then related a dream. Said that he saw Joseph the second night after his death, and that he looked as natural as life, and bore the same self-commanding look. Elder Phelps thought the Kingdom appeared to be on wheels, and Joseph asked him why he did not speak to the drivers and have them go ahead with it. He asked Joseph if the Kingdom was on wheels, and he said "yes", and told him to drive ahead. Elder Phelps then spoke to the drivers and they drove ahead. He saw the Kingdom move around the Temple. Joseph spoke to him as they came round and said, "You see it moves and receives no harm. Now drive across the river into Iowa." Brother Phelps replied that if they did that they would be obliged to cross Devil Creek. "Never mind Devil Creek," said Joseph, "drive ahead."

President Young again arose and spoke concerning the endowments of the elders. Said that if they did not get them in the temple, they should have them if they had to receive them in the wilderness, for the devil could not cheat them out of them. He then called upon the Saints to know if they would receive the Twelve and let them stand in their place as the First Presidency of the Church in the absence of Joseph. The vote was unanimous in the affirmative. On this day it was plainly manifest that the mantle of Joseph had rested upon President Young. The voice of the same spirit by which he, Joseph, spake was this day sounded in our ears, so much so that I once, unthoughtedly, raised my head to see if it was not actually Joseph addressing the assembly. The assembly was dismissed by President Young after being blessed in the name of the Lord (*The Private Journal of William Hyde* [L. Tom Perry Special Collections, Harold B. Lee Library, Brigham Young University, Provo, Utah], 13–15).

Brigham Young

I do not care who leads the church . . . but one thing I must know, and that is what God says about it. I have the keys and the means of obtaining the mind of God on the subject. . . Joseph conferred upon our heads all the keys and powers belonging to the Apostleship which he himself held before he was taken away, and no man or set of men can get between Joseph and the Twelve in this world or in the world to come.

How often has Joseph said to the Twelve, "I have laid the foundation and you must build thereon, for upon your shoulders the kingdom rests."

All that want to draw away a party from the church after them, let them do it if they can, but they will not prosper (*History of the Church,* 7:230–32).

Transfiguration of Brigham Young at the Succession Meeting

William Adams

There was a great multitude attending the meeting, more than one half the crowd could not find seats, and stood on their feet. Never were so many at one meeting that I ever saw. I was sitting down and could not see the speakers on the stand. I was listening very attentively, so that I could hear every word.

I heard a voice speaking, I was surprised, and jumping to my feet, expecting to see Joseph the Prophet was speaking, having heard him often in public and private, so that I was quite acquainted with his voice. This was a strong testimony that the Twelve Apostles were the rightful leaders of the Church and that the mouth of Joseph had fallen on Brigham Young. Out of that vast multitude about twenty votes for Rigdon to be guardian of young Joseph until he should come of age, he then being a boy of ten or eleven years of age. Rigdon, Marks, and these that sustained him [Sidney] were cut off from the Church, and the Twelve were sustained as the successors of Joseph the Prophet (*Autobiography of William Adams,* 4–15).

Orrin Rockwell

I was nine years old when the Prophet was martyred. I well remember the excitement at the time. The people hardly knew what to do. The prophet was gone and Sidney Rigdon wanted a guardian put in for the Church. Brother Thomas Grover, one of the High Council, spoke and told the people not to be in a hurry: the Twelve would be home soon and they would tell the people what to do. When Brigham Young came home he held a meeting, at which time the mantle of Joseph fell on him. It was a manifestation to let the people know who was to lead the Church. His looks and ways were like the Prophet. I, as a boy, was quite well acquainted with the Prophet. I was sitting with my mother in the meeting and I thought it was the Prophet and told my mother so. There are a good many who have heard my mother tell this ("In the Valley of the Saints," *Our Pioneer Heritage*, comp. Kate B. Carter, 20 vols. [Salt Lake City: Daughters of Utah Pioneers, 1958–77], 6:204).

Eliza Ann Haven

The question was a general one: "What shall we do without our Prophet?" I was then 15 years of age and we all felt so sad. I was at the meeting when Sidney Rigdon arose and declared himself our true Prophet and leader. Very few responded to his declaration. I am happy to say that not one of my father's family felt he was the right one. Soon after, President Brigham Young came home from the East, where he had been on a mission. I was at the meeting when the mantle of Bro. Joseph [*sic*] encircled him. . . . When he spoke, it was in Brother Joseph's voice. I arose to my feet and said to my mother: "Our prophet has come to life, mother we have Bro. Joseph back," for there he stood as plain as I ever saw him in life; and his voice and features were truly those of our beloved Prophet. Shortly a mist seemed to pass from Bro. Brigham's face and there stood Brother Young talking in his natural voice, but we knew he was to be our leader. Hundreds witnessed the same thing, but not all that were there had that privilege (Janet Burton Seegmiller, *Be Kind to the Poor: Life Story of Robert Taylor Burton* [United States: Robert Taylor Burton Family Organization, 1988], 50).

Mary Ann Stearns Winters

I was at the great meeting when the mantle of Brother Joseph rested upon Brigham Young until his whole being seemed changed and his voice was like that of the Prophet. The people around me, rising to their feet to get a better chance to hear and see, I and my little companion of the day, Julia Felshaw, being small of stature, stood upon the benches that we, too might behold the wonderful transformation, and I know that from that time on the power of that change remained with Brother Brigham Young as long as he lived on earth ("An Autobiographical Sketch of the Life of the Late Mary Ann Sterns Winters," typescript [LDS Church Archives, The Church of Jesus Christ of Latter-day Saints, Salt Lake City], n.p.).

Robert Burton Taylor

The occasion that I now refer to was a general meeting of the Latter-day Saints, soon after the return to Nauvoo of President Brigham Young and other members of the Quorum of Twelve Apostles, from their missions. The meeting had been called to order, and after the usual opening exercises President Brigham Young arose to address the assembly.

At that time I was not acquainted with President Young, but his voice, manner, expression, and in fact, his personal appearance was so strikingly that of the martyred Prophet, that I rose from my seat, as did hundreds of others, to look at the Prophet Joseph Smith Jr. The likeness was so marked that I could hardly make myself believe that the Prophet had not himself returned; not that there was a resemblance between the two men. I am not going to say why this was other than I received it, as an evidence to the people that God had chose Brigham Young as successor to the Prophet Joseph Smith Jr. There were dozens, even hundreds of others, who were impressed just the same as I was at that time, and I have heard many, many who are now gone make similar statements or expressions to that I am here making (Seegmiller, *Be Kind to the Poor: Life Story of Robert Taylor Burton*, 49).

Homer Duncan

I must make mention on one [more] manifestation of the Lord's goodness to me. At the special meeting held at Nauvoo after the Prophet Joseph Smith's death at the time that the mantle of the Prophet of the Lord fell upon Brigham Young. I sat listening to someone speaking with my head down, my face in the palms of my hands and my elbows on my knees. While in this position, Brigham Young came to the stand and commenced to speak with the voice of Joseph the Prophet. Being so well acquainted with the Prophet's voice, I nearly sprang from my seat through astonishment, but I sat and heard the Prophet's [Joseph's] voice as long as Brigham Young was speaking. Not only did the voice of Brigham [sound] like that of Joseph, but the very gestures of his right hand when he was saying anything very positive reminded me of Joseph. My decision was then made as to who should lead The Church of Jesus Christ of Latter Day Saints for surely the mantle of Joseph has fallen upon Brigham (Homer Duncan, *Autobiographical Sketch*, holograph [LDS Church Archives, The Church of Jesus Christ of Latter-day Saints, Salt Lake City], 22–23).

George Morris

In the afternoon, President Young replied to what had been said, and when he arose to speak I was sitting holding down my head, reflecting upon what had been said by Rigdon—when I was startled by hearing Joseph's voice. He had a way of clearing his throat before he began to speak—by a peculiar effort of his own—like Ahhem, but it had a different sound to him than to anyone else—I raised my head suddenly and the first thing I saw was Joseph—as plain as I ever saw him in my life. He was dressed in a light linen suit with a light leghorn hat such as he used to wear in the warm weather and the first words he said were, "Right here is the authority to lead this Church" at the same time striking his hand on his bosom and went on to utter several sentences in Joseph's voice as clear and distinct as I ever heard Joseph speak and his gestures and appearance were perfect. It was Brigham Young. That was testimony enough to convince me where the proper authority rested (George Morris, *Autobiography*, in *Writings of Early Latter-day Saints*, 26).

Mary Field

I, with my mother, was present at the meeting in the bowery when the mantle of Joseph fell upon Brigham Young while he was talking with the people. Mother had the baby on her knee, who was playing with a tin cup. He dropped it, attracting our attention to the floor. Mother stooped over to pick it up, when we startled by hearing the voice of Joseph. Looking up quickly we saw the form of the Prophet Joseph standing before us. Brother Brigham looked and talked so much like Joseph that for a minute we thought it was Joseph. There was no doubt in the hearts of the Saints from that moment on who was to be their inspired leader (Mary Field Garner, *Autobiographical Sketch*, typescript [L. Tom Perry Special Collections, Harold B. Lee Library, Brigham Young University, Provo, Utah], 6–7).

Benjamin Franklin Johnson

I sat in the assembly near President Rigdon, closely attentive to his appeal to the conference to recognize and sustain his claims as "Guardian for the Church." . . . And as he closed his address and sat down, my back was partly turned to the seat occupied by Apostle Brigham Young and other Apostles, when suddenly, and as from Heaven, I heard the voice of the Prophet Joseph, that thrilled my whole being, and quickly turning around I saw in the transformation of Brigham Young, the tall, straight, and portly form of the Prophet Joseph Smith, clothed in a sheen of light, covering him to his feet; and I heard the real and perfect voice of the Prophet, even to the whistle, as in years past caused by the loss of a tooth said to have been broken out by a mob at Hyrum. This view or vision although but for seconds, was to me as vivid and real as the glare of lightening or the voice of thunder from the heavens ("An Interesting Letter: From Patriarch Benjamin F. Johnson to Elder Geo S. Gibbs" [L. Tom Perry Special Collections, Harold B. Lee Library, Brigham Young University, Provo, Utah], 30).

Orson Hyde

I will tell you that as long as God has a Church on the earth, He will govern it. Now I will tell you a little of my feelings in relation to it. I know that when President Young returned with the Twelve to Nauvoo, he gathered them around him, and said he: "I want you to disperse among the congregation and feel the pulse of the people while I go upon the stand and speak."

We went among the congregation and President Young went on the stand. Well, he spoke; and his words went through me like electricity. "Am I mistaken?" said I, "or is it really the voice of Joseph Smith?" This is my testimony, it was not only the voice of Joseph, but there were the features, the gestures and even the stature of Joseph before us in the person of Brigham. And though it may be said that President Young is a complete mimic, and can mimic anybody, I would like to see the man who can mimic another in stature who was about four or five inches higher than himself.—Everyone in the congregation, every one who was inspired by the Spirit of the Lord—felt it. They knew it. They realized it. . . . Now, this was a manifestation of the power of the Almighty—it was the power of God resting on an individual in the eyes of all the people; not only in feature and voice, but actually in stature. This is my testimony. . . . Did it require proof that Joseph was there in the person of Brigham, speaking with an angel's voice? It required no argument; with those who feared God and loved truth, it required none (*Journal of Discourses*, 26 vols. [London: Latter-day Saints' Book Depot, 1854–86], 13:181).

Wilford Woodruff

If I had not seen him with my own eyes, there is no one that could have convinced me that it was not Joseph Smith (*History of the Church*, 7:236).

Zina D. Huntington Young

Never can it be told in words what the saints suffered in those days of trial; but the sweet spirit—the comforter—did not forsake them; and when the twelve returned, the mantle of Joseph fell upon Brigham.

When I approached the stand (on the occasion when Sidney Rigdon was striving for the guardianship of the Church), President Young was speaking. It was the voice of Joseph Smith—not that of Brigham Young. His very person was changed. The mantle was truly given to another. There was no doubting this in the minds of that vast assembly. All witnessed the transfiguration, and even to-day thousands bear testimony thereof. I closed my eyes. I could have exclaimed, I know that is Joseph Smith's voice! Yet I knew he had gone. But the same spirit was with the people; the comforter remained.

The building of the [Nauvoo] temple was hurried on. The saints did not slacken their energies. They had a work to do in that temple for their dead, and blessings to obtain for themselves (Edward W. Tullidge, *Women of Mormondom* [Salt Lake City: n.p., 1975], 326–327, L. Tom Perry Special Collections, Harold B. Lee Library, Brigham Young University, Provo, Utah).

URGENCY TO COMPLETE THE NAUVOO TEMPLE

With the Twelve sustained as the head of the Church, the Saints could again renew their efforts in building the temple. They worked feverishly to obey the Lord's command to build the temple and receive those promises which the Lord had in store for them. While the temple was under construction, portions were dedicated and put to immediate use. In November 1841, a wooden baptismal font had been constructed in the basement and enclosed in a small wood-frame structure, while the exterior temple walls were still being built. When the attic was finished in December 1845, Brigham Young dedicated it and began giving endowments. Finally by May 1846, the whole building was completed and dedicated.

George Whitaker

Counsel was given to go to work and finish the temple according to the revelation given to Joseph Smith, so that we might receive our washings and anointings and the keys and powers of the Holy Priesthood, and also the Holy Anointings and Sealings that the power of God might rest upon his servants ("Life of George Whitaker, A Utah Pioneer, as written by himself," typescript, 8–9, Utah State Historical Society, Salt Lake City).

Brigham Young

This morning Elder Heber C. Kimball related the following dream: last evening, before retiring to bed he asked God to enlighten his mind with regard to the work of endowment. While sleeping he beheld a large field of corn that was fully ripe, he and a number of others were commanded to take baskets and pick off the corn with all possible speed, for there would soon be a storm that would hinder the gathering of the harvest. The hands engaged in gathering the harvest, were heedless and unconcerned and did not haste, as they were commanded; but he and the man he assisted had a much larger basket than the rest, and picked with all their might of the largest ears of the field, they once in a while would pick an ear that had a long tail on each end and but a few grains scattering over the center of the cob, which were very light.

The interpretation of the dream is, that the field represented the church, the good corn represented good saints, the light corn represented the light and indifferent saints, the laborers are those appointed to officiate in the Temple, the storm is trouble that is near upon us, and requires an immediate united exertion of all engaged in giving the endowments to the saints, or else we will not get through before we will be obliged to flee for our lives (*History of the Church*, 7:561).

Brigham Young

(President Young counseled the Saints to both finish the temple and then use their means to also go forward and help prepare the way for those to follow.)

Let there be no feelings about who shall go first; those who go first will lay a foundation for those who shall come after, and none will be neglected in their time. I have one request to make of all the Saints that expect to immigrate with us, that they be subject to their leaders, with their property and means, and if this is done I can say there never will be a lack in the church. . . . I propose that all the Saints lay down their property to be used in building the Temple, the Nauvoo House and helping the poor away, such as must go in the first company (*History of the Church*, 7:575).

Norton Jacobs

[Heber C. Kimball] said he had rather go into the wilderness with a pack on his back, and his wife, with a bundle of clothes under his arms, and have the temple finished than to go with his wagon loaded down with gold and the temple not finished ("Norton Jacobs Autobiography," 20; as cited in David R. Crockett, *Saints in Exile: A Day-By-Day Pioneer Experience* [Tuscon, Arizona: LDS-Gems Press, 1996], 42).

ENDOWMENTS

The attic story of the temple was dedicated on November 30, 1845, by President Brigham Young. For the next two months he and other Church leaders worked tirelessly to endow as many members as possible with the ordinances of the temple. The sisters had originally planned on washing temple clothes on Saturday, but such was the urgency to endow the members that they began washing the temple clothes during the night. When the Saints began their exodus in February of the following year, 5,615 Saints had received their temple blessings.

George Whitaker

About the last of November the temple was so far along, having the upper rooms finished, that they began to give endowments. Those who had paid their property tithing, that is, one tenth of the property they had brought with them, and also one-tenth of their increase or labor, had the privilege of going through the temple. Everyone seemed to be trying to work and settle up their tithing that they might have the privilege of getting their endowments and blessings in the temple. Many thousands got their blessings and endowments in the space of about ten weeks. I paid my property tithing and also my labor tithing and got my receipts for it, and had the privilege of going through the temple and getting my endowments a few days before they closed. They were at work night and day from the time they commenced until they closed, which was about the sixth day of February, 1846 ("Life of George Whitaker," 9).

Brigham Young

Such has been the anxiety manifested by the saints to receive the ordinances [of the Temple], and such the anxiety on our part to administer to them, that I have given myself up entirely to the work of the Lord in the Temple night and day, not taking more than four hours sleep, upon an average, per day, and going home but once a week (as cited in *History of the Church*, 7:567).

Brigham Young

(February 3, 1846)

Notwithstanding that I had announced that we would not attend to the administration of the ordinances, the House of the Lord was thronged all day, the anxiety being so great to receive, as if the brethren would have us stay here and continue the endowments until our way would be hedged up, and our enemies would intercept us. But I informed the brethren that this was not wise, and that we should build more Temples, and have further opportunities to receive the blessings of the Lord, as soon as the Saints were prepared to receive them. In this Temple we have been abundantly rewarded, if we receive no more. I also informed the brethren that I was going to get my wagons started and be off. I walked some distance from the Temple supposing the crowd would disperse, but on returning I found the house filled to overflowing.

Looking upon the multitude and knowing their anxiety, as they were thirsting and hungering for the word, we continued at work diligently in the House of the Lord. [February 8, 1846] I met with the Council of the Twelve in the southeast corner room of the attic of the Temple. We knelt around the altar, and dedicated the building to the Most High. We asked his blessing upon our intended move to the west; also asked him to enable us some day to finish the Temple, and dedicate it to him, and we would leave it in his hands to do as he pleased; and to preserve the building as a monument to Joseph Smith. We asked the Lord to accept the labors of his servants in this land. We then left the Temple (as cited in *History of the Church*, 7:579–80).

Orson Hyde

If we moved forward and finished this House we should be received and accepted as a church with our dead, but if not we should be rejected with our dead. These things have inspired and stimulated us to action in the finishing of it which through the blessings of God we have been enabled to accomplish and prepared it for dedication. In doing this we have only been saved as it were by the skin of our teeth (Wilford Woodruff, *Wilford Woodruff's Journal, 1833–1898*, ed. Scott G. Kenney, 9 vols. [Midvale, Utah: Signature Books, 1983], 3:43; May 8, 1846).

Wilford Woodruff

The Saints have labored faithfully and finished the Temple and were now received as a Church with our dead. This is glory enough for building the Temple and thousands of the Saints have received their endowment in it. And the light will not go out (*Wilford Woodruff's Journal*, 3:46–47; May 8, 1846).

NAUVOO TEMPLE DEDICATION

Families were assigned to remain in Nauvoo and finish the temple when the main body of Saints left in February. The temple was completed by the end of April, but because of a fear that the mobs would interfere with the dedication, a private dedication was held on the 30th. Brigham Young's brother Joseph Young offered the final dedicatory prayer and presented the temple to the Lord as a witness of His people's sacrifice to keep His commandments. The next day, May 1, Orson Hyde offered the dedicatory prayer in a public meeting.

Orson Hyde
(Nauvoo Temple dedication—dedicatory prayer, May 1, 1846)

Holy and Everlasting Father, before Thee this morning we present ourselves and acknowledge thy mercy that has been extended to us since we have been on thy footstool, and of the Holy Priesthood now dedicating this house . . . by the authority of the Holy Priesthood now we offer this building as a sanctuary to Thy Worthy Name. We ask Thee to take the guardianship into Thy hands and grant that Thy Spirit shall dwell here and may all feel a sacred influence on their hearts that His Hand has helped in the work. Accept of our offering this morning . . . let Thy Spirit rest upon those who have contributed to the building of this temple, the laborers on it that they may come forth to receive kingdoms and dominions and glory and immortal power. Accept of us we pray Thee, inspire every bosom to do Thy will, cause that truth may lead them for the glorious coming of the Son of God when you come in the name of the King, the Lord of Hosts shall be the King. Gather us in thy Kingdom through Jesus Christ, our Lord, Amen ("Minutes of Thomas Bullock of the Dedication of the Nauvoo Temple," [Historic Sites File, Church Historical Library, Salt Lake City]; see also *Manuscript History of Brigham Young*, ed. Elden J. Watson [Salt Lake City: Elden J. Watson, 1971], 148).

Wilford Woodruff

Notwithstanding the many false prophecies of Sidney Rigdon and others that the roof should not go on nor the House be finished, and the threats of the mob that we should not dedicate it, yet we have done both and we had an interesting time (*Wilford Woodruff's Journal*, 3:41).

Sarah DeArmon Pea Rich

(Sarah commented on the sustaining power the Saints felt during the trek west as a result of receiving their temple blessings.)

Many were the blessings we had received in the house of the Lord, which has caused us joy and comfort in the midst of all our sorrow and enabled us to have faith in God, knowing he would guide us and sustain us in the unknown journey that lay before us. For if it had not been for the faith and knowledge that was bestowed upon us in that Temple by the influence and help of the Spirit of the Lord, our journey would have been like one taking a leap in the dark, to start out on such a journey in the winter as it were, and in our state of poverty, it would seem like walking into the jaws of death (Sarah DeArmon Pea Rich, *Autobiography*, in *Writings of Early Latter-day Saints*, 42).

Nauvoo Temple
(Courtesy of the Church Archives,
The Church of Jesus Christ of Latter-day Saints)

⚈ 3 ⚈

A PREMATURE DEPARTURE

As work on the temple progressed, persecution in Nauvoo increased. In September 1845, the leaders of the Church signed an agreement with the citizens of Quincy, promising them that the Saints would leave Nauvoo in the spring if persecutions would cease. Both parties accepted the terms, and the Saints immediately began preparations for the trek west. Since they were still trying to finish the temple, they often had to convert their homes into work stations and work through the night constructing wagons. Persecution, however, continued to plague the Saints, and they were forced to leave earlier than planned. The first group of Saints ferried across the Mississippi River on February 4, 1846, and established a temporary camp at Sugar Creek. Weeks later, bitter cold temperatures froze the Mississippi, enabling subsequent groups to walk on the ice bridge. The impoverished Saints continued to congregate at Sugar Creek, where Brigham Young organized the camp.

INCREASING STRIFE AGAINST THE MORMONS

S. M. Bartlett

(In September 1845, the citizens of Quincy met to appoint a committee to confer with Church leaders and learn their intentions for leaving Illinois. The citizens of Quincy believed that the only way to establish peace in the state was to force the Mormons to leave. Mr. Bartlett attended this meeting and was the editor of the Quincy Whig.*)*

It is a settled thing that the public sentiment of the state is against the Mormons, and it will be in vain for them to contend against it; and to prevent bloodshed, and the sacrifice of many lives on both sides, it is their duty to obey the public will, and leave the state as speedily as possible. That they will do this we have a confident hope—and that too, before the last extreme is resorted to—that of force (B. H. Roberts, *A Comprehensive History of The Church of Jesus Christ of Latter-day Saints*, 7 vols. [Salt Lake City: Deseret News Press, 1930], 2:504).

Gov. Thomas Ford

(Even the governor of Illinois, in a letter to Church leaders, conveyed his unwillingness to prevent injustices against the Mormons.)

I wish you to say to the Mormons for me, that I regret very much, that so much excitement and hatred against them should exist in the public mind. Nevertheless, it is due to truth to say that the public mind everywhere is so decidedly hostile to them that public opinion is not inclined to do them common justice. Every bad report against them is greedily swallowed, whilst nothing can be heard in their favor; under these circumstances, I fear that they will never be able to live in peace with their neighbors of Hancock and the surrounding counties. There is no legal power in the state to compel them to leave, and no such power will be exercised during my administration.

The spirit of the people, however, is up and the signs are very evident that an attempt will be made by the surrounding counties to drive them out. Such an attempt may fail once or even twice, but if undertaken in earnest and persevered in, it must finally succeed. Those who may think it wrong to drive out the Mormons cannot be made to fight in their defense, and indeed the people of the state will never tolerate the expense of frequent military expeditions to defend them. The Mormons may think themselves strong enough to defend themselves; but do they want to live in a state of continued war? They may overcome their enemies; but those enemies will rally again, and murders will be committed and mischief done from this time out, as each party may find itself able.

I desire that you will impress these facts upon the Mormons, and that you will counsel and promote peaceable means of accommodation whereby the Mormons may be induced to leave the state. It is acknowledged by me that the state has no power to insist upon their removal, that it is a great hardship on them to remove from their comfortable homes and the property which they have accumulated by years of toil; but is it not better that they should do so voluntarily than to live in a state of continual war? (*Nauvoo Neighbor,* October 29, 1845; see also *Comprehensive History of the Church,* 2:506.)

Brigham Young

(President Young responded to Governor Ford's letter by promising that the Saints would leave in the spring if persecutions would cease.)

We would say to the committee above mentioned, and to the governor, and all the authorities and people of Illinois, and the surrounding states and territories; that we propose to leave this county next spring, for some point so remote, that there will not need to be a difficulty with the people and ourselves, provided certain propositions necessary for the accomplishment of our removal shall be observed, as follows, to wit:

That the citizens of this, and the surrounding counties, and all men, will use their influence and exertions, to help us to sell or rent our properties, so as to get means enough that we can help the widow, the fatherless and destitute to remove with us;

That all men will let us alone with their vexatious law suits, so that we may have the time, for we have broken no law; and help us to cash, dry goods, groceries, good oxen, milch cows, beef cattle, sheep, wagons, mules, harnesses, horses, etc., in exchange for our property, at a fair price, and deeds given at payment, that we may have the means to accomplish a removal, without the suffering of the destitute, to an extent beyond the endurance of human nature . . .

That we will use all lawful means, in connection with others to preserve the public peace while we tarry, and shall expect decidedly that we be no more molested with house burning, or any other depredations, to waste our property and time and hinder our business;

That it is a mistaken idea that we "have proposed to remove in six months" for that would be so early in the spring, that grass might not grow nor water run, both of which would be necessary for our removal, but we propose to use our influence, to have no more seed-time nor harvest among our people in this county, after gathering our present crops.

By order of the Council
Brigham Young, President
Willard Richards, Clerk.
(*Comprehensive History of the Church*, 2:509–10.)

George Whitaker

They [the mob] were afraid to come to Nauvoo as they knew we were ready for them, but they began to harass our brethren in the outside settlements by burning their houses and stacks of wheat, threatening women and children, and frightening them and driving them from their homes. Their husbands and fathers had to get out of their way or they would have been killed. Hundreds of families came into Nauvoo destitute. We prepared ourselves for self defense the best we could, but the mob dared not come into Nauvoo. They were afraid some of them would get hurt. They knew they were in a bad cause. The Latter-day Saints were on the defensive to protect themselves, their wives and children and their property. . . . Some of the leading men of the state and the authorities of the Church held councils. It was agreed that the mob should cease their hostilities and that the Saints should go somewhere beyond the Rocky Mountains when the spring opened. After this treaty was made, the mob to some extent ceased their burnings and drivings in the outside settlements ("Life of George Whitaker, A Utah Pioneer, as written by himself," typescript, 8, Utah State Historical Society, Salt Lake City).

THE BLESSINGS OF AN EXODUS

Heber C. Kimball

(Elder Kimball insightfully commented that all the Saints, eventually, would desire to join the trek rather than remain in Nauvoo.)

I am glad the time of our exodus is come; I have looked for it for years. It is necessary for us to be faithful and humble, and if we listen to counsel we shall prosper. And although we leave all our fine houses and farms here, how long do you think it will be before we shall be better off than we are now? . . . There may be individuals who will look at their pretty houses and gardens and say, "It is hard to leave them;" but I tell you, when we start, you will put on your knapsacks and follow after us (Heber C. Kimball, "General Conference," *Millennial Star* [January 15, 1846], 7:21).

Orson Pratt

(Elder Pratt addressed the importance of sacrifice and unity in his farewell talk to the Saints in the Eastern States.)

If we die in the dens and caves of the Rocky Mountains, we shall die where freedom reigns triumphantly. Liberty in a solitary place, and in a desert, is far more preferable than martyrdom in these pious States. . . . The Lord requires a sacrifice, and he that is not willing, will fail of the blessing. Brethren now is the time for you to be up and doing, for unless you can get to Nauvoo this winter, it will be entirely needless for you to go in the spring, for you could not arrive in time to leave with the Saints ("Farewell Message of Orson Pratt," *Times and Seasons* [December 1, 1845], 6:1042).

Parley P. Pratt

The people of God always were required to make sacrifices and if we have a sacrifice to make, [I am] in favor of its being something worthy of the people of God. . . . The people must enlarge in numbers and extend their borders; they cannot always live in one city, nor in one country. . . . In short, this people are fast approaching that point which ancient prophets have long since pointed out as the destiny of the saints of the last days (Joseph Smith, *History of The Church of Jesus Christ of Latter-day Saints*, ed. B. H. Roberts, 7 vols. [Salt Lake City: Deseret Book, 1964], 7:463–64).

Amasa Lyman

It has been said, that we should leave this country next spring, if the Lord is willing and the people have no objections. And we don't care much whether they have or not, we calculate to go about next spring. And we calculate to go the same people we are now, preserving the same principles which have caused us to grow and expand as we have done. This people have grown until there is not room for them to grow, and now they need transplanting where they can have more room, and however much the people may seem disposed not to go, the sails are set, the wind is fair, and we are bound to weather the point, whether we will or not, *for we are not at the helm* (Amasa Lyman, "General Conference," *Millennial Star* [January 15, 1846], 7:22).

Brigham Young

The mob seems determined to drive us to our duty in gathering, and then drive us to carry the fullness of the gospel from among them and carry it to Israel (*History of the Church*, 7:445).

Amasa Lyman

(Brother Lyman had a vision that the hosts of heaven, including Joseph, would guide and protect them on their westward journey.)

At the beginning of the last winter we spent in Illinois, about the time the clouds were gathering so thick and the last storm began to break upon us, we heard the thunders and threatenings of our enemies wherein they stated that we were to be driven away.

At that time I was confined to my bed with sickness, but I heard the report of the proceedings day after day. . . . To get away was impossible with me at that time, and we knew that the longer we stayed the more we should be oppressed by our enemies.

After I had commenced to recover my health, one morning, while lying in my bed in open day, as wakeful as I am at this moment, the surrounding objects which I could see when in my natural condition all in an instant disappeared, and, instead of appearing to keep my bed, I found myself standing in a place where those acquainted with Nauvoo and the location of the Printing Office, subsequent to the death of the Prophets, will remember. There was a vacant lot in front of the Printing Office; I stood there, and I heard a rumbling noise. . . . I turned round to look in the direction of Main Street, and behold! The whole country was filled with one moving mass of people that seemed to be traveling directly to the point where I stood. As they approached somewhat nearer, they seemed not to be traveling on the ground, but somewhat near the altitude of the tops of the buildings.

At the head of the company were three personages clothed with robes of white, something like those which many of us are acquainted with. Around their waist was a girdle of gold, and from this was suspended the scabbard of a sword—the sword being in the hand of the wearer.

They took their places with their faces directly west; and as they stopped, the individual in advance turned and looked over his shoulder to me with a smile of recognition. It was Joseph; and the others were his two brothers, Hyrum and Carlos. . . . To tell my feelings would be impossible. I leave you to guess them; for it would be futile to attempt a description.

After contemplating the scene a few moments, I was again in my bed as before, and the vision had disappeared. This was my assurance, in the commencement of our troubles there, that I received of the guardianship that was around us and the protection that we were receiving from the hosts of heaven (*Journal of Discourses*, 26 vols. [London: Latter-day Saints' Book Depot, 1854–86], 5:58–59).

PREPARATIONS

During the fall general conference of 1845, members of the Church accepted the call to move west. They also covenanted with Church leaders that they would "give all to help take the poor; and every honest industrious member who wants to go" (*History of the Church*, 7:464–65). When the conference convened, an increased effort was made to organize into companies and have sufficient supplies for the spring exodus.

George Whitaker

When the [October 1845] conference was over we went to our homes and began to prepare for the great journey before us. The thing on hand was the finishing of the temple. There was a great deal of work to be done in a little time. Meetings were called in different parts of the city to organize companies for manufacturing wagons. Men went into the woods to get out timber, and seasoned it the best way they could, while every man who could use a tool worked at some part of the business. My brother Moses went to work in the blacksmith shop making the irons and setting the tires on the wagons. I went to work on the temple. I turned all my labor in on tithing ("Life of George Whitaker," 9).

Irene Hascall Pomeroy

(In a letter to her father, who was living in Massachusetts, Sister Pomeroy described the preparations being made for the exodus.)

The church as a body intend[s] removing in the spring. . . . They have their arrangements made. They are going in companies consisting of one hundred families each, every company half a mile apart, every wagon two rods apart [thirty-three feet]. They make calculations for twenty-five hundred families. The rich [members] promise to sacrifice all except what they need themselves—to help the poor so all can go that wish. . . . You must come—how can I go and leave you on this side of the mountains—and yet I cannot stay when God calls to go. The twelve and Joseph received revelations concerning [the westward exodus] before Joseph died. We expect to go in the first company (letter of Irene Azula Hascall Pomeroy, Nauvoo, Illinois, October 1845, to Captain Ashbell Green Hascall, North New Salem, Franklin County, Massachusetts, as found in "Letters of Irene B. Hascall Pomeroy to her parents and relatives in North New Salem, Massachusetts, covering the period: May 1845–August 1841," microfilm, Utah State Historical Society, Salt Lake City).

History of the Church

(Church leaders recommended what supplies each family of five and each company would need for the trek west.)

Each family consisting of five adults, will require one good strong wagon, well covered. Three good yokes of oxen between the ages of four and ten. Two or more cows. One or more good beeves, some sheep if they have them.

One thousand pounds of flour or other bread stuff and good sacks to put it in.

One bushel of beans.

One hundred pounds of sugar.

One good musket or rifle to each man.

One pound of powder and three lbs. lead (or perhaps more).

Two lbs. tea, five lbs. coffee.

Twenty-five pounds of salt.

A few pounds of dried beef, or bacon, as they choose.

A good tent and furniture to each two families.

From ten to fifty pounds of seed to a family.

And from twenty-five to one hundred pounds of farming or other tools.

Clothing and bedding to each family of five persons not to exceed five hundred pounds.

One or more sets of saw and gristmill irons to each company of one hundred families.

Cooking utensils to consist of a bake-kettle, frying-pan, coffee pot, tin cups, plates, and forks, spoons, pans, etc., etc., as few as will do.

A few goods to trade with the Indians.

A little iron and steel, a few pounds of nails.

Each wagon supposed to be loaded on the start with one ton without the persons or twenty-eight hundred including them. . . .

A few horses will be necessary for each company. Also a few cannon [sic] and ammunition for the same. The journey to the coast will require some four or five months, being upwards of two thousand miles.

There was also added two sets of pulley blocks and rope for crossing rivers to each company.

Two ferry boats to each company.

One keg of alcohol of five gallons for each two families.

Ten pounds of dried apples for each family.

Five pounds of dried peaches.

Twenty pounds of dried pumpkin.

Two pounds of black pepper.

One pound of cayenne.

One-half pound mustard.

Twelve nutmegs. One fish seine for each company. Hooks and lines for each family (*History of the Church*, 7:454–55).

Louisa Barnes Pratt

(Sister Pratt expressed her heartache at trying to pack up and move without her husband, who was then serving a mission in Tahiti.)

In the autumn of 1845 the Saints entered into a treaty to leave Nauvoo the ensuing spring. No pen can paint the anguish of my heart when I heard the news. It fell on my ear like the funeral knell of all departed joy. What could I do I thought, with my little means, and my helpless family in launching out into the howling wilderness: I had no male relative to take charge of my affairs, My brother-in-law and family were not prepared to go at the time, were struggling hard to make preparation. I was almost in despair when I reflected on the burden I had to bear, and my companion on the opposite side of the globe. An indescribable melancholy came over me at times, when I thought of my devotion to that beautiful City! Oh! how sorrowful I was! But the watchword was "go!" Like the pilgrim, "take your stuff and travel on. . . ."

At length the time came that we must leave our beloved Temple, Our City, our homes. I forbear to dwell upon the solemn dread which took possession of my mind. Almon Babbit called to see me. I asked him if he could divine the reason why those who had sent my husband to the ends of the earth, did not call to inquire whether I could prepare myself for such a perilous journey, or if I wished to go or stay? His reply was, "Sister Pratt, they expect you to be smart enough to go yourself without help, and even to assist others." The remark awakened in me a spirit of self reliance. I replied, "Well, I will show them what I can do. . . ."

I swept out my pleasant house, closed the doors and bid farewell to it. I had sold one yoke of cattle for forty-five dollars; fifty [dollars], Mr. Haywood paid me, which fitted us up for provision and clothing. I had two yoke of oxen, two cows, and a good new wagon. I was comparatively rich; and by this time began to be in fine spirits (*Reminiscences of Louisa Barnes Pratt [1879]* [LDS Church Archives, The Church of Jesus Christ of Latter-day Saints, Salt Lake City], n.p.).

RENEWED PERSECUTION IN NAUVOO

Even though the Saints strived to gather the needed supplies and be ready to depart by the spring, their efforts didn't appease their enemies and persecution began anew. Neighbors refused to buy their homes, land, and other goods, knowing that within months they could have them at no cost. Church leaders even heard that the federal government would prevent the Saints as an armed mass from leaving the United States since they could pose a threat to the U.S. by forming an alliance with another country. The Saints then realized that they needed to leave much sooner than the spring. Yet again, they were forced to leave in the middle of the winter.

George Whitaker

The greatest portion of our summer's work was lost. The kiln of bricks which we had made we could not sell. Everybody wanted to sell their property, therefore nobody wanted to build or improve their property. The Saints in Nauvoo were as a general thing very poor. Some thousands had emigrated from England and from the Eastern States, and had spent most of their means in getting here. We lived mostly on corn meal and milk, vegetables, and sometimes a little meat and flour. Our enemies tried to starve us out by stopping everything they could from coming into Nauvoo. Money was very scarce. I never got one cent in money from the time I arrived at Nauvoo until I left ("Life of George Whitaker," 9).

William Clayton

In mid-December 1845, Brigham Young received a letter from Samuel Brannan. This New York publisher had visited with the United States secretary of war and other cabinet members. Brannan reported that these men objected to the departure of an armed band of men from the United States either to California or Oregon. Nor, said Brannan, were they inclined to let the Saints remain in the United States. It sounded to Brannan like another effort at extermination (William Clayton, *Journals*, 195, December 11, 1845; see also *History of the Church*, 7:544).

Eliza R. Snow

We better live in tents and smoke
Than wear the cursed Gentile yoke—
We better from our country fly
Than by mobocracy die. . . .
Our homes were dear—we lov'd them well,
Beneath our roofs we hop'd to dwell;
And honor the great God's commands,
By mutual rights of Christian lands.
Our persecutors will not cease
Their murd'rous spoiling of our peace
And have decreed that we must go
To wilds where reeds and rushes grow.
The Camp,—the Camp,—its numbers swell
Shout, shout, O Camp of Israel!
The King, the Lord of hosts is near,
His armies guard our front and rear.
("The Camp of Israel," *Improvement Era*
[March 1943], 46:142)

CROSSING THE MISSISSIPPI RIVER

Charles Shumway commenced the exodus on February 4, 1846, by ferrying his wagons across the Mississippi River. Hundreds of wagons and Saints began lining up along Parley Street, waiting for a chance to cross as well. Parley Street became known as the "trail of tears" as the Saints bid farewell to their homes, property, and the temple in their beloved Nauvoo. Cold weather caused portions of the river to freeze and send chunks of ice crashing through the river, making it treacherous and more difficult to cross. By the 25th, temperatures had plummeted so much that the Mississippi River froze, and the Saints began crossing it in wagons and on foot.

John Taylor

About two thousand are ready and crossing the Mississippi to pioneer the way, and make arrangements for summer crops at some point between this and the "Pacific," . . . To see such a large body of men, women and children, compelled by the inefficiency of the law, and potency of mobocracy, to leave a great city in the month of February, for the sake of the enjoyment of *pure religion* fills the soul with astonishment, and gives the world a sample of fidelity and faith, brilliant as the sun, and forcible as a tempest, and as enduring as eternity.

May God continue the spirit of fleeing from false freedom, and false dignity, till every Saint is removed to where he "can sit under his own vine and fig tree" without having any to molest or make afraid. Let us go—let us go (John Taylor, *Times and Seasons* [February 1, 1846], 6:1114).

John R. Young

(John was eight years old when he crossed the Mississippi River.)

It is the month of February, 1846. The sun is shining brightly, yet the air is keen and cutting. The wheels ring as we drive over the frozen snow. In our home since early morning, all has been hurry and bustle; two wagons stand in our front yard, and my father with two other men, strangers to me, are carrying out our household goods. My mother looks pale, and when I ask her, "What is the matter?" she takes me in her arms, kisses me, and says, "We are going to leave our home, and will never see it again!"

Just then some other teams come along, and one of the brethren calls to my father to be sure to put out the fire, and to hurry up, for it is getting late. In a few minutes mother and the children are lifted tenderly into the wagon. Father next takes his place on the front seat, turns his face to the west, and his back upon the home, which it had taken seven years of sacrifice and toil to build.

At the river are three flat boats, or scows. Here and there on the banks of the river stand pale-faced mothers cuddling their little ones, while husbands and fathers quietly, yet resolutely, roll the wagons on to the boats, then with long poles, push from the shore out upon the bosom of the mighty river. No farewells are uttered, no words spoken. Each man knows his duty, and performs it energetically; for they are not hirelings, these men of stout hearts and muscular arms. Nor is it a light task to guide those unwieldy scows through drifting ice, across that mile-wide river (John R. Young, *Memoirs of John R. Young, Utah Pioneer* [Salt Lake City: The Deseret News, 1920], 12–13).

Tamma Durfee Miner

At last a great many left, not knowing where they were going [except] to hunt a place in the wilderness among the savages and wild beasts over the desert beyond the Rocky Mountains where white men had never lived (*Voices From the Past: Diaries, Journals, and Autobiographies*, comp. Campus Education Week Program [Provo, Utah: Brigham Young University Press, 1980], 80).

Eliza Maria Partridge Smith Lyman

In February 1846, we left Nauvoo and crossed the Mississippi River with many of the Saints and started to go to the Rocky Mountains where we hoped to be free to serve the Lord as we thought best. While crossing the river the ice came down in large pieces and threatened to sink our boat, but at this time as well as many others, we were preserved by the power of God (Eliza Maria Partridge Smith Lyman, "Life and Journal of Eliza Maria Partridge (Smith) Lyman," typescript, in *Writings of Early Latter-day Saints and Their Contemporaries, A Database Collection*, comp. Milton V. Backman [Provo, Utah: BYU Religious Studies Center, 1996], 8).

Brigham Young

A number of brethren were crossing the river in a flatboat, when in their rear a man and two boys were in a skiff in a sinking condition, on account of being overloaded and the unskillfulness of the helmsman. They hailed to the flatboat, which soon turned, and rendered them assistance. As soon as they got the three on board the flatboat, a filthy wicked man squirted some tobacco juice into the eyes of one of the oxen attached to Thomas Grover's wagon, which immediately plunged into the river, dragging another ox with him, and as he was going overboard he tore off one of the sideboards which caused the water to flow into the flatboat, and as they approached the shore the boat sank to the bottom, before all the men could leap off. Several of the brethren were picked up in an exhausted condition. Two oxen were drowned and a few things floated away and were lost. The wagon was drawn out of the river with its contents damaged (*Manuscript History of Brigham Young 1846–1847*, ed. Elden J. Watson [Salt Lake City: Elden J. Watson, 1971], 30).

Brigham Young

The great severity of the weather and not being able to sell any of our property, [and] the difficulty of crossing the river during many days of running ice all combined to delay our departure, though for several days the bridge of ice across the Mississippi greatly facilitated the crossing and compensated, in part, for the delay caused by the running ice (*History of the Church*, 7:602).

FAREWELL TO NAUVOO

Brigham Young

(Encampment on Sugar Creek, Iowa—February 26, 1846)

The fact is worthy of remembrance that several thousand persons left their homes in midwinter and exposed themselves without shelter, except that afforded by a scanty supply of tents and wagon covers, to a cold which effectually made an ice bridge over the Mississippi river which at Nauvoo is more than a mile broad. We could have remained sheltered in our homes had it not been for the threats and hostile demonstrations of our enemies, who, notwithstanding their solemn agreements had thrown every obstacle in our way, not respecting either life, liberty or property, so much so, that our only means of avoiding a rupture was by starting in midwinter.

Our homes, gardens, orchards, farms, streets, bridges, mills, public halls, magnificent Temple, and other public improvements we leave as a monument of our patriotism, industry, economy, uprightness of purpose and integrity of heart; and as a living testimony of the falsehood and wickedness of those who charge us with disloyalty to the Constitution of our country, idleness and dishonesty (*History of the Church*, 7:603).

Col. Thomas L. Kane

(Months after the Saints left Nauvoo, Kane visited the desolate city and marveled at how quickly it had changed.)

I looked, and saw no one. I could hear no one move, though the quiet everywhere was such that I heard the flies buzz, and the water-ripples break against the shallow of the beach. I walked through solitary street. The town lay as in a dream, under some deadening spell of loneliness, from which I almost feared to wake it, for plainly it had not slept long. There was no grass growing up in the paved ways; rains had not entirely washed away the prints of dusty footsteps.

Yet, I went about unchecked as I went into empty workshops, ropewalks and smithies. The spinner's wheel was idle; the carpenter had gone from his workbench and shavings. . . . The blacksmith's shop

Thomas L. Kane
(Public Domain, Courtesy of BYU Online Collection)

was cold; but his coal heap and ladling pool, and crooked water horn were all there, as if he had just gone off for a holiday. No work-people anywhere looked to know my errand . . . no one called out to me from any opened window, or dog sprang forward to bark an alarm.

I could have supposed the people hidden in the houses, but the doors were unfastened, and when at last I timidly entered them, I found dead ashes white upon the hearths, and had to tread a tiptoe, as if walking down the aisle of a country church to avoid rousing irreverent echoes from the naked floors. On the outskirts of the town was the city graveyard; but there was no record of plague there, nor did it anywise differ much from other Protestant American cemeteries. Some of the mounds were not long sodded; some of the stones were newly set, their dates recent, and their black inscriptions glossy in the mason's hardly-dried lettering ink. Beyond the graveyard, out in the fields, I saw, in one spot hard by where the fruited boughs of a young orchard had been roughly torn down, the still smouldering remains of a barbecue fire, that had been constructed of rails from the fencing around it. It was the latest sign of life there. Fields upon fields of heavy-headed yellow grain lay rotting ungathered upon the ground. No one was there to take in their rich harvest.

As far as the eye could reach, they stretched away—they sleeping too in the hazy air of autumn (*Journal of Discourses*, 13:115–16).

Lewis Barney

On reaching the summit between the Mississippi and Des Moines Rivers the company made a halt for the purpose of taking a last and peering look at the Nauvoo Temple, the spire of which was then glittering in the bright shining sun. The last view of the temple was witnessed in the midst of sighs and lamentations, all faces in gloom and sorrow bathed in tears, at being forced from our homes and Temple that had cost so much toil and suffering to complete its erection (Lewis Barney, *Autobiography*, in *Writings of Early Latter-day Saints*, typescript, 28).

Luman Shurtliff

Our way led through a prairie country and as we passed along I carried a heavy heart. I had now been a member of this Church nearly ten years and had been compelled to move my family four times and start anew. I had lived in Nauvoo the longest by half of any other place since I belonged to the Church. This place was endeared to me for the sweet association I had enjoyed with the Prophet, patriarch and the apostles of the most high. Here I was leaving the body of my dear wife and child, never to behold those places again in the flesh. I turned my back to the west and took a last look at the Nauvoo Temple and its surroundings and bade them goodbye forever (Luman Andros Shurtliff, "Biographical Sketch of the Life of Luman Andros Shurtliff," typescript, *Writings of Early Latter-day Saints*, 66).

Wilford Woodruff

(Because of his missionary service, it took Wilford Woodruff three years to build his two-story brick home, yet he was only able to spend about sixty-four nights in this home before he had to bid it farewell.)

I left Nauvoo for the last time perhaps in this life. I looked upon the Temple and City of Nauvoo as I retired from it and felt to ask the Lord to preserve it as a monument of the sacrifice of His Saints

Wilford Woodruff's house in Nauvoo
(Public Domain, Courtesy of BYU Online Collection)

(*Wilford Woodruff Journal*, 3:49, May 22, 1846).

MAKING CAMP AT SUGAR CREEK

Since the Saints who first crossed the Mississippi River didn't know where they were going, they made camp along Sugar Creek where they waited for their leaders and further instruction. Sugar Creek was the first of dozens of Mormon settlements throughout Iowa, Nebraska, and Wyoming.

Lewis Barney

We camped on Sugar Creek, eight miles west of Nauvoo. There we stayed three weeks exposed to the most severe storms of snow and cold weather that occurred that winter. All most in sight of our own homes that were now in the hands of our persecutors. Our women and children trailing from one wagon to another knee deep in snow, many times nearly frozen to death (Lewis Barney, *Autobiography*, in *Writings of Early Latter-day Saints*, typescript, 27).

Joseph Fielding Smith

(February 1846)

The campground is by Sugar Creek where they have plenty of wood and water, a good place for such a purpose. On the night of the 13th, the snow fell and covered the ground and the 14th was a very rough day, snowing all the day long. I felt much for them. Some had tents and some wagon covers and some neither of them. This day is also rough, snowing all the day from the north, but it is not very cold, when I think that men, with some women and children, should be exposed (Joseph Fielding, *Diary*, as quoted in "Nauvoo Journal," *BYU Studies* [1979], 19:161).

William Pace

Our camp was made in the snow about 8 inches deep and was a rather uncomfortable introduction into camp life without tent or any shelter save it be a wagon cover made from common sheeting. Here we stayed [for] some time waiting the arrival of all those who could possibly supply themselves with teams (William Pace, *Autobiography*, in *Writings of Early Latter-day Saints*, 9).

ORGANIZING THE CAMP OF ISRAEL

Andrew Jenson

(February 15, 1846)

Apostles Brigham Young and Willard Richards, with their families, and Apostle George A. Smith crossed the Mississippi river for the West. They traveled nine miles, and camped on Sugar Creek, where President Young spent the following day organizing the camps of the Saints (*Church Chronology: A Record of Important Events Pertaining To The History Of The Church Of Jesus Christ Of Latter-Day Saints*, comp. Andrew Jenson, 2nd ed. [Salt Lake City: Deseret News, 1914], 29).

Brigham Young

At 5:00 in the morning the bugle is to be sounded as a signal for every man to arise and attend prayers before he leaves his wagon. Then cooking, eating, feeding teams, etc., until seven o'clock, at which time the camp is to move at the sound of the bugle. Each teamster to keep beside his team, with his loaded gun in his hands or in his wagon where he can get it in a moment. The extra men, each to walk opposite his wagon with his loaded gun on his shoulder, and no man is to be permitted to leave his wagon unless he obtains permission from his officer. In case of an attack from Indians or hostile appearances, the wagons to travel in double file. The order of encampment to be in a circle with the mouth of the wagon to the outside, and the horses and stock tied inside the circle. At 8:30 p.m. the bugle to be sounded again at which time all to have prayers in their wagons and to retire to rest by nine o'clock (William Clayton's journal, entry for April 18, 1847, *International Society Daughters of Utah Pioneers* [Salt Lake City: Utah Printing Co., 1994]; as cited in *Comprehensive History of the Church*, 3:165–66).

George Whitaker

We all felt very happy and joyful. Our camp ground took up some acres of ground. We could see grouped all around the camp fires men, women and children; some were singing, some were dancing, some were playing music, everyone seemed full of life and joy. We felt as though we had been released from bondage and were free, where there was no one to make us afraid ("Life of George Whitaker," 14).

～4～

JOURNEY TO WINTER QUARTERS

Once they crossed the Mississippi River, the Saints were no longer in the United States but had entered the Iowa Territory. Despite the relatively short distance between Nauvoo, situated on the Mississippi River, and Winter Quarters, on the Missouri River, this stretch across Iowa quickly became one of the most difficult parts of the trek. Constant snow and rain turned the trail into one long and frustrating mud hole, making progress unbearably slow. Sometimes the Saints would labor all day, only to gain a single mile. However, because of the violent mobs in Nauvoo, the Saints had no choice but to press forward through the bitter cold and downpouring rain of the northern wilderness.

A PLEA FOR PROTECTION

Brigham Young

(Before the Saints left Sugar Creek, the following correspondence was sent to the governor of the Iowa Territory.)

Honored Sir: The time is at hand in which several thousands of free citizens in this great Republic are to be driven from their peaceful homes and firesides, their property and farms and their dearest constitutional rights, to wander in the barren plains and sterile mountains of western wilds, and linger out their lives in wretched exile far beyond the pale of professed civilization; or else be exterminated upon their own lands by the people and authorities of the State of Illinois. As life is sweet, we have chosen banishment rather than death. But, sir, the terms of our banishment are so rigid that we have not sufficient time allotted us to make the necessary preparations to encounter the hardships and difficulties of these dreary and uninhabited regions. We have not time allowed us to dispose of our property, dwellings and farms; consequently, many of us will have to leave them unsold, without the means of procuring the necessary provisions, clothing, teams, etc., to sustain us but a short distance beyond the settlements; hence, our persecutors have placed us in very unpleasant circumstances.To stay is death by fire and sword, to go into banishment unprepared is death by starvation. But yet, under these heartrending [circumstances], several hundreds of us have started upon our dreary journey, and are now encamped in Lee county, Iowa, suffering much from the intensity of the cold. Some of us are already without food, and others have barely sufficient to last a few weeks; hundreds of others must shortly follow us in the same unhappy condition.

Therefore, We, the presiding authorities of The Church of Jesus Christ of Latter-day Saints, as a committee in behalf of several thousand suffering exiles, humbly ask your Excellency to shield and protect us in our constitutional rights, while we are passing through the Territory over which you have jurisdiction. And should any of the exiles be under the necessity of stopping in this Territory for a time, either in the settled or unsettled parts, for the purpose of raising crops, by renting farms, or upon the public lands, or to make the necessary preparations for their exile in any lawful way, we humbly petition your Excellency to use an influence and power in our behalf; and thus preserve thousands of American citizens, together with their wives and children, from intense suffering, starvation, and death. And your petitioners will ever pray (signed Brigham Young et al.) (Joseph Smith, *History of The Church of Jesus Christ of Latter-day Saints*, 7 vols., ed. B. H. Roberts [Salt Lake City: Deseret Book, 1964], 7:601).

MUSIC IN THE WILDERNESS

When the ancient prophet Isaiah saw the Latter-day Saint pioneer trek in vision, he sensed the importance music would hold for them, saying, "Therefore the redeemed of the Lord shall return, and *come with singing* unto Zion; and everlasting joy shall be upon their head" (Isaiah 51:11; emphasis added). Amidst their poverty and afflictions, the Saints managed to continue to have music in their camps as they traveled to Zion. In fact, they seemed to rely on it. Music revived the weary travelers, both rousing their spirits and setting the stage for dances that provided much needed warmth through movement.

Jane B. Taylor

Sabbath morning. March 1st, a meeting was called for the purpose of giving general instructions to the brethren regarding their journey. Bro. Kimball exhorted the Saints to be diligent in prayer to Almighty God all the day long. He called especially upon heads of families to attend daily to family worship, and to give heed to counsel, assuring them that if they did so God would bless them, and angels of God would go before them, and would be the breakers up of our way. He left the camp with family shortly after meeting was dismissed . . . There was a great amount of sympathy manifested by the people as we traveled through Iowa. Many visited our camps, and wherever the companies stopped our men were able to find employment. The splendid music made by the Nauvoo Brass Band quite surpassed anything that had been heard in that part and they were cordially invited to play at every settlement, and requested to give a number of concerts—this they did after consulting the Presidency, and for which they were generously recompensed. Thus we see that God did fulfill the predictions made that day by my father, and truly His angels went before us, and He was the breaker up of our way (Helen Mar Whitney, *A Woman's View: Helen Mar Whitney's Reminiscences of Early Church History*, ed. Jeni Broberg Holzapfel and Richard Neitzel Holzapfel [Provo, Utah: BYU Religious Studies Center, 1997], 341–42).

Helen Mar Kimball Whitney

Camp life in February [1846] was quite a novel experience . . . The band played every evening. . . . I there took my first lesson in the Danish waltz. The weather was so cold that it was impossible to keep warm without exercise (Whitney, *A Woman's View: Helen Mar Whitney's Reminiscences*, 339–40).

Col. Thomas L. Kane

Well as I knew the peculiar fondness of the "Mormons" for music, their orchestra in service on this occasion astonished me by its numbers and fine drill. The story was that an eloquent Mormon missionary had converted its members in a body at an English town, a stronghold of the sect, and that they took up their trumpets, trombones, drums, and hautboys together, and followed him to America. When the refugees from Nauvoo were hastening to part with their tableware, jewelry, and almost every other fragment of metal wealth they possessed that was not iron, they had never a thought of giving up the instruments of this favorite band. And when the battalion was enlisted some of the performers were to accompany it; but they all refused. Their fortunes went with the Camp of the Tabernacle. They had led the Farewell Service in the Nauvoo Temple. Their office now was to guide the monster choruses and Sunday hymns; and like the trumpets of silver, made of a whole piece, "for the calling of the assembly, and for the journeying of the camp," to knoll the people into church. Some of their wind instruments, indeed, were uncommonly full and pure-toned, and in that clear dry air could be heard to a great distance. It had the strangest effect in the world, to listen to their sweet music winding over the uninhabited country. Something in the style of a Moravian death-tune blown at daybreak, but altogether unique. It might be when you were hunting a ford over the Great Platte, the dreariest of all wild rivers, perplexed among the far-reaching sand bars, and curlew shallows of the shifting bed;—the wind rising would bring you the first faint thought of a melody; and as you listened, borne down upon the gust that swept past you a cloud of the dry sifted sands, you recognized it—perhaps a home-loved theme of Henry Proch or Mendelssohn. Mendelssohn-Bartholdy, away out there in the Indian Marshes! (Susa Young Gates, *The Life Story of Brigham Young* [New York: MacMillan Company, 1930], 242–43).

Brigham Young

For some weeks past I could not wake up at any time of the night but I heard the axe at work; and now my feelings are, dance all night if you desire to do so. . . . The world considers it very wicked for a Christian to hear music and to dance. Many preachers say that fiddling and music come from hell; but I say there is no fiddling, there is no music in hell. Music belongs to heaven, to cheer God, angels and men. If we could hear the music there is in heaven, it would overwhelm us mortals. Music and dancing are for the benefit of holy ones, and all of those who come here tonight who are not holy and righteous and do not worship God have no right to be here (Gates, *The Life Story of Brigham Young*, 81–82).

Col. Thomas L. Kane

(In speaking of a ball held prior to the departure of a number of the brethren joining the Mormon Battalion, Colonel Kane observed the festivities.)

A more merry dancing rout I have never seen, though the company went without refreshments and their ball room was of the most primitive kind (a "bowery," with Mother Earth for a floor). To the canto of debonair violins, the cheer of horns, the jingle of sleigh bells, and the jovial snoring of the tambourine, they did dance! None of your minuets or other mortuary processions of gentles in etiquette, tight shoes, and pinching gloves, but . . . French fours, Copenhagen jigs, Virginia reels, and the like forgotten figures executed with the spirit of people too happy to be slow, or bashful, or constrained. Light hearts, lithe figures, and light feet, had it their own way from an early hour till after the sun had dipped behind the sharp skyline of the Omaha hills. Silence was then called, and a well cultivated mezzo-soprano voice, belonging to a young lady with fair face and dark eyes, gave with quartette accompaniment a little song, the notes of which I have been unsuccessful in repeated efforts to obtain since—a version of the text, touching to all earthly wanderers: By the rivers of Babylon we sat down and wept. We wept when we remembered Zion (Wallace Stegner, *The Gathering of Zion*, *The Story of the Mormon Trail* [New York: McGraw-Hill, 1964], 81–82).

RICHARDSON'S POINT

Erastus Snow

The company, crossing the Des Moines river at Bonaparte succeeded in reaching a point of timber 20 miles above called Richardson's

Point. . . . Here they were compelled to remain until the 16th [they had left Sugar Creek on March 1st]. During this time it rained almost incessantly and the roads were rendered impassable, and our encampment being trod into a perfect Mortar bed by ourselves and stock was far from being a pleasant one (Erastus Snow, "A Journal or Sketch of the Life of Erastus Snow," in *Writings of Early Latter-day Saints and Their Contemporaries, A Database Collection,* comp. Milton V. Backman [Provo, Utah: BYU Religious Studies Center, 1996], 97–98).

Eliza R. Snow

My Good friend Sister Markham brought me a slice of beautiful white light bread and butter, that would have done honor to a more convenient bakery than an out-of-door fire in the wilderness (*Extracts from Eliza R. Snow's Private Journals,* March 4, 1846, typescript [n.d.], microfilm [LDS Family and Church History Department Archives], 6).

Horace K. Whitney

The weather continued showery till the 18th, when it cleared off pleasant. . . . The corpse of Bro. Edwin Little was brought into camp and interred today. He was taken sick here a few days ago, and conveyed into the country in order to have a skillful treatment and to be shielded from the inclemency of the weather; but notwithstanding all was done for his relief that human aid could afford, he died today while in the wagon on the way to the camp. His disease was the quick consumption. He appeared to be reconciled to his death, and died in the full faith of the gospel (Whitney, *A Woman's View: Helen Mar Whitney's Reminiscences,* 347–48).

Brigham Young

With some 200 teams then scattered over the wet, flat prairies for three miles, the rain increased, the roads soon became impassable. Teams were stalled in every direction, men doubling the trebling teams but to no effect. With many wagons left stalled in the mud in every direction, many families remained on the prairie over the night without fire, with their clothing wet and cold. . . . Spent one of the most uncomfortable nights that so many of the church ever suffered in. One night rained steady all night, very cold and a high wind. The ground filled with water, the mud knee deep around our tents, and little or no feed. One cow, through fatigue, laid down by the wagon on the prairie, chilled, and died A general scene of suffering for man and beast (Stegner, *The Gathering of Zion*, 61–62).

George Whitaker

It was now about the middle of March. We had only traveled about sixty miles. The weather was cold and very rainy. It rained almost every day. Brother Pratt and myself had to be out in the rain mostly all of the time. Fires had to be made, water had to be brought, cows had to be milked, the cooking had to be done, and the teams had to be seen to. The women could not get around much on account of the rain and mud, although they wanted to get out of their wagons and help around, but I told them I would get supper, which consisted in cooking a large kettle of mush. I was willing to do all I could for the comfort of the women and children. The other men did not feel so interested as they might have done. They kept in their wagons as much as they could to keep out of the rain. Brother Pratt was always around doing all he could and when he wanted help he always called on me. He was always in a good humor and would be singing and talking and encouraging us all he could. I always felt very cheerful, although it was very cold and disagreeable. We would go to bed in our wet clothes as there was no chance of drying them. It seemed as though the Lord was with us and His angels around about us to keep us from getting colds and from sickness, as we were all well and hearty ("Life of George Whitaker, A Utah Pioneer, as written by himself," typescript, 15–16, Utah State Historical Society, Salt Lake City).

George Whitaker

Having had so much rain, our wagons would sink down and there we would have to stay until we were helped out. Some of the wagons would turn out of the track and try to cross at another place, but would sink down and there were times when there were as many as half a dozen stuck at once. We would then double teams and get the company across, and then get those out that were stuck in the mud.

We traveled in this way all through the month of March and part of the month of April. The rains were almost incessant. We could only travel a few miles a day. Our teams were weak and we made very slow progress ("Life of George Whitaker," 16).

Jonathan Crosby

About the middle of the day we came to [a] slew, and in crossing it [the wagon] got stuck. [We] unhitched the team and commenced unloading the wagon, when on looking back, [we] saw a yoke of oxen coming all yoked up. So I hitched them on with my own and pulled out, turned them loose again, put in things we took out [of the wagon], and went on. We looked upon that as [a] favor and blessing from Father (Jonathan Crosby, *The Writings of Jonathan Crosby Autobiography: A Biographical Sketch of the Life of Jonathan Crosby written by himself,* typescript, 19, Utah State Historical Society, Salt Lake City).

CHARITON RIVER CROSSING

Orson Pratt

The heavy rains had rendered the prairies impassable; and our several camps were very much separated from each other. We were compelled to remain as we were for some two or three weeks, during which time our animals were fed upon the limbs and bark of trees, for the grass had not yet started, and we were a number of miles from any inhabited country, and therefore, it was very inconvenient to send for grain. The heavy rains and snows, together with frosty nights, rendered our situation very uncomfortable. Our camps were now more perfectly organized, and captains were appointed over hundreds, over fifties, and over tens, and over these all, a president and counselors, together with other necessary officers (Orson Pratt, "Extracted from the Private Journal of Orson Pratt," *Millennial Star* [December 15, 1849], 11:370).

George Whitaker

As Brother Pratt was always busy and wanted to be doing something, he would have all hands turn out and cut down some timber and build a log house or two. He said it might be a resting place for somebody. He was thinking about those who would follow, and as there was good land there, he thought perhaps some persons who could not get any further would stay there and cultivate the land and the houses would come in very useful, and which we found out afterwards was the case ("Life of George Whitaker," 16).

Zina D. Huntington Young

Zina D. Huntington Young

(Courtesy of the Church Archives, The Church of Jesus Christ of Latter-day Saints)

On the banks of the Chariton an incident occurred ever eventful in the life of woman. I had been told in the temple that I should acknowledge God even in a miracle in my deliverance in woman's hour of trouble, which hour had now come. We had traveled one morning about five miles, when I called for a halt in our march. There was but one person with me—Mother Lyman, the aunt of George A. Smith; and there on the bank of the Chariton I was delivered of a fine son. . . . Occasionally the wagon had to be stopped, that I might take breath. Thus I journeyed on. But I did not mind the hardship of my situation, for my life had been preserved, and my babe seemed so beautiful (Zina Huntington Young, as quoted in Edward W. Tullidge, *The Women of Mormondom* [New York: Tullidge and Drandall, 1877], 328).

Sarah DeArmon Pea Rich

We left the Chariton on our march towards the Rocky Mountains, leaving all the settlements behind, so from there on we had to pick our way without any road, only as we made it (Sarah DeArmon Pea Rich, *Autobiography*, in *Writings of Early Latter-day Saints*, 51).

Locust Creek Camp

William Clayton

Saturday, 4th. This morning all our clothing, beds and bed clothing were drenched and it has continued to rain all day. I have been sick again all day especially towards night. I was so distressed with pain it seemed as though I could not live. I went to bed and put a bag of hot salt on my chest which seemed to give me some ease but I suffered much through the night, and it continued to rain until after midnight. We put an extra cover on our sleeping wagon, which kept out the rain. We have only slept in the wagon three nights but have slept under a tent on the wet ground. Haw's company are now formed with us, making our 50 nearly complete. A number of the company feel unwell on account of the rain and wet (William Clayton, *William Clayton's Journal: A Daily Record of the Journey of the Original Company of Mormon Pioneers from Nauvoo, Illinois, to the Valley of the Great Salt Lake* [New York: Arno Press, 1973], 12; April 4, 1846).

Heber C. Kimball

I did not think there had ever been a body of people since the days of Enoch, placed under the same unpleasant circumstances that this people have been, where there was so little grumbling, and I was satisfied that the Lord was pleased with the majority of the Camp of Israel (*History of the Church*, 7:608).

William Clayton

This morning Ellen Kimball came to me and wishe[d] me much joy. She said (my wife) Diantha has a son. I told her I was afraid it was not so, but she said Brother [Stillman] Pond had received a

William Clayton
(Public Domain, Courtesy of BYU Online Collection)

letter. I went over to Pond's and he read that she had a fine fat boy on the 30th ult. [of last month], but she was very sick with ague and mumps. Truly I feel to rejoice at this intelligence but feel sorry to hear of her sickness. . . . In the evening . . . [several] persons retired to my tent to have a social christening. . . . We named him William Adriel Benoni Clayton. . . . This morning I composed a new song—"All is Well." I feel to thank my heavenly father for my boy and pray that he will spare and preserve his life and that of his mother and so order it so that we may soon meet again (Clayton, *William Clayton's Journal*, 19; April 15, 1846).

William Clayton

Come, come, ye Saints, no toil nor labor fear;
But with joy wend your way.
Though hard to you this journey may appear,
Grace shall be as your day.
'Tis better far for us to strive
Our useless cares from us to drive;
Do this, and joy your hearts will swell—
All is well! All is well!

Why should we mourn or think our lot is hard?
'Tis not so; all is right.
Why should we think to earn a great reward
If we now shun the fight?
Gird up your loins; fresh courage take.
Our God will never us forsake;
And soon we'll have this tale to tell—
All is well! All is well!

We'll find the place which God for us prepared,
Far away in the West,
Where none shall come to hurt or make afraid;
There the Saints will be blessed.
We'll make the air with music ring,
Shout praises to our God and King;
Above the rest these words we'll tell—
All is well! All is well!

And should we die before our journey's through,
Happy day! All is well!
We then are free from toil and sorrow, too;
With the just we shall dwell!
But if our lives are spared again
To see the Saints their rest obtain,
Oh, how we'll make this chorus swell—
All is well! All is well!
("Come, Come Ye Saints," *Hymns*, no. 30)

GARDEN GROVE

Parley P. Pratt

All things being harmonized and put in order, the camps moved on. Arriving at a place on a branch of Grand River we encamped for a while, having traveled much in the midst of great and continued rains, mud and mire. Here we enclosed and planted a public farm of many hundred acres and commenced settlement for the good of some who were to tarry and of those who should follow us from Nauvoo. We called the place *Garden Grove* (*Autobiography of Parley P. Pratt*, ed. Parley P. Pratt Jr. [Salt Lake City: Deseret Book, 1985], 307).

George Whitaker

It was a beautiful place for a settlement. The Twelve held a council and decided to stay there about two weeks and make a settlement for the benefit of those who were coming who could not get any further that season.

The whole camp was then reorganized. It was concluded that we would fence in a large field of about six hundred acres and plant it in corn and vegetables. Every man was put in his proper place to work. Some worked at cutting house logs, some at building houses, some at cutting timber for rails, some at splitting rails, some at plowing, some at planting corn and vegetables, while others commenced to put up the fence, and a certain number were sent out to herd and take care of the stock. Every man went to work with a will. There were no idlers amongst us. We were all full of life and spirit. . . . In about 14 or 15 days we had quite a little town built up. We had about 600 acres of land fenced in, plowed and planted ("Life of George Whitaker," 19).

Hosea Stout

When I came to the edge of the timber I found a number of men at work clearing and cutting house logs. It was a pleasantly situated place from the first appearance and presented a beautiful thick wood of tall shell bark hickory. The soil uncommonly rich and so loose now that our teams could but draw their loads through. Farther in the timber commenced white oak land and a harder soil where I found the camp. All seemed to be engaged at work. I had already been classed in a company of plough makers . . . I was well pleased with the good order and businesslike appearance which the camp had assumed so quick in the "Magic City of the Woods" as it seemed to be (Hosea Stout, *The Diary of Hosea Stout*, 3 vols. [Provo, Utah: Brigham Young University Harold B. Lee Library, 1941–43], 1:156).

Hancock Eagle

A mail carrier arrived here on Monday last from the Camp, and reported the pioneer party, or bend of the Column, as having crossed the tributaries of the Chariton, over 150 miles distant. . . . Thus far, everything has gone favorably with the exception of the breaking down of a few over laden wagons. The party is in good health and spirits—no dissentions exist; and the Grand Caravan moves slowly and steadily and peacefully. This progress has been materially retarded by the want of fodder for their live stock;—the grass not having fairly started, reduced them to the necessity of laboring for the farmers on the route to supply the deficiency.

They travel in detached companies, from five to ten miles apart and in point of order, resemble a military expedition ("The 'Camp of Israel,'" *Hancock Eagle*, April 10, 1846, as reprinted in the *Illinois Gazette*, May 6, 1846).

Eliza R. Snow

Our location is a beautiful, undulating grove, which apparently may become a garden of fruits in a short time, *but my spirit rests not here* ("Pioneer Diary of Eliza R. Snow," *Improvement Era*, April 26, 1943, 46:253).

Mount Pisgah

Parley P. Pratt

After assisting to fence this farm [Garden Grove] and build some log houses, I was dispatched ahead by the Presidency with a small company to try to find another location. Crossing this branch of

Grand River, I now steered through the vast and fertile prairies and groves without a track or anything but a compass to guide me—the country being entirely wild and without inhabitants. Our course was west, a little north. We crossed small streams daily, which, on account of deep beds and miry banks, as well as on account of their being swollen by the rains, we had to bridge. After journeying thus for several days, and while lying encamped on a small stream which we had bridged, I took my horse and rode ahead some three miles in search of one of the main forks of Grand River, which we had expected to find for some time. Riding about three or four miles through beautiful prairies, I came suddenly to some round and sloping hills, grassy and crowned with beautiful groves of timber; while alternate open groves and forests seemed blended in all the beauty and harmony of an English park. While beneath and beyond, on the west, rolled a main branch of Grand River, with its rich bottoms of alternate forest and prairie. As I approached this lovely scenery several deer and wolves, being startled at the sight of me, abandoned the place and bounded away till lost from my sight amid the groves.

Being pleased and excited at the varied beauty before me, I cried out, "this is *Mount Pisgah*." I returned to my camp, with the report of having found the long sought river, and we soon moved on and encamped under the shade of these beautiful groves. It was now late in May, and we halted here to await the arrival of the President and council. In a few days they arrived and formed a general encampment here, and finally formed a settlement, and surveyed and enclosed another farm of several thousand acres. This became a town and resting place for the Saints for years, and is now known on the map of Iowa as a village and post-office named *"Pisgah"* (*Autobiography of Parley P. Pratt*, 307–08).

Hancock Eagle

Hancock Eagle, on Friday last, notices the arrival there of Mr. S. Chamberlain, who left the most distant camp of the Mormons at Council Bluffs on the 26th, and on his route passed the whole line of Mormon emigrants. He says that the advance [Vanguard] company of the Mormons, with whom were the Twelve, had a train of one thousand wagons, and were encamped on the east bank of the Missouri River, in the neighborhood of the Council Bluffs. They were employed in the constriction of boats, for the purpose of crossing the river.

The second company had encamped temporarily at station No. 2, which has been christened Mount Pisgah. They mustered about three thousand strong, and were recruiting [resting and feeding] their cattle preparatory to a fresh start. A third company had halted for a similar purpose at Garden Grove, on the head waters of Grand river, where they have put in about 2000 acres of corn for the benefit of the people in general. Between Garden Grove and the Mississippi river, Mr. Chamberlain counted over one thousand wagons en route to join the main bodies in advance.

The whole number of teams attached to the Mormon expedition, is about three thousand seven hundred, and it is estimated that each team will average at least three persons and perhaps four. The whole number of souls now on the road may be set down in round numbers at twelve thousand. From two to three thousand have disappeared from Nauvoo in various directions. Many have left for Council Bluffs by the way of the Mississippi and Missouri rivers—others have dispersed to parts unknown; about eight hundred or less still remain in Illinois. This comprises the entire Mormon population that once flourished in Hancock [County]. In their palmy days they probably numbered between fifteen and sixteen thousand souls, most of whom are now scattered upon the prairies, bound for the Pacific slope of the American continent ("Late from the Mormon Camp," *Hancock Eagle*, as reprinted in the *Illinois Gazette, Sangamo Journal* [Springfield, IL], July 23, 1846).

George Whitaker

(The Indians were sometimes hostile, but they were often friendly and helpful to the Saints.)

The camps all moved down to the river to a place which was called the Point, where some Indian agents lived who kept supplies for the Pottowatamie Indians, living about 30 miles east from there. They were the first Indians I ever saw and they seemed to be quite intelligent. They wanted to know where we were going. We told them we were going beyond the Rocky Mountains, that we were driven out from the United States and were seeking a home far away in the west. They seemed to be very friendly and thought it very strange that we could not live with the white people. We showed them the Book of Mormon and told them it was a record of their forefathers. They seemed very pleased and wanted to know more about it ("Life of George Whitaker," 23).

Chief Pied Riche

(On one occasion, Chief Pied Riche of the Pottawattamies remarked on the common bond between the Native Americans, who were being forced off their lands, and the Saints.)

We must help one another and the Great Spirit will help us both. Because one suffers and does not deserve it is no reason he shall suffer always. We may live to see it right yet. If we do not, our children will (statement appears on a monument at Mount Pisgah, Iowa; as cited in Carol Cornwall Madsen, *Journey to Zion* [Salt Lake City: Deseret Book, 1997], 32–33).

George Whitaker

President Young called a meeting of the brethren and spoke to them in relation to our traveling and getting over the Rocky Mountain that season. We had then been on the road about three months and had only traveled about 225 miles. President Young wanted the brethren to fit out the Twelve and make up a company large enough to travel in safety through the Indian country, cross the Rocky Mountains and form a colony that season, but the people did not see it in this light. They did not seem willing for him to go ahead without them, and he was not willing to go with such a large company, so many women and children, as he knew they were not fitted out for a journey of a thousand miles. Quite a number of the Saints could not travel any further, and so it was decided that a settlement should be made there and that it should be a resting place for the Saints until they were able to continue their journey. Brother Charles C. Rich was appointed to preside.

President Young and the rest of the company started out for the Missouri River which was supposed to be about 75 miles. It was not past the middle of May. We traveled about ten or twelve miles a day through a beautiful and well watered country ("Life of George Whitaker," 20–21).

Nishnabonta River Crossing

David Moore

Traveled to little Nishnabotina ferry, had to pay 25 cents per wagon here, and swim our cattle. The settlers here (half apostates) told us that we had better not go on to Council Bluffs, for the saints were dying off very fast with the colery at that place. We did not give any heed to their stories, but traveled ahead and camped at highland grove (David More, *Journal*, June 1, 1849, typescript [LDS Church Archives, The Church of Jesus Christ of Latter-day Saints, Salt Lake City], n.p.).

Lorenzo Dow Young

Bro. Brigham and wife came over in their carriage and Bro. Kimball, Bro. Whitney and myself with our wives went a strawberring, and had a rich repast, being liberated from the bustle and cares of the camp. We returned sun about an hour high. Found a table spread with the luxuries of life such as biscuit and butter . . . plenty of strawberries sweetened, together with a little pickled pork ("Diary of Lorenzo Dow Young," *Utah Historical Quarterly* (1946) 14:141, Utah State Historical Society, Salt Lake City).

Mosquito Creek

Robert Gardner

Iowa was a new and thinly settled territory, and many of the Saints were poor and not having teams to travel with were counseled to stop where the land was not taken up and put in crops until they could help themselves. They had settled a place called Garden Grove and another called Mount Pisgah and other places. Some of our camp began to drop off at some of these places and others went on. We overtook what was known as Orson Hyde's camp near Mosquito Creek close by the Missouri River. Here I began to see some of the suffering of the Saints. The first night we come to Hyde's camp there come up a storm. [It] thundered and the wind blew very hard, also very hard rain next morning. It was painful to see the Saints with tents . . .

blown down and wagon covers tore off and everything wet with the rain. I went to one tent that was blown down and found a woman sitting on the ground and a very young baby both shaking with the ague and a number of larger children sitting around in their wet clothes, shaking with the same disease, no one able to help the rest. I asked where her husband was and she said he was called to go to Mexico to fight for Uncle Sam who had driven us to the wilderness [to] endure these hardships. I tried to gather up her tent but I could not; it was wore out. They had been driven from Nauvoo in the dead of winter, in the depth of poverty, traveling through deep snow. The men having to leave part of their family by the wayside, and travel on perhaps for a week, then leave that part and go back for the rest with the same team, until themselves nearly everything they had was worked out. And many died by the way from hardships (Robert Gardner, *Autobiography*, in *Writings of Early Latter-day Saints*, 13).

GRAND ENCAMPMENT

Col. Thomas L. Kane

(Summer 1846)

This landing, and the large flat or bottom on the east side of the river, were crowded with covered carts and wagons; and each one of the Council Bluff hills opposite, was crowned with its own great camp, gay with bright white canvas, and alive with busy stir of swarming occupants. In the clear blue morning air, the smoke streamed up from more than a thousand cooking fires. Countless roads and bypaths checkered all manner of geometric figures on the hillsides. Herd boys were dozing upon the slopes; sheep and horses, cows and oxen, were feeding around them, and other herds in the luxuriant meadow of the then swollen river. From a single point I counted four thousand head of cattle in view at one time. As I approached, it seemed to me the children there were to prove still more numerous (B. H. Roberts, *A Comprehensive History of The Church of Jesus Christ of Latter-day Saints*, 7 vols. [Salt Lake City: Deseret News Press, 1930], 3:132–33).

Council Bluffs

Brigham Young

It will be wisdom and necessary to establish schools for the education of children during the coming winter in this region, and we wish you to see that this is done. Done in Council, at Council Bluffs, this 21st day of July, 1846 (*Comprehensive History of the Church*, 3:149–50) ("History of Brigham Young," *Journal History*, July 21, 1846, 16:91).

Parley P. Pratt

In July we arrived at the Missouri River, near Council Bluffs. There we encamped for several weeks; opened a trade with upper Missouri, exchanging wagons, horses, harness and various articles of furniture, cash, etc., for provisions, oxen, cows, etc. In the meantime we built a ferry boat, fixed landings, made dugways, etc., and commenced ferrying over the Missouri. The ferry ran night and day for a long time, and still could not complete the crossing of the camps till late in the season (*Autobiography of Parley P. Pratt*, 308).

Battle of Nauvoo

Although almost all of the Saints had fled Nauvoo, a few had been forced to stay. These last few were mostly women and children who had not been able to leave, due to sickness, pregnancy, poverty, or the command to finish the temple. Still, the ruthless mobs would not tolerate their presence and violently drove them from the city.

Tamma Durfee Miner

In the spring the mob began to get together once a week and threatened to drive out what was left. The first of May we moved to town, sold our place for a yoke of cattle and a wagon, thinking to start on in two or three weeks, but the mob gathered every week right on the public square close by the house. The Mormons told them they would go as fast as they could get ready and get teams to go with. It was mostly women and children that were there, and they did not want any more of the men to leave for fear of what might happen. So we stayed, and my oldest brother and family was with us.

Till at last the mob gathered in full and reports came that they were camped outside the town about a mile, about 2,000 of them. One afternoon they started to come into town, cross-lots. There were only fifty of our men to go out to meet them, but they drove them back that night. In the morning at 2 o'clock it was moonlight, and the Mormons went and fired right in their camp. They fired guns and cannons on both sides till 2 o'clock in the afternoon. They killed three Mormon men. One man was named Anderson, and he and his son were both killed by one cannon ball. One man was killed with a cannon ball in a blacksmith shop. Three men were slightly wounded. My brother was wounded by a gun between the cords of his heel. There were only 50 of the Mormons against 2,000 of them in the mob. Ten of them had to be on guard, two on the top of the temple with spy glasses. They went into Law's cornfield and there they had their battle. They were seen to fill three wagons with the wounded and killed. And the next morning a woman stood in the second story of a house and saw the mob put seventy-six bodies in calico slips with a drawstring around the neck and feet before they left for home.

The Mormon women rolled the cannon balls up in their aprons, took them to our boys, and they would put them in the cannon and would shoot them back again when they were hot. It was a fearful time. I could have crossed the river, but I would not leave my husband. In about two days the men had to surrender, lay down their arms. I saw the mob all dressed in black ride two by two on horseback. It looked frightful. They said there was about 2,000 of them rode around the Temple in Nauvoo (*Voices From the Past: Diaries, Journals, and Auto-biographies,* comp. Campus Education Week Program [Provo, Utah: Brigham Young University Press, 1980], 80).

Thomas Bullock

If you was to see me and my family at this moment, you would say we had either been whitewashed or had risen out of our graves—we have not the least idea where our next meal is to come from. . . . Some subsist by selling their clothes for food. There have been many saints who were preparing as fast as they could to go to the West who have gone to the grave, many literally dying for want—two or three dying in a house (Thomas Bullock to Willard Richards, September 10, 1846, Brigham Young office files, LDS Family and Church History Department Archives, Salt Lake City).

Sarah Burbank

They had to hurry and get all the Saints through the temple, for the mob said they would burn it down. One night they got shavings and matches and were going to set fire to it when our guard came onto them with guns and saved it that time, but not long after that they burned it to the ground [October 9, 1848]. To see it burn to the ground, after working so long, was a great trial.

[The mob] went in people's homes, dragged out men, women, and children, and burned their houses and left them in the street. A young man went to fight with them with his gun to save his widow mother. While he was gone they went in and killed his sick mother. He had to hide until they got away, then he secured help and buried his mother. While doing this they stole his clothes and bedding and burned his house. That was the way they did to scores of people. They drove them across the river in the night in leaking boats. This happened in the beautiful city of Nauvoo.

In this flight we had to cross the Mississippi River in the night on a flat boat to save our lives. The people were camped by the river, some of which were without tents and many sick and some dying. We did not know where we were going but got word from Brigham Young that we were going west (*Voices From the Past*, 27).

RESCUE MISSION

The destitute Saints fled for their lives across the Mississippi River. Once the Saints were in Iowa, they formed impoverished, make-shift camps since they lacked the means to join the Saints at Winter Quarters. On September 14, 1846, Capt. Orval M. Allen led a group of eleven men back toward Nauvoo, to help the refugee Saints. Captain Allen's men reached the distressed Saints on the banks of the Mississippi River on October 6th (Madsen, *Journey to Zion*, 37–38).

Brigham Young

I have felt sensibly there was a good deal of suffering among the saints in Nauvoo, and there has been amongst us, but the Lord God who has fed us all the day long, has his care still over us and when the saints are chastened enough, it will cease. I have never believed the Lord would suffer a general massacre of this people by a mob. If ten thousand men were to come against us, and no other way was open for our deliverance, the earth would swallow them up (*Journal History of The Church of Jesus Christ of Latter-day Saints*, September 27, 1846 [LDS Church Archives, The Church of Jesus Christ of Latter-day Saints, Salt Lake City]).

Josiah B. Convers

(Dr. Convers was not a member of the Church but strongly disapproved of the illegal anti-Mormon actions taking place in Hancock County.)

In every part of the city [Montrose, Iowa] scenes of destitution, misery and woe met the eye. Families were hurrying away from their homes, without a shelter, without means of conveyance, without tents, money, or a day's provision, with as much of their household stuff as they could carry in their hands. Sick men and women were carried upon their beds, weary mothers with helpless babes dying in their arms hurried away—all fleeing they scarcely knew or cared whither, so it was from their enemies, whom they feared more than the waves of the Mississippi, or the heat and hunger and lingering life and dreaded death of the prairies in which they were about to be cast. The ferry boats were crowded, and the river bank was lined with anxious fugitives, sadly awaiting their turn to pass over and take up their solitary march to the wilderness (Josiah B. Convers, *A Brief History of the Hancock Mob in the Year 1846* [St. Louis: Cathcart and Prescott, 1846], 17–21).

Brigham Young

(While instructing teams to return to rescue the Saints stranded at Sugar Creek, Brigham Young reminded those with him of the covenant they had made in the Nauvoo Temple, wherein they had promised to do all they could to gather all who desired to come to Zion.)

Let the fire of the covenant which you made in the House of the Lord, burn in your hearts, like flame unquenchable till you, by yourselves or delegates . . . [can] rise up with his team and go straightway and bring a load of the poor from Nauvoo ... [for] this is a day of action and not of argument (*Journal History*, September 28, 1846).

Henry S. Buckwalter

(Henry Buckwalter describes a miracle the Saints at Sugar Creek experienced after the rescue teams arrived, the morning they were about to leave for Winter Quarters. Unexpectedly, an enormous flock of quail landed in their camp, providing much needed food for the starving and destitute Saints.)

[I] witnessed the approach and attack of the Mob in September 1846 upon us few remaining Saints that was too poor in this worlds goods to admit of emigrating along with our brethren and sisters when the first start was made but was forced to remain behind to be driven out by them which occurred about the 10th of the Month a few days after their attack upon us; Our Family along with all of the few remaining Saints fled across the mighty Mississippi River into the Territory of Iowa and camped upon its banks Leaving our Houses ... taking but very little with us only what very few things we could run and Carry with us. ... [I] can bare testimony to the goodness of our Heavenly Father and watch care [*sic*] over his Saints in sending large flocks of apparently tame quails into our Camps for our sustenance in our destitute Condition So tame were they that one could pick them right up alive And I assure you that they where greatly appreciated by one and all as what few effects of this worlds goods they where in possession of where mostly left behind in their bustle to get away from Nauvoo (Henry Shuler Buckwalter, *Biographical Sketch of Henry Shuler Buckwalter* [Provo, Utah: Brigham Young University Library, 1956], 3–4).

Thomas Bullock

On the 9th of October, several wagons with oxen having been sent by the Twelve to fetch the poor Saints away, were drawn out in a line on the river banks ready to start. But hark! What noise is that? See! The quails descend. They alight close by our little camp of twelve wagons, run past each wagon tongue, when they arise, fly around the camp three times, descend and again run the gauntlet past each wagon. See! The sick knock them down with sticks and the little children catch them alive with their hands! Some are cooked for breakfast.

While my family were seated on the wagon tongue and ground, having a washtub for a table . . . One descends upon our tea-board in the midst of our cups, while we were actually around the table eating our breakfast, which a little boy eight years old catches alive with his hands. They rise again, the flocks increase in number, seldom going seven rods from our camp, continually flying around the camp, sometimes under the wagons, sometimes over, and even into the wagons where the poor, sick Saints are lying in bed; thus having a direct manifestation from the Most High that although we are driven by men He has not forsaken us, but that His eyes are continually over us for good. At noon, having caught alive about fifty and killed about fifty more, the captain gave orders not to kill any more, as it was a direct manifestation and visitation from the Lord. In the afternoon hundreds were flying at a time. When our camp started at three p.m. there could not have been less than five hundred, some said there were fifteen hundred, flying around the camp.

Thus am I a witness to this visitation. Some Gentiles who were at the camp marveled greatly. Even passengers on a steamboat going down the river looked with astonishment (as cited in James A. Little, *From Kirtland to Salt Lake City* [Salt Lake City: James A. Little, 1890], 74–75).

Col. Thomas L. Kane

I have seen the site of Nauvoo before it was a city, and in nearly all the stages of progress, from the planning of the first colony to this time. I have been present at some of the most exciting scenes that have occurred within its limits, and I had a desire to see it as it now is, shorn of its glory and in other hands. The change has been very great. A few months ago, I rode through it . . . and there was the appearance of business and activity in every direction. The Temple, the greatest and chief ornament of Nauvoo, was then, on Sundays, crowded to suffocation. Everywhere . . . there were signs of enjoyment and contentment.

Now, how changed the scene. The streets are deserted—the houses are empty, the hum and bustle of the city has passed away—the faces and voices lately seen and heard are gone. All is changed, and a gloomy depression, as appalling as the low whispers of the death-chamber, is palpable to every sense (E. Cecil McGavin, *Nauvoo the Beautiful* [Salt Lake City: Stevens & Wallis, 1946], 254).

5

THE MORMON BATTALION

In April 1846, Mexican cavalry ambushed American troops. Congress responded by declaring war on Mexico. President James K. Polk appointed Col. Stephen W. Kearny as commander of the Army of the West and ordered Kearny to overtake the United States' new adversary and extend the country's borders to the Pacific Ocean. Although the Saints were currently being driven from the borders of the United States, Jesse Little, whom Brigham Young authorized to seek government aid in Washington, convinced President Polk to help the Mormons. Because of the need for soldiers, President Polk authorized the formation of a Mormon battalion. Under Kearny's command Capt. James Allen went to Iowa to recruit the services of the exiled Latter-day Saints. Although hesitant at first, 541 Latter-day Saint men eventually enlisted. The battalion began their march on July 21, 1846, from Council Bluffs. Traveling through Fort Leavenworth, Missouri; Santa Fe, New Mexico; and Tucson, Arizona, the battalion reached Los Angeles, California, on March 23, 1847, having traveled a total of 2,030 miles—the longest infantry march in U.S. military history. Because the United States had already overtaken California, the troops were not required to fight, and true to Brigham Young's prophecy, no one in the battalion died in battle. However, even after completing the longest march in United States military history, the battalion had not finished leaving its mark on the American legacy. As the discharged men worked their way back to the main body of Saints through northern California and Nevada, they helped discover gold, which launched the 1849 gold rush to California, bringing countless miners and desperately needed supplies through the Salt Lake Valley.

THE DECISION TO FORM
THE MORMON BATALLION

Brigham Young

*(On January 26, 1846, President Young wrote a letter to
Jesse C. Little, who presided over the New England Saints,
and instructed him to seek financial government aid to
help the Saints migrate west.)*

If our Government should offer facilities for emigrating to the western coast, embrace those facilities if possible. As a wise and faithful man,
take every honorable advantage of the times you can. Be thou a savior
and a deliverer of the people, and let virtue, integrity, and truth be your
motto—salvation and glory the prize for which you contend (as cited in
Daniel Tyler, *A Concise History of the Mormon Battalion in the Mexican
War, 1846–1847* [Glorieta, NM: Rio Grande Press, 1969], 111).

Col. Stephen W. Kearny

*(Colonel Kearny penned the following to Capt. James Allen in a
letter instructing him to enlist a battalion of Mormons to help
win the war against Mexico.)*

Sir—It is understood that there is a large body of "Mormons" who
are desirous of emigrating to California for the purpose of settling in
that country, and I have, therefore, to direct that you will proceed to
their camps, and endeavor to raise from among them five companies
of volunteers to join me in my expedition to that country; each company to consist of any number between 73 and 109. . . . The companies,
upon being organized thus, will be mustered by you into the service
of the United States, and from that day will commence to receive the
pay, rations and other allowances given to the other infantry volunteers,
each according to his rank. . . . You will give the "Mormon" distinctly to
understand that I wish to have them as volunteers for twelve months;
that they will be marched to California, receiving pay and allowances
during the above time, and at its expiration they will be discharged,
and allowed to retain, as their private property, the guns and accoutrements furnished to them at the post ("The Loyalty of Brigham Young,"
Improvement Era, May 1911, 14:606).

Capt. James Allen

(In a meeting with the Saints at Mount Pisgah, Captain Allen called on the Mormon pioneers to supply men to aid the war efforts.)

I have come among you, instructed by Colonel S. F. Kearney, of the U. S. Army, now commanding the Army of the West, to visit the Mormon camps, and to accept the service, for twelve months, of four or five companies of Mormon men who may be willing to serve their country for that period in our present war with Mexico; this force to unite with the Army of the West at Santa Fe, and be marched thence to California, where they will be discharged.

They will receive pay and rations, and other allowances, such as volunteers or regular soldiers receive, from the day they shall be mustered into the service, and will be entitled to all comforts and benefits of regular soldiers of the army, and when discharged, as contemplated, at California, they will be given, gratis, their arms and accoutrements, with which they will be fully equipped at Fort Leavenworth. This is offered to the Mormon people now.

This gives an opportunity of sending a portion of their young and intelligent men to the ultimate destination of their whole people, and entirely at the expense of the United States, and this advanced party can thus pave the way and look out the land for their brethren to come after them. Those of the Mormons who are desirous of serving their country, on the conditions here enumerated, are requested to meet me without delay at their principal camp at Council Bluffs, whither I am now going to consult with their principal men, and to receive and organize the force contemplated to be raised.

I will receive all healthy, able-bodied men of from eighteen to forty-five years of age (as cited in Daniel Tyler, *Concise History of the Mormon Battalion* [Waynesboro, VA: M & R Books, 1964], 114–15).

REACTION TO THE GOVERNMENT'S REQUEST

Hosea Stout

We were all very indignant at this requisition and only looked on it as a plot laid to bring trouble on us as a people. For in the event that we did not comply with the requisition we supposed they would now make a protest to denounce us as enemies to our country and if we did comply that they would then have 500 of our men in their power to be destroyed as they had done our leaders at Carthage. I confess that my feelings was uncommonly wrought up against them. This was the universal feeling at Pisgah and General Rich sent me word by Brother Wright to keep a sharp look out for him [Captain Allen] as he passed and see that he did not get any knowledge of the public arms which I had (*The Diary of Hosea Stout*, 2 vols. [Provo, Utah: Brigham Young University Harold B. Lee Library, 1941–43], 1:171–72).

Sarah DeArmon Pea Rich

A more cruel demand could not have been made upon us at this time of our affliction and poverty (Sarah DeArmon Pea Rich, *Autobiography*, in *Writings of Early Latter-day Saints and Their Contemporaries, A Database Collection*, comp. Milton V. Backman [Provo, Utah: BYU Religious Studies Center, 1996], 33–34).

Brigham Young

As hard as it is to write it—it must ever remain a truth on the page of history—that while the flower of Israel's camp were sustaining the wings of the American eagle, by their influence and arms in a foreign country [Mexico], their brothers, sisters, fathers, mothers, and children, were driven by mob violence from a free and independent State of the same national Republic (Brigham Young, "General Epistle from the Council of Twelve Apostles," *Millennial Star* [March 15, 1848], 10:82).

Hosea Stout

I confess that I was glad to learn of war against the United States and was in hopes that it might never end until they were entirely destroyed for they had driven us into the wilderness and was now laughing at our calamities (Juanita Brooks, ed., *On the Mormon Frontier: The Diary of Hosea Stout, 1844–1861*, 2 vols. [Salt Lake City: University of Utah Press, 1964], 1:163–64).

A CALL TO COMPLY

Brigham Young realized that the request to form the battalion was extended because of Jesse Little's efforts in Washington. He saw the advantages to such a request and encouraged the Saints to comply. Companies were organized, captains appointed, and within days their march began. Before they left, however, Brigham Young promised them that if they were faithful, the Lord would spare their lives.

Brigham Young

Now, suppose we refuse this privilege what will we do? If you won't go, I will go and leave you. We told you sometime ago we would fit you out to go, and now we are ready to fit you out with Captain Allen as the agent of the U.S. to help us. The President of the United States has now stretched out his hand to help us and I thank God and him too (B. H. Roberts, *A Comprehensive History of The Church of Jesus Christ of Latter-day Saints*, 7 vols. [Salt Lake City: Deseret News Press, 1930], 3:83).

Drusilla Hendricks

(Drusilla's son William wanted to enlist in the battalion but Drusilla was hesitant to allow him to go since her husband had been crippled at Haun's Mill and William had become her mainstay.)

I got ready to get breakfast, and when I stepped up on the wagon tongue to get my flour I was asked by the same spirit that had spoken to me before, If I did not want the greatest glory and I answered with my natural voice, Yes, I did. Then how can you get it without making the greatest sacrifice, said the voice. I answered Lord, what lack I yet. Let your son go in the Battalion, said the voice. I said it is too late, they are to be marched off this morning. That spirit then left me with the heart ache. I got breakfast and called the girls and their Father to come for the tent for prayers. William came wet with dew from the grass and we sat down around the board and my husband commenced asking the blessing on

James and Drusilla Hendricks

(Courtesy of the Church Archives, The Church of Jesus Christ of Latter-day Saints)

our food, when Thomas Williams came shouting at the top of his voice, saying "Turn out men, Turn out, for we do not wish to press you but we lack some men yet in the Battalion." William raised his eyes and looked me in the face. I knew then that he would go . . . I went to milk the cows. . . . I thought the cows would be shelter for me and I knelt down and told the Lord if he wanted my child to take him, only spare his life and let him be restored to me and to the bosom of the church. I felt it was all I could do. Then the voice that talked with me in the morning answered me saying, It shall be done unto you as it was unto Abraham when he offered Isaac on the altar. I don't know whether I milked or not for I felt the Lord had spoken to me ("Historical Sketch of James Hendricks and Drusilla Dorris Hendricks," typescript copy [LDS Church Archives, The Church of Jesus Christ of Latter-day Saints, Salt Lake City], 26–27).

Brigham Young

[I] instructed the Captains [of the battalion] to be fathers to their companies, and manage their affairs by the power and influence of their priesthood, then they would have power to preserve their lives and the lives of their companies and escape difficulties. I told them I would not be afraid to pledge my right hand that every man will return alive, if they will perform their duties faithfully, without murmuring and go in the name of the Lord, be humble and pray every morning and evening in their tents. A private soldier is as honorable as an officer, if he behaves as well. No one is distinguished as being better flesh and blood than another. Honor the calling of every man in his place. All the officers, but three, have been in the Temple. Let no man be without his under garment and always wear a coat or vest; keep neat and clean, teach chastity, gentility and civility; swearing must not be admitted, insult no man; have no contentious conversation with the Missourians, Mexicans or any class of people; do not preach, only where people desire to hear, and then by wise men, impose not your principles on any people; take your bibles and books of Mormon (*Journal History of The Church of Jesus Christ of Latter-day Saints*, July 18, 1846 [LDS Church Archives, The Church of Jesus Christ of Latter-day Saints, Salt Lake City]).

James S. Brown

Just before our last farewell to friends at the Missouri River, and preparatory to taking up our line of march, we were formed into a hollow square, and President Brigham Young, with Heber C. Kimball and others of the Apostles, came to our camp, rode into the square, and gave us parting blessings and instructions. The words of President Young, as they fastened themselves upon my memory, were in substance as follows: "Now, brethren, you are going as soldiers at your country's call. You will travel in a foreign land, in an enemy's country; and if you will live your religion, obey your officers, attend to your prayers, and as you travel in an enemy's land, hold sacred the property of the people, never taking anything that does not belong to you only in case of starvation; though you may be traveling in an enemy's country, do not disturb fruit orchards or chicken coops or beehives, do not take anything but what you pay for—although it is customary for soldiers to plunder their enemies in time of war, it is wrong—always spare life when possible; if you obey this counsel, attending to your prayers to the Lord, I promise you in the name of the Lord God of Israel that not one soul of you shall fall by the hands of the enemy" (James Brown, *Life of a Pioneer Being the Autobiography of James S. Brown* [Salt Lake City: Geo. Q. Cannon & Sons Co., 1900], 28).

Beginning the March

From Council Bluffs, the Mormon Battalion, which consisted of 541 soldiers, 35 women, and 42 children under the direction of Lt. Col. James Allen, journeyed to Fort Leavenworth, Missouri, where they were outfitted with guns, supplies, and money for clothing. Parley P. Pratt collected some of this money and brought it back to Council Bluffs to help support battalion members' families. At Fort Leavenworth the weather was really hot and many in the battalion became sick, including Colonel Allen. He died a few weeks after the battalion began their march to Santa Fe. First Lt. A. J. Smith took Colonel Allen's position and quickened their pace to Mexican territory. With this persistent push, many of the soldiers increasingly became more ill. The battalion's doctor, George B. Sanderson, unsuccessfully tried to cure all their sufferings with arsenic and calomel: three detachments of the sick and ill were sent to Pueblo, Colorado, by the time the battalion reached California. In Santa Fe, Lt. Col. Philip St. George Cooke replaced Lieutenant Smith as commanding officer and followed orders to have a new wagon trail blazed to California. Lack of water and sandy trails plagued the battalion and impeded their progress. When they arrived at Tucson, they encountered a herd of abandoned wild bulls. The bulls stampeded and wounded three of the soldiers. The Battle of the Bulls was the only time the Mormon Battalion had to fight. On January 29, 1847, the weary battalion finally reached Mission San Diego and ended their 2,030 mile march.

Edward H. Anderson

The Mormon Battalion rendered financial aid to the pioneers. . . . Upon enlisting each soldier received from the government, besides his accoutrements, which he was to retain after his term of service had expired, forty-two dollars in cash, as clothing money for the year. The clothing was not purchased, and a good portion of the money was sent back to Council Bluffs for the use of the people there; and thus doubtless assisted in completing the equipment of the pioneers who entered Salt Lake Valley July 24, 1847. Under the command of Col. Philip St. George Cooke the Battalion made an infantry march of 2,000 miles from the Missouri river to the Pacific coast. On account of the sacrifice which they had made in not purchasing appropriate clothing and shoes for the long, strenuous march, they endured excruciating hardships (Edward H. Anderson, "Mormon Battalion and its Monument," *Improvement Era*, January 1920, 23:239).

Daniel Tyler

(As the battalion traveled through Missouri on its way to Fort Leavenworth, battalion members talked to several Missourians who regretted the atrocities committed against the Saints during the 1830s.)

Passing on from the Nodaway River [in Missouri], we found the country poor and broken, the road bad and the inhabitants very miserable. A great many of the settlers in this part of the country, were old mobocrats, as several of them admitted. They said that they had been misled by false rumors, and very much regretted having persecuted the

Saints. They would have been glad to take their old "Mormon" neighbors back. They had not prospered since the Saints were banished from the State, and the men they then hired to labor for them accomplished only about one half the amount of work in a day that the "Mormons" did (Tyler, *A Concise History of the Mormon Battalion in the Mexican War, 1846–1847*, 132–33).

Daniel Tyler

(He described some of the hardships faced by the Mormon Battalion as they marched—including hunger and starvation.)

Our course now lay down the Rio Del Norte. We found the roads extremely sandy in many places, and the men while carrying blankets, knapsacks, cartridge boxes (each containing thirty-six rounds of ammunition), and muskets on their backs, and living on short rations, had to pull at long ropes to aid the teams. The deep sand alone, without any load, was enough to wear out both man and beast. Upon one occasion, several wild geese were killed by some of the hunters, which proved a treat to them and their immediate comrades or messmates. Once in awhile, also, as we passed the Mexican villages, those who had money or anything to trade found opportunities for purchasing Spanish grapes. . . . The men were ready to eat anything that would furnish them any nourishment, the rations issued to them being insufficient to satisfy the cravings of hunger. When we left Santa Fe we supposed the few fat cattle taken along were intended for beef, but we were soon undeceived upon that point. When one of them was slaughtered the second day out, the Colonel gave positive orders that no more of them should be killed, as they must be used as work animals, and only such killed for beef as were unable from sheer weakness and exhaustion to work. From that time on it was the custom to kill the work animals as they gave out and issue the carcasses as rations. Nor was any portion of the animal thrown away that could possibly be utilized for food. Even to the hides, tripe and entrails, all were eagerly devoured, and that, too, in many cases without water to wash them in. The marrow bones were considered a luxury, and were issued in turns to the various messes (Tyler, *A Concise History of the Mormon Battalion in the Mexican War, 1846–1847*, 180–81).

Levi W. Hancock

(Levi Hancock wrote the following song to illustrate the battalion's desert route.)

While here, beneath a sultry sky,
Our famished mules and cattle die;
Scarce aught but skin and bones remain
To feed poor soldiers on the plain.

CHORUS.
How hard, to starve and wear us out,
Upon this sandy, desert route.

We sometimes now for lack of bread,
Are less than quarter rations fed,
And soon expect, for all of meat,
Naught less than broke-down mules, to eat.

Now, half-starved oxen, over-drilled,
Too weak to draw, for beef are killed;
And gnawing hunger prompting men
To eat small entrails and the skin.

Sometimes we quarter for the day,
While men are sent ten miles away
On our back track, to place in store
An ox, given out the day before.

And when an ox is like to die,
The whole camp halts, and we lay by:
The greedy wolves and buzzards stay,
Expecting rations for the day.

Our hardships reach their rough extremes,
When valiant men are roped with teams,
Hour after hour, and day by day,
To wear our strength and lives away.

The teams can hardly drag their loads
Along the hilly, sandy roads,
While trav'ling near the Rio Grande,
O'er hills and dales of heated sand.

We see some twenty men, or more,
With empty stomachs, and foot-sore,
Bound to one wagon, plodding on
Thro' sand, beneath a burning sun.

A Doctor which the Government
Has furnished, proves a punishment!
At his rude call of "Jim Along Joe,"
The sick and halt, to him must go.

Both night and morn, this call is heard;
Our indignation then is stirr'd,
And we sincerely wish in hell,
His arsenic and calomel.

To take it, if we're not inclined,
We're threatened, "You'll be left behind:"
When bored with threats profanely rough,
We swallow down the poisonous stuff.

Some stand the journey well, and some
Are by the hardships overcome;
And thus the "Mormons" are worn out
Upon this long and weary route.
(Tyler, *A Concise History of the Mormon Battalion in
the Mexican War, 1846–1847*, 182–83)

James A. Scott

March! march! march! is the daily task. Day break brings the reveille, sick or well must go either to roll call or to the Doctor; next boys get your breakfast and strike your tents with all possible speed; then left, left, all day over the sand through dust over hills and across valleys, sometimes twelve, fifteen and eighteen miles. Halt, stack arms, pitch tents, run over all creation gathering buffalo chips or a little brush and getting water, draw rations, cook supper, eat, then roll call, and by the time the evening chores are finished it is dark. Attend to evening duties, go to bed and sleep on the rough, cold ground with only one blanket and a thin tent to shelter from the cold. Say, sympathetic reader, is not the condition of the Mormon soldier hard? (*Journal History*, September 26, 1846.)

David R. Crockett
(Friday, December 11)

During the morning, the Mormon Battalion experienced the only skirmish of its long march—"The Battle of the Bulls." As the battalion marched down to the San Pedro river bottom, a few wild bulls charged toward the ranks. One bull trapped Sgt. Albert Smith with his horns. Sgt. Smith's ribs were severely bruised, but the horns passed harmlessly on both sides of his body. After these bulls were killed, as the men were watering their mules at the river, many more wild bulls charged.

Great confusion soon reigned as guns were fired and soldiers ran for the protection of wagons or trees. Levi Fifield was pursued by a bull, but could not find safety. His only choice was to throw himself flat on the ground. The bull jumped over Pvt. Fifield and left him unharmed.

When the dust cleared, Battalion members counted about 20 bulls lying on the battle field. Cpl. Thomas Dunn predicted, "This is a day that will long be remembered by some and perhaps most of the Battalion" (David R. Crockett, comp., "Battalion Fights 'Battle of the Bulls," *LDS Church News*, December 14, 1996.)

Eliza R. Snow
(Sister Snow summarized the trek with the following poem.)

> When "Mormon" trains were journeying thro'
> To Winter Quarters, from Nauvoo,
> Five hundred men were called to go
> To settle claims with Mexico—
> To fight for that same Government
> From which, as fugitives we went.
> What were their families to do—
> Their children, wives, and mothers too,
> When fathers, husbands, sons were gone?
> Mothers drove teams, and camps moved on.

And on the brave Battalion went,
With Colonel Allen who was sent
As officer of Government.
The noble Colonel Allen knew
His "Mormon boys" were brave and true,
And he was proud of his command,
As he led forth his "Mormon Band."
He sickened, died, and they were left
Of a loved leader, soon bereft!
And his successors proved to be
The embodiment of cruelty,
Lieutenant Smith the tyrant, led
The Cohort on, in Allen's stead,
To Santa Fe, where Colonel Cooke,
The charge of the Battalion, took.

'Twas well the vision of the way,
Was closed before them on the day
They started out from Santa Fe.
'Tis said no infantry till then,
E'er suffered equal to those men.
Their beeves were famished and their store
Was nigh exhausted long before
They neared the great Pacific shore.
Teams e'en fell dead upon the road,
While soldiers helped to draw the load.
'Twas cruel, stern necessity
That prompted such severity;
For General Kearney in command
Of army in the western land,
Expressly ordered Colonel Cooke,
The man who failure could not brook,
To open up a wagon-road
Where wheels, till then, had never trod;
And Colonel Cooke was in command
Across that desert waste and sand:
He, with a staunch and iron will,
The general's orders to fulfill,
Must every nerve and sinew strain
The expedition's points to gain.
Tho' stern, and e'en at times morose,
Strict sense of justice marked his course.

He, as his predecessors, knew
The "Mormon" men were firm and true.

They found road-making worse by far
Than all the horrors of the war:
Tried by the way—when they got thro'
They'd very little more to do:
The opposing party, panic struck,
Dare not compete with "Mormon" pluck,
And off in all direction fled—
No charge was fired—no blood was shed.

Our God who rules in worlds of light,
Controls by wisdom and by might.

If need, His purpose to fulfill,
He moves the nations at His will—
The destinies of men o'errules,
And uses whom He will as tools.
The wise can see and understand,
While fools ignore His guiding hand.

Ere the Battalion started out
Upon that most important route,
'Twas thus predicted by the tongue
Of the Apostle, Brigham Young,
"If to your God and country true,
You'll have no fighting there to do."

Was General Kearney satisfied?
Yes, more—for he with martial pride
Said, "O'er the Alps Napoleon went,
But *these men cross'd a continent."*

And thus, with God Almighty's aid
The conquest and the road were made,
By which a threatning storm was staved,
And lo! the Saints of God were saved.
(As cited in Tyler, *A Concise History of the Mormon
Battalion in the Mexican War, 1846–1847,* 107–8)

Col. Phillip St. George Cooke

(Colonel Cooke, the battalion's commanding officer, praised the Saints for their feats.)

History may be searched in vain for an equal march of infantry. Half of it has been through a wilderness, where nothing but savages and wild beasts are found, or deserts where, for want of water, there is no living creature. There, with almost hopeless labor, we have dug deep wells, which the future traveler will enjoy. Without a guide who had traversed them we have ventured into trackless tablelands where water was not found for several marches. With crowbar and pick and axe in hand, we have worked our way over mountains, which seemed to defy aught save the wild goat, and hewed a pass through a chasm of living rock more narrow than our wagons. . . . Thus, marching half naked and half fed, and living upon wild animals, we have discovered and made a road of great value to our country (*A Comprehensive History of the Church*, 3:120).

DISCOVERING GOLD

When the battalion completed their one-year enlistment, most of them started for northern California with the intention of traveling east to the Salt Lake Valley, while others reenlisted for another six months. In the Tahoe Valley, Capt. James Brown intercepted those returning to Salt Lake and delivered a message from Brigham Young which instructed those without families to remain in California and work. John Sutter employed several of these men to construct a sawmill. While building the sawmill, gold dust was discovered. This discovery led to the 1849 California gold rush.

Gordon B. Hinckley

It was the men of the Battalion whose efforts for the most part built the mill, where gold was found, and they were the men who recorded the find for future historians and greatly extended the original discovery for thousands of anxious men who followed. . . .

On August 26 [the discharged battalion] camped near the fort of John Sutter, the enterprising Swiss immigrant who had established

New Helvetia with headquarters at the present site of Sacramento. On learning that Brigham Young and the pioneers had reached the Salt Lake Valley and that supplies were scarce there, some of them decided to remain in California until the following spring, thereby adding to their own resources and at the same time assisting in building up the country.

They indicated to Sutter and his foreman-partner, Marshall, that they had among their number skilled millwrights, carpenters, and wheel-wrights. This was apparently good news to the Californians, for Sutter and Marshall concluded to go ahead with the flour mill and the sawmill they had wanted to build.

The sawmill site was some forty-five miles up the South Fork of the American River. Marshall, six men of the Mormon Battalion, three other white men, and some Indians began work in September. The river was dammed with brush to turn the water into a dry channel which was cleared for a race. The mill was built over this, and then a tailrace was fashioned to return the water to the main stream.

Between the 15th and 20th of January water was turned in the race to test the mill, but the operation was not satisfactory and further work was undertaken.

On January 24, [Henry Bigler wrote] "while sauntering along the tailrace inspecting the work, Mr. Marshall noticed yellow particles mingled with the excavated earth. He told the others what he had found" (Gordon B. Hinckley, "Gold or God's Kingdom," *Improvement Era*, March 1948, 51:149–50).

Henry W. Bigler

(Henry Bigler was one of the discharged battalion members and was responsible for recording when gold was discovered in California.)

Monday 24 [January]: This day some kind of metal was found in the tail race that looks like *gold*.

January 30: Clear, and has been all the last week. Our metal has been tried and proves to be *gold*. It is thought to be rich. We have picked up more than a hundred dollars worth this week (facsimile from Henry W. Bigler's Journal; as cited in *Comprehensive History of the Church*, 3:362).

Brigham Young

(Brigham Young noted how gold fever afflicted some of the Saints in the Salt Lake Valley.)

Some few have caught the gold fever. I counseled such, and all the Saints to remain in these valleys of the mountains and make improvements, build comfortable houses and raise grain against the days of famine and pestilence with which the earth would be visited (*Journal History*, December 7, 1848).

James Brown

(During the winter of 1848–49, many of the Saints desired to mine gold in California because the lack of food and cold weather made living in Utah hard and uncomfortable. Brigham Young promised the Saints that if they remained in Utah, they would be better off than those who would go to California.)

The winter of 1848–49 was quite cold. Many people had their feet badly frozen. For one, the writer suffered so severely from this cause that he lost every nail from the toes of both feet. In February and March there began to be some uneasiness over the prospects, and as the days grew warmer the gold fever attacked many so that they prepared to go to California. Some said they would go only to have a place for the rest of us; for they thought Brigham Young too smart a man to try to establish a civilized colony in such a "God-forsaken country," as they called the valley. They further said that California was the natural country for the Saints; some had brought choice fruit pips and seed, but said they would not waste them by planting in a country like the Great Salt Lake Valley; others stated that they would not build a house in the valley, but would remain in their wagons, for certainly our leaders knew better than to attempt to make a stand in such a dry worthless locality, and would be going on to California, Oregon or Vancouver's Island; still others said they would wait awhile before planting choice fruits, as it would not be long before they would return to Jackson County, Missouri. . . .

It was at this time of gloom that President Young stood before the whole people, and said, in substance, that some people had misgivings, and some were murmuring, and had not faith to go to work and make their families comfortable; they had got the gold fever and were going to

California. Said he: "Some have asked me about going. I have told them that God has appointed this place for the gathering of His Saints, and you will do better right here than you will by going to the gold mines. Some have thought they would go there and get fitted out and come back, but I told them to stop here and get fitted out. Those who stop here and are faithful to God and His people will make more money and get richer than you that run after the god of this world; and I promise you in the name of the Lord that many of you that go, thinking you will get rich and come back, will wish you had never gone away from here, and will long to come back but will not be able to do so. Some of you will come back, but your friends who remain here will have to help you; and the rest of you who are spared to return will not make as much money as your brethren do who stay here and help build up the Church and Kingdom of God; they will prosper and be able to buy you twice over. Here is the place God has appointed for his people. We have been kicked out of the frying pan into the fire, out of the fire into the middle of the floor, and here we are and here we will stay. God has shown me that this is the spot to locate his people, and here is where they will prosper; He will temper the elements for the good of His Saints; He will rebuke the frost and the sterility of the soil, and the land shall become fruitful. Brethren, go to, now, and plant out your fruit seeds." Stretching his arms to the east and to the west, with his hands spread out, he said: "For in these elements are not only all the cereals common to this latitude, but the apple, peach and plum; yea, and the more delicate fruits, the strawberry and raspberry; and we will raise the grapes here and manufacture wine; and as the Saints gather here and get strong enough to possess the land, God will temper the climate, and we shall build a city and a temple to the Most High God in this place. We will extend our settlements to the east and west, to the north and to the south, and we will build towns and cities by the hundreds, and thousands of the Saints will gather in from the nations of the earth. This will become the great highway of the nations. Kings and emperors and the noble and wise of the earth will visit us here, while the wicked and ungodly will envy us our comfortable homes and possessions. Take courage, brethren. I can stand in my door and can see where there is untold millions of the rich treasures of the earth—gold and silver. But the time has not come for the Saints to dig gold. It is our duty first to develop the agricultural resources of the country, for there is no country on the earth that is more productive than this. We have the finest climate, the best water, and the purest air that can be found on earth; there is no healthier climate anywhere. As for gold and silver, and the rich minerals of the earth, there is no other country that equals this; but let them alone; let others seek them, and we will cultivate the soil; for if the mines are opened first, we are a thousand miles from any base of supplies, and the people would rush in here in such great numbers that they would breed a famine; and gold would not do us or them any good if there were no provisions in the land. People would starve to death with barrels of gold; they would be willing to give a barrel of gold for a barrel of flour rather than starve to death. Then, brethren, plow your land and sow wheat, plant your potatoes; let the mines alone until the time comes for you to hunt gold, though I do not think this people ever will become a mining people. It is our duty to preach the Gospel, gather Israel, pay our tithing, and build temples. The worst fear that I have about this people is that they will get rich in this country, forget God and His people, wax fat, and kick themselves out of the Church and go to hell. This people will stand mobbing, robbing, poverty, and all manner of persecution, and be true. But my greater fear for them is that they cannot stand wealth; and yet they have to be tried with riches, for they will become the richest people on this earth (Brown, *Life of a Pioneer*, 122–23).

Heber C. Kimball

(Brother Kimball prophesied that the poor and starving Saints in the Salt Lake Valley would be blessed. Little did he know that the Mormon Battalion's discovery of gold in California would prove to be the Saints' salvation in the Salt Lake Valley.)

I have predicted things I did not foresee, and did not believe anybody else did, but I have said it, and it came to pass even more abundantly than I predicted; and that was with regard to the future situation of the people who first came into this valley. Nearly every man was dressed in skins, and we were all poor, destitute, and distressed, yet we all felt well. I said, "it will be but a little while, brethren, before you shall have food and raiment in abundance, and shall buy it cheaper than can be bought in the cities of the United States." I did not know there were any Gentiles coming here, I never thought of such a thing; but after I spoke it I thought I must be mistaken this time. Brother Rich remarked at the time, "I do not believe a word of it." And neither did I; but, to the astonishment and joy of the Saints, it came to pass just as I had spoken it, only more abundantly. The Lord led me right but I did not know it (*Journal of Discourses*, 26 vols. [London: Latter-day Saints' Book Depot, 1854–86], 3:111–12).

Gordon B. Hinckley

Thinking to get rich with the sale of goods in California, eastern merchants had loaded great wagon trains with clothing, tools, and other items for which there would be demand at the gold diggings. But on reaching Salt Lake City they learned that competitors had beaten them by shipping around the Cape.

Their only interest then was to unload what they had for what price they could get, and go on to California as quickly as possible. Auctions were held from their wagons on the streets of Salt Lake City. Cloth and clothing sold for less than they could be bought for in New York. Badly needed tools could be had for less than in St. Louis. Fine teams, jaded from the long journey, were eagerly traded for the fatter but less valuable stock of the Mormons. Good, heavy wagons, in great demand in the mountain colony, were traded for lighter vehicles with which the gold seekers could make better time (Gordon B. Hinckley, *What of the Mormons?* [Salt Lake City: Deseret Book Co., 1947], 185).

Brigham Young

(In September 1849, President Young described the condition of the Saints returning from the gold rush.)

That there is plenty of gold in Western California is beyond doubt, but the valley of the Sacramento is an unhealthy place, and the Saints can be better employed in raising grain and building houses in this vicinity, than digging for gold in the Sacramento, unless they are counseled to do so.

The true use of gold is for paving streets, covering houses, making culinary dishes; and when the Saints shall have preached the Gospel, raised grain, and built up cities enough, the Lord will open up the way for a supply of gold to the perfect satisfaction of his people; until then, let them not be over anxious for the treasures of the earth are in the

Lord's storehouse, and he will open the doors thereof, when and where he pleases (*History of Brigham Young*, Ms., for 1849, 144; as cited in *Comprehensive History of the Church*, 3:347).

~6~

PASSING THE WINTER

Brigham Young did not want to wait until the spring to cross the Missouri River, since the spring runoff would make traversing it more difficult. Instead, he negotiated with the Omaha and Otoe Native Americans for a place to stay west of the river and later wrote to United States president James K. Polk requesting his approval. The Saints originally settled at Cutler's Park, some three miles from the river, but realized the area was too small for the thousands of Saints en route along the trail. They moved farther east and established Winter Quarters. Homes were immediately constructed, ranging from comfortable log homes to mere dugouts in the bluff. Sickness infested the cramped area and many died. While they waited out the winter, the Saints continued to improve Winter Quarters: they built a ferry, a post office, schools, and mills. After the long and trying winter, the Saints that were able to began making final preparations for the trek to the Rocky Mountains.

REQUESTING PERMISSION TO REMAIN ON NATIVE AMERICAN LANDS

Big Elk, Standing Elk, Little Chief

(Church leaders signed a treaty with Omaha leaders on August 31, 1846. This treaty gave the Saints permission to remain on Omaha lands for the next two years, by which time they hoped to travel to the Rockies.)

We the undersigned chiefs and braves representative of the Omaha nation of Indians, do hereby grant to the Mormon people the privilege of tarrying upon our lands for two years or more, or as long as may suit their convenience, for the purpose of making the necessary preparations to prosecute their journey west of the Rocky Mountains, provided that our great father, the president of the United States, shall not counsel us to the contrary.

And we also do grant unto them the privilege of using all the wood and timber that they shall require.

And furthermore agree that we will not molest their cattle, horses, sheep, or any other property.

Big Elk

Standing Elk

Little Chief

(B. H. Roberts, *A comprehensive History of The Church of Jesus Christ of Latter-day Saints*, 7 vols. [Salt Lake City: Deseret News Press, 1930], 3:146.)

Brigham Young

(After five hundred men left with the Mormon Battalion, President Young wrote President Polk of the United States and requested permission to remain on Indian lands until the Saints could find a permanent place to settle.)

To James K. Polk, President of the United States.

Sir: A large portion of The Church of Jesus Christ of Latter-day Saints, having passed from the nation of our nativity, and the republic over which you have the honor to preside, and finding ourselves on the western shore of the great Missouri [River], while others of our friends are following close in our rear, beg your Excellency's indulgence for a moment while we pour out the pure feelings of our souls before you.

The cause of our exile we need not repeat, it is already with you, suffice it to say that a combination of fortuitous, illegal and unconstitutional circumstances have placed us in our present situation, on a journey which we design shall end in a location west of the Rocky Mountains, and within the basin of the Great Salt Lake, or Bear River Valley, as soon as circumstances shall permit, believing that to be a point where a good living will require hard labor, and consequently will be coveted by no other people, while it is surrounded by so unpopulous but fertile country.

While on our way thither and beyond the borders of the states, we were met by Captain J. Allen of your army of the West, proffering us the enrolment of five hundred men to be marched into California ... To this offer we promptly responded, though it has left five hundred of our loaded teams standing on the prairies of the Pottawatomie and Omaha nations, and nearly as many families destitute of their head and guardians. . . . [We] received assurances from Lieutenant Colonel Allen of the Mormon battalion, that we should be safe and that it would be proper for us to stop on any Indian lands, while it was necessary, considering our hindrance in filling his command. . . . Please give us your views of Colonel Allen's permit for us to stop on Indian lands as soon as your convenience will permit (*Comprehensive History of the Church*, 3:88–90).

WINTER QUARTERS

While waiting for permission from President Polk, the Saints crossed the Missouri and started preparing their winter settlement at Cutler's Park, three miles west of the Missouri River. The Saints soon learned, however, that the area was too small and that they needed to settle a wider area. They searched for a new location, closer to the river, and settled at what they called Winter Quarters.

Major Thomas H. Harvey

(Major Harvey described Winter Quarters while visiting in the late fall.)

[Winter Quarters] is situated on the South bank of the Missouri River 18 miles above Bellevue in the Omaha country, upon a beautiful table land, rising I would judge about fifty feet above common water, running back about 600 yards to the Bluffs, and extending down the river ... about 1 ½ miles; the Bluff or rather the high land rises beautifully above the table land. The camp is a regularly laid out town embracing the width of the table land and extending along the river a mile or more (Thomas H. Harvey to William Medill, Commissioner of Indian Affairs, December 3, 1846; as cited in Oscar G. Winther, ed., *The Private Papers and Diary of Thomas Leiper Kane: A Friend of the Mormons* [San Francisco: Gelber-Lilienthal, Inc., 1937], 25–29).

Brigham Young

The city was laid off into 41 blocks; and there were 820 lots (*Comprehensive History of the Church*, 3:88–90).

Helen Mar Kimball Whitney

We arrived in our winter quarters about one o'clock P.M., which is about 3 miles from Cutler's Park. We are located on the second shelf of the river bottoms. It is laid out in the form of a city, five acres in each block consisting of 20 lots. The city as laid out occupies from six to eight hundred acres of ground (Helen Mar Whitney, *A Woman's View: Helen Mar Whitney's Reminiscences of Early Church History*, ed. Jeni Broberg Holzapfel and Richard Neitzel Holzapfel [Provo, Utah: BYU Religious Studies Center, 1997], 415).

Thomas Bullock

[I] went through the City—where, nine weeks ago there was not a foot path, or a Cow track, now may be seen hundreds of houses, and hundreds in different stages of completion—impossible to distinguish the rich from the poor. The Streets are wide and regular and every prospect of a large City being raised up here (Thomas Bullock, *Journal*, November 28, 1846; as cited in Richard Bennett, *Mormons at the Missouri, 1846–1852: "And Should We Die"* [Norman: University of Oklahoma Press, 1987], 80–81).

BUILDING HOMES

Franklin D. Richards

Upward of 1,000 houses were built—700 of them in about 3 months, upon a pretty plateau overlooking the river and neatly laid out with highways and byways and fortified with breastwork and stockade (B. H. Roberts, *A Comprehensive History of The Church of Jesus Christ of Latter-day Saints*, 7 vols. [Salt Lake City: Deseret News Press, 1930], 3:148, see footnote 3).

Helen Mar Kimball Whitney

(Helen was seventeen years old when she married and immediately began the trek west. She spent her honeymoon on the plains, and it wasn't until Winter Quarters that she had her own home.)

This, like the majority of the houses, was covered with sod, and the chimneys were built of the same. Each room had one door and a window, with four panes of glass, but no floor. I was rather unfortunate, first, in having a chimney that seldom drew the smoke, particularly when the weather was cold enough to need a roaring fire in front of a good sized backlog . . . but I shed many unbidden tears during the smoking period, lasting one month, when, finding that our fireplace, built of sod, was about to tumble down. [The brethren] had some brick brought from the rubbish of the Old Fort of Council Bluffs and built a new one. Thus ended our troubles from that quarter. We had been accustomed to trials from smoke, heat, wind and dust, and many others things of an unpleasant nature during camp life, and we took considerable pleasure in fixing up our little homes. Our floors we managed to cover with canvas or pieces of carpeting, which had outlived the storm and the wear and tear while journeying from the states. We made curtains serve as partitions to divide the bedrooms, repositories, etc. from the kitchen. Most of our furniture we had made to order—such as cupboards and bedsteads—they being attached to the house, also tables, chairs and stools, and an occasional rocking chair, relics of other days, graced our ingleside [fireside]. . . . And here I received my "setting out" in crockery ware, etc., which, though not very extensive, was deemed quite immense for those times. Our marriage taking place just as we were about starting from the states, the presenting of these needful articles was postponed till a future time, expecting, as we then did, to cross the Rocky Mountains before building houses to inhabit. . . . The larger houses were generally shingled and had brick chimneys and puncheon floors, with a six lighted window in each room. Father's [Heber C. Kimball] largest house contained four good sized rooms on the ground and two upstairs (Helen Mar Whitney, "Scenes and Incidents at Winter Quarters," *Women's Exponent*, 13:139).

Brigham Young

The buildings of the city were generally of logs, averaging from twelve to eighteen feet long, a few of which were split; the floors were laid with puncheon (logs split about three inches thick and hewed on one side.) The timber used for floors was principally lynn and cotton-wood; a great many roofs were made by splitting oak timbers into boards called shakes, six inches wide and about three feet long and half an inch thick, which were kept to their places by weight poles, a few were nailed on. Many roofs were made with willows, straw and earth, about a foot thick, while others had puncheon. Many of the cabins had no floors. A few persons who could not procure logs made dugouts on the side hills, cutting out a fireplace at the upper end, the ridge pole of the roof was supported by the uprights in the center. Such were generally roofed with willows, straw and earth. The most of the chimneys were built of prairie sods, and the doors made of shakes pinned together, wooden hinges and finished with a string latch. The log houses were daubed inside with clay; a few rather more aristocratic cabins had fireplaces made of clay pounded in for jams and back. A few persons had stoves. The building of these houses was prosecuted with unremitting energy; at any hour of the evening the sound of the ax or the saw relieved the still-ness of the night (*Manuscript History of Brigham Young 1846–1847*, ed. Elden J. Watson [Salt Lake City: Elden J. Watson, 1971], 487–88).

Eliza Maria Partridge Lyman

[September] 26—Removed to our Winter Quarters on the bank of the Missouri River.

[October] 15—We have taken possession of our log house today. The first house my babe was ever in. I feel extremely thankful for the privilege of sitting by a fire where the wind cannot blow in every direc-tion and where I can warm one side without freezing the other. Our house is minus floor and many other comforts but the walls protect us from the wind if the sod roof does not from the rain (*Journal of Eliza Maria Partridge Lyman, 1846 February–1885 December* [LDS Church Archives, The Church of Jesus Christ of Latter-day Saints, Salt Lake City], n.p.).

Hosea Stout

(Hosea Stout expressed his happiness at living in a twelve-by-twelve foot home without windows or even a covering over the doorway.)

Tonight, myself and family had the pleasure of once more sleeping in our own house for the first time since we left Nauvoo on the 9th day of last February (*Journal of Hosea Stout*, September 25, 1846).

Ursalia Hascall

We have lived in our log cabin through the winter very comfortably. We have a brick chimney and hearth . . . a window with four lights of glass . . . the furniture consists of sacks, barrels, chests, trunks and two bedsteads with curtains from eaves to floor, my chest for a table. We have plenty of provisions except vegetables. . . . I think we shall get along first rate ("Letters of a Proselyte, The Hascall-Pomeroy Correspondence," *Utah Historical Quarterly*, July 15, 1957, 133–51, 237–57).

SICKNESS AND DEATH AT WINTER QUARTERS

After enduring the expulsion from Nauvoo, continual storms, the strenuous trek across Iowa, and inadequate provisions and shelter, the exiled Saints arrived at Winter Quarters exhausted. In their weakened and exposed condition, they were susceptible to such diseases as pneumonia, malaria, and tuberculosis. A plague of scurvy also raged in the camp because of the lack of fresh vegetables in the area. During their two-year stay at Winter Quarters, about six hundred Saints died.

George Whitaker

There was a great deal of sickness in the camp during the winter, partly on account of not having the proper food and partly from hunger and exposure. The disease of scurvy was prevalent. Hundreds died and were buried on the hill above the city. It was a time of mourning among the Saints ("Life of George Whitaker, A Utah Pioneer, as written by himself," typescript, 27, Utah State Historical Society, Salt Lake City).

William Clayton

Fever prevailed to such an extent that hardly any escaped it. They [the sick] let their cows go unmilked, they wanted for voices to raise the psalm of Sundays. The few who were able to keep their feet, went about among tents and wagons with food and water, like nurses through the wards of an infirmary. Here at one time the digging [of graves] got behind hand: burials were slow; and you might see women sit in the open tents keeping the flies off their dead children, sometimes after decomposition had set in (*Comprehensive History of the Church*, 3:153).

Lewis Barney

I nursed my wife as well as I could. Yea, I did stand by her bed and did minister herbs and mild foods and prayed over her. I was sick myself. I had a high fever and shook all over. My wife could not take any food, only a little water. . . . About 10 o'clock in the evening Father Kimball came to the tent door and asked how we were. I told him I was better and I thought my wife was, for she was asleep. I went to sleep again. When I awoke later, although I was very ill, the first thing I did was to go to the bed of Martha to see how she was. She was partly uncovered and cold. I spoke to her but she could not speak. I persevered, but she was so stopped up in the throat she could not speak. She was unconscious and did not move. Her eyes were half shut, and she breathed very hard. Her pulse was low, and she was cold as death in her lower limbs. I concluded she was struck with death. I could not do much for her, as she could not swallow. I sent for Father Kimball. He came and laid hands on her. He asked her if she knew him, but she made no signs that she knew him. I presume the dampness of the night and the bed clothes being partly off, and not having anyone to watch and give her some warm drinks and keep her warm, she took her death of cold (Lewis Barney, "Excerpts From a Journal of the Trek," in *Voices From the Past: Diaries, Journals, and Autobiographies*, comp. Campus Education Week Program [Provo, Utah: Brigham Young University Press, 1980], 32–33).

John R. Young

And die many of them did. As previously remarked, Winter Quarters was the Valley Forge of Mormondom. Our home was near the burying ground; and I can remember the small mournful-looking trains that so often passed our door. I also remember how poor and same-like our habitual diet was: cornbread, salt bacon, and a little milk. Mush and bacon became so nauseating that it was like taking medicine to swallow it; and the scurvy was making such inroad amongst us that it looked as if we should all be "sleeping on the hill" before spring, unless fresh food could be obtained (John R. Young, *Memoirs of John R. Young Utah Pioneer 1847* [Salt Lake City: Deseret News Press, 1920], 41).

Wilford Woodruff

I have never seen the Latter Day Saints in any situation where they seemed to be passing through greater tribulations or wearing out faster than at the present time (*Wilford Woodruff Journals*, 3:95–96; November 17–21, 1846).

Emmeline B. Wells

Yes, we had our hardships there on the Missouri. There was a great deal of sickness and many deaths, especially of babies and the older folk. Yet, the Lord did not forget us. We had our brighter moments. The brethren built larger log houses in which we could worship and have our social gatherings to sing our troubles away (*Manuscript History of Brigham Young,* 1846–47, 297).

Emmeline B. Wells

(Courtesy of the Church Archives, The Church of Jesus Christ of Latter- day Saints)

A SEVERE WINTER

Hosea Stout

January 7, 1847. Towards day the howling Northwind . . . began to howl with renewed strength and filled our little shanty full of its cold and piercing breath. The weather had increased in coldness and when morning light came I found one of those intolerable cold clear days that bids the most industrious to cease his labors and keep within.

Saturday Feb. 20th 1847. Today was the most snowy day we have had this winter. It was hurled full force with a hard wind from the sides of the North where old Lucifer sits, falling fast and bids fair to be a deep one. I was around town about as usual. The traveling was very uncomfortable.

Sunday Feb. 21st 1847. This morning the snow had blown and drifted until it was near half way to the top of my door and I could scarcely get it opened and had to throw away the snow to make roads before I could get around. It was decidedly one of the deepest snows that has fallen for some years and is still blowing and drifting all day, the air still full as in a snow storm.

Those who are caught out in a large prairie are in a bad snap for the deep ravines will be filled level full and impassable. But little stir this morning (*The Diary of Hosea Stout*, 3 vols. [Provo, Utah: Brigham Young University Harold B. Lee Library, 1941–43], 3:46, 73–74).

ESTABLISHING A CITY

Winter Quarters was more than just a stopover community: it provided the Saints with many of the comforts of city life. During the two-year stay, the Saints established schools for singing, dancing, and writing. They also entertained themselves through parties and socials. They constructed a post office and were able to keep in touch with family members back east. They also built flour and corn mills, stores, and a ferry. Such projects kept the Saints busy during the long winter months and made living in Winter Quarters more enjoyable. It also prepared them for the city that they would establish a few months later.

B. H. Roberts

At first the city was divided into thirteen wards with a bishopric appointed to preside over each, with instructions to look after both the spiritual and temporal welfare of the people, to suggest industrial activities, and look to the maintenance of the sanitary conditions so needful to the health of the community. Before the winter set in, the number of wards increased to twenty-two. A high council was also selected for Winter Quarters which was in this case authorized to exercise the functions both of an ecclesiastical high council, and also a municipal council. . . . The nature of the duties of these high councils may be learned from the instructions to Father Morley, the president of the one when installed at Kanesville: "The council was instructed to oversee and guard the conduct of the saints, and counsel them that the laws of God and good order are not infringed." (*Comprehensive History of the Church*, 3:149–50; see *History of Brigham Young*, Ms., 1846–1847, book 2, 91.)

Brigham Young

Our great city . . . sprang up in a night as it were, like Jonah's gourd. . . . No one suffers for food or raiment unless it be through their own fault, that is, in not asking for it, or being well and too lazy to work; but the fact of so many houses been built in so short a time, is proof of the general industry of the people, which will bear comparison with the history of all the nations of the earth, and in all the periods of time (Brigham Young, "Letter to Elders Hyde, Pratt and Taylor," *Millennial Star* [April 1, 1847], 9:97).

Emmeline B. Wells

I taught one of the schools. You see, I was born and reared in Massachusetts, and was trained for teaching when Horace Mann was a teacher at one of our schools there, and I did teach for two years. Afterward, I joined The Church of Jesus Christ of Latter-day Saints and went west to Nauvoo. When we left our beautiful city on the Mississippi, I was one of those who got over the Missouri River into the land of the Omaha Indians. Of course I wanted to help, and seeing the number of barefooted boys and girls running about the town, I asked our leaders to build a schoolhouse and let me teach the lively youngsters the best I could. They were glad to provide the house. It had only a dirt floor, with just logs for seats. We did not have many books and mice ate up some we did manage to gather, but the boys and girls were ready to learn. They recited with me, read what they could, and sang songs. Best of all, they were out of the cold and were kept busy (*Manuscript History of Brigham Young*, 297).

Vilate Kimball

(After the birth of her seventh son, Heber C. Kimball's wife also tried her hand at poetry.)

> The Lord blessed us with another son
> Which is the seventh I have born

May he be the father of many lives
But not the husband of many wives.
(Kenneth W. Godfrey, Audrey M. Godfrey, Jill Mulvay
Derr, *Women's Voices* [Salt Lake City: Deseret Book,
1982], 181)

Ursalia Hascall

(In a letter to her sister living in the East, describing the social ambiance of Winter Quarters.)

Thales [Ursalia's teenage son] attended dancing school this winter, [the Mormons] open their school with prayer and so they always do at their dancing parties or feasts. They have all the good and fat things they can procure for supper, I never saw a larger supply at any place. Each grade had a feast until they went through the camp. . . . There is some of the smartest and best men and women here there is in the world ("Letters of a Proselyte, The Hascall-Pomeroy Correspondence," *Utah Historical Quarterly* [April 1957]: 133–51; [July 1957]: 237–57).

Claire Noall

(Willard Richards built an octagon-shaped house that served not only as his home but also as a community gathering place, council house, and post office. He served as the city's postmaster.)

On a snow-whitened day in January, Amelia was petting the children, keeping them as warm as possible in the eight-sided room with its small cross-barred windows in two faces, and with a smoke hole at the peak of the octagon. A bed occupied each of the six walls for the women and children.

Willard placed his bed along one wall of the extension, next to the outside door of the inner room of the wing, one of two compartments. In the front room of the wing, he set up a postoffice, with a counter, and under a window he arranged a log table for a desk, with chairs for his two clerks, Thomas Bullock and Robert Campbell. Boards were set up as benches when the council met. Frequently, Willard ate his supper with the twelve in his office, his wives waiting upon the men from the main room of the octagon. Until the council house could be finished, the "Doctor's Tabernacle" served as the community center (Claire Noall, *Intimate Disciple: A Portrait of Willard Richards* [Salt Lake City: University of Utah Press, 1957], 514).

George Whitaker

A brother by the name of John Neff and family from Pennsylvania, came to Winter Quarters early in the spring. He was a miller and farmer, and had acquired considerable means. President Young thought it would be a good plan to build a grist mill on a little stream that ran on the north side of the town, as it would make work for a great many men who had nothing to do and very little to eat. The mill was needed to grind our wheat and corn that we were to take with us the ensuing summer. He wanted Brother Neff to take hold of it and build it, which he agreed to do. Accordingly, quite a number of men were wanted to go to work. There was a dam to be built across the creek to hold the water. Brother Frank Pullen and myself were appointed to superintend that work. There was also a mill race to be dug, two or three hundred yards long and from eight to twelve feet deep. Carpenters, millwrights and sawyers were employed. They had to saw all the lumber by hand or what we would call pit sawing. This work seemed to revive and stimulate people. We now had more provisions and the people felt better as the spring opened. It had been a very severe winter, such a winter as I had never experienced before ("Life of George Whitaker," 28–29).

PREPARING FOR THE 1847 TREK
TO THE ROCKY MOUNTAINS

George Whitaker

(Spring, 1847)

There were now some thousands gathered at Winter Quarters and many hundreds camped up and down the river and on the bluffs. All were anxious to know what they should do. Spring was now opening upon [us]. A great many of the Saints had lost part of their stock during the winter, some of it having been stolen by the Indians and some having died. This naturally broke up the arrangements of a good many who had intended to cross the plains that season, and they were compelled to get what little stock they had left and go to farming or anything else they could do and wait until they could get another outfit ("Life of George Whitaker," 28).

Joseph F. Smith

(As the Saints prepared to leave Winter Quarters, trips were often made to Missouri to purchase provisions. Joseph recalled the following experience on his way back to Winter Quarters from Missouri.)

Once I accompanied [my mother] along with my uncle Joseph Fielding, at which time we went to St. Joseph Missouri, and purchased corn and had it ground at Savannah, and on our way home we camped in the edge of a wood, in the neighborhood of a large herd of cattle that were being driven to market. In the morning our best yoke of cattle were gone. My uncle and I hunted far and near but could not find them. We enquired of the herdsmen and followed their directions but could not find our oxen. This broke up our team so that we could not travel and would have been under the necessity of purchasing or trading in some way for another yoke before we could have moved on.

After some delay . . . [Mother] started out to find the cattle. Uncle thought it was useless for her to go. I confess I thought so too, but I had more faith that she would find them, if findable, than I had in either my or my uncle's finding them. While Mother was walking along through the tall grass, one of the herdsmen rode up to her and said he had seen her cattle over in the opposite direction to what she was going. Strange to say she passed right on, not heeding what had been said at all. He repeated, she paid no attention but passed on as tho' she were in "the strait and narrow path." Suddenly she came upon a slight ravine filled with tall willows, and in a dense cluster of large willows she found the oxen, where they had been fastened up during the night by the herdsmen with the intention of stealing them and driving them to the market, for they were in good condition. After the cattle were found these worthy herdsmen suddenly rode off, perhaps in search of honesty, which I trust they found (Joseph F. Smith, *Reminiscent account*, holograph, in *Joseph F. Smith Papers* [LDS Church Archives, The Church of Jesus Christ of Latter-day Saints, Salt Lake City]; as cited in Susan Arrington Madsen, *I Walked to Zion: True Stories of Young Pioneers on the Mormon Trail* [Salt Lake City: Deseret Book, 1994], 36).

Doctrine and Covenants 136:1–8, 10–11, 15, 21–22

(Just as the ancient Israelites had been, the Saints were organized by revelation into groups of tens, fifties, and hundreds. Compare Deuteronomy 1:15.)

The Word and Will of the Lord concerning the Camp of Israel in their journeyings to the West:

Let all the people of The Church of Jesus Christ of Latter-day Saints, and those who journey with them, be organized into companies, with a covenant and promise to keep all the commandments and statutes of the Lord our God.

Let the companies be organized with captains of hundreds, captains of fifties, and captains of tens, with a president and his two counselors at their head, under the direction of the Twelve Apostles.

And this shall be our covenant—that we will walk in all the ordinances of the Lord.

Let each company provide themselves with all the teams, wagons, provisions, clothing, and other necessaries for the journey, that they can.

When the companies are organized let them go to with their might, to prepare for those who are to tarry.

Let each company, with their captains and presidents, decide how many can go next spring; then choose out a sufficient number of able-bodied and expert men, to take teams, seeds, and farming utensils, to go as pioneers to prepare for putting in spring crops.

Let each company bear an equal proportion, according to the dividend of their property, in taking the poor, the widows, the fatherless, and the families of those who have gone into the army, that the cries of the widow and the fatherless come not up into the ears of the Lord against this people. . . .

Let every man use all his influence and property to remove this people to the place where the Lord shall locate a stake of Zion.

And if ye do this with a pure heart, in all faithfulness, ye shall be blessed; you shall be blessed in your flocks, and in your herds, and in your fields, and in your houses, and in your families. . . .

And appoint presidents, and captains of hundreds, and of fifties, and of tens. . . .

Brigham Young

(On February 22, 1847, while in Winter Quarters, President Young related to the brethren the following dream relative to their westward migration.)

While sick, and asleep, about noon-day of the 17th . . . I dreamed that I went to see Joseph. He looked perfectly natural, sitting with his feet on the lower round of his chair. I took hold of his right hand and kissed it many times, and said to him, "Why is it that we cannot be together as we used to be? You have been away from us a long time, and we want your society, and I do not like to be separated from you."

Joseph, rising from his chair and looking at me with his usual earnest, expressive and pleasing countenance, said, "It is all right."

I replied, "I do not like to be away from you."

Joseph said, "It is all right; we cannot be together yet; we shall be, by-and-by; but you will have to do without me awhile, and then we shall be together again."

. . . I said, "Brother Joseph, . . . if you have a word of counsel for me, I should be glad to receive it."

Joseph stepped toward me, and, looking very earnestly, yet pleasantly, said, "Tell the people to be humble and faithful, and be sure to keep the Spirit of the Lord, and it will lead them right. Be careful and not turn away the small, still voice; it will teach what to do and where to go; it will yield the fruits of the kingdom. Tell the brethren to keep their hearts open to convictions, so that when the Holy Ghost comes to them, their hearts will be ready to receive it. They can tell the Spirit of the Lord from all other spirits; it will whisper peace and joy to their souls; it will take malice, strife and hatred, and all evil, from their hearts; and their whole desire will be to do good, bring forth righteousness, and build up the kingdom of God. Tell the brethren if they will follow the Spirit of the Lord, they will go right. Be sure to tell the people to keep the Spirit of the Lord; and if they will, they will find themselves just as they were organized by our Father in heaven, before they came into the world. Our Father in heaven organized the human family, but they are all disorganized and in great confusion" (Susa Young Gates, "Reminiscences of Brigham Young," *Improvement Era*, June 1908, 11:619–20).

BEGINNING THE JOURNEY
OF A THOUSAND MILES

CAMP OF ISRAEL

The "Camp of Israel" was an appropriate label for Brigham Young's first company of pioneers. In January 1847, the Lord revealed to Brigham Young that the Saints were to travel under the same organization that was revealed to Moses for the children of Israel (see Deuteronomy 1:15). Like the years of wandering in the wilderness were for the Israelites, the trek west was to be as much a spiritual journey as it was a physical journey. Before departing, Brigham Young warned the Saints that their success depended on their willingness to heed the Lord's directions in spiritual matters, as much as it would depend on their willingness to obey instructions for physical guidance.

Carol Cornwall Madsen

For [the pioneers] the Nauvoo exodus found its prototype in the flight of ancient Israel. The fleeing Saints called themselves the Camp of Israel; their Sinai was Nauvoo; the freezing of the Mississippi, the parting of the Red Sea; their sacred books and records, the Ark of the Covenant; and the miracle of the quail among the poor camps, the appearance of the quail to the Israelites. They were the Lord's covenant people delivered from their enemies by a modern Moses and led to a promised land where they would build a temple to the God who had preserved them (Carol Cornwall Madsen, *Journey to Zion* [Salt Lake City: Deseret Book, 1997], 10–11).

I am the Lord your God, even the God of your fathers, the God of Abraham and of Isaac and of Jacob.

I am he who led the children of Israel out of the land of Egypt; and my arm is stretched out in the last days, to save my people Israel.

Sarah Burbank

(The similarities between ancient Israel and the Lord's people in the latter-days were not lost on the pioneers.)

To look around upon the camp and see the tents in motion and hear the large herds of cattle lowing, it caused me to meditate upon the Camp of Israel in the days of Moses. Says I to myself, "Can it be possible that we have been driven from the land of our fathers who did lay down their lives for our liberty that we might worship God according to the dictates of our conscience?" (*Voices From the Past: Diaries, Journals, and Autobiographies*, comp. Campus Education Week Program [Provo, Utah: Brigham Young University Press, 1980], 32.)

Eliza R. Snow

Eliza R. Snow
(Courtesy of the Church Archives, The Church of Jesus Christ of Latter-day Saints)

Lo! a num'rous host of people
Tented on the western shore
Of the noble Mississippi
They for weeks were crossing o'er
At the last day's dawn of winter,
Bound with frost and wrapt in snow,
Hark! the sound is onward, onward!
Camp of Israel! rise & go.
All at once is life in motion—
Trunks and beds & baggage fly;
Oxen yok'd and horses harness'd,
Tents roll'd up, are passing by,
Soon the carriage wheels are rolling
Onward to a woodland dell,
Where at sunset all are quarter'd—
Camp of Israel! All is well.
Thickly round, the tents are cluster'd
Neighb'ring smokes together blend—
Supper served—the hymns are chanted

And the evening pray'rs ascend.
Last of all the guards are station'd—
Heav'ns! Must guards be serving here?
Who would harm the houseless exiles?
Camp of Israel! Never fear.
Where is freedom? Where is justice?
Both have from this nation fled;
And the blood of martyr'd Prophets,
Must be answer'd on its head!
Therefore to your tents, O Jacob!
Like our Father Abr'm dwell—
God will execute his purpose—
Camp of Israel! All is well.
(Eliza R. Snow, "Song for the Pioneers—No. 2,"
Improvement Era [March 1943], 46:142–43)

Helen Mar Kimball Whitney

Our history is a wonder and a marvel to those who have taken the trouble to hunt us and review it in all its ups and downs. . . . And our experience, I think, comes nearest to that of the children of Israel after their departure out of the land of Egypt than any other people of whom we have record, though I believe we were a more patient people. . . . God had . . . brought us deliverance every time; and it is our wish and purpose to trust Him still (Helen Mar Kimball Whitney, "Travels Beyond the Mississippi," *Women's Exponent* [May 1, 1884], 12: 182).

"OF ONE HEART AND ONE MIND"

Brigham Young knew that the establishment of a new Zion would take more than a change in physical location. As was the case with the people of Enoch, establishing Zion was more a matter of where the pioneers's hearts were. In Enoch's day, "the Lord called his people Zion, because they were of one heart and one mind, and dwelt in righteousness" (Moses 7:18). Because President Young knew that the success of the pioneers would depend on their spiritual worthiness, his sights were set not only on the western horizon but also on the spiritual standing of his people.

Brigham Young

(Brigham Young described his expectations of those pioneers who desired to journey with his company.)

Make up your minds one way or the other—if we penetrate into the wilderness and do not do right and keep the commandments of God it is better to tarry here. You need not think that you are going to creep into my company and commit iniquity without being punished for it. . . . Remember when you leave the Gentiles you will only have yourself to imagine evil. If one man steals, another commits adultery and another swear and curse the authorities of the church [they] had better stay here and go to Missouri for there they will be whipt . . . don't come into my company unless you can obey the Word and Will of the Lord. I want all to live in all honesty, build up temples, and go and purify the people that they may build up the Kingdom on the earth (*Journal of Willard Richards*, January 18, 1847 [LDS Church Archives, The Church of Jesus Christ of Latter-day Saints, Salt Lake City], n.p.).

Brigham Young

(In his journal, Willard Richards recorded the following statement made by Brigham Young.)

I would rather cross the mountains with the Twelve and not another person with them than be accompanied by a set of wicked men and those who continued to lie and steal and swear and commit iniquity. . . . If the Saints will reform and act upon the knowledge which they now possess, flood gates of knowledge will be open to them and they will be filled with light and intelligence (*Journal of Willard Richards*, December 20, 1846).

Brigham Young

Return unto the Lord and get the Holy Ghost . . . pray for me and my Brethren that we carry off the Kingdom of God. We must not indulge in negligence, slothfulness, coldness. . . . We are looking for glory immortal, and eternal lives. Go at it that we may turn away disease from the camp, that we may live and redeem Zion . . . pray that we may live to do a great work in the Earth. Pray for me, hang on one to another, never slacken your exertions, don't give up. Be wide awake. . . . I feel all the time like Moses . . . [I] would to God that all these brethren were Prophets, Seers, and Revelators (*Journal of Willard Richards*, March 14, 1847).

Mary Pugh Scott

(Sister Scott's account is a testament of the strict rules that demanded obedience in physical actions, in addition to the need to be spiritually obedient.)

Finally May 30, 1848, John Scott and family started in Heber Kimball's Co. John [Mary's husband] was Captain over 10 wagons. His company included 662 people, 266 wagons, 150 loose cattle, 25 mules, 737 oxen, 57 horses, 299 chickens, 96 pigs, 52 dogs, 17 cats, 3 hives of bees, 3 doves, 1 squirrel.

Rules of a camp: Each had a captain, a captain of the guard, a Chaplin, and clerk.

All names were enrolled.

1. Noise and confusion will not be allowed after 8 p.m.
2. Camp will be called by trumpet for prayer meeting morning and night.
3. Arise at 4:30 a.m. Assembly for prayers 5:30 a.m. Card playing will not be allowed.
4. Dogs must be tied up at night.
5. Profane language will not be tolerated.
6. Each man will help driving the cattle.
7. Rate of travel for oxen [will be] 3 miles an hour (The corral made by wagons will not be broken until all of the cattle have been yoked).

John's responsibility for ten wagons made it difficult at times to help his own families (LaRee Barson McCauley, *Life Story of Mary Pugh*, typescript, 4, Utah State Historical Society, Salt Lake City).

THE DEPARTURE

Brigham Young did not think it wisdom to attempt the trek in one large body. There were too many to make the journey fast enough and too few who were sufficiently prepared. Instead, he organized a smaller party—consisting mainly of ten of the Twelve Apostles and others with the pioneering skills necessary for making the trek. This advance company would travel ahead of their families and the main body of Saints, in order to find a place for the Saints to gather, and plant crops to sustain them through the coming winter. The company, known as the Vanguard Company, was composed of 143 men, 3 women, and 2 children. Parley P. Pratt and John Taylor, who returned from missions in the British Isles shortly before the Vanguard Company left, remained and led the main body of Saints to the West, two months later.

Brigham Young

In a few days I start with my brethren, the Twelve, and as many more as can get ready as pioneers to find the place where a stake of Zion shall be located over the mountains, leaving all our families at this place [Winter Quarters], with the anticipation of returning here to winter and taking our families over one year hence (as cited in Richard E. Bennett, *We'll Find the Place: The Mormon Exodus 1846–1848* [Salt Lake City: Deseret Book, 1997] chapter 1).

Erastus Snow

I loaded my wagon and prepared for starting. . . . I called my family together and dedicated them unto the Lord, and commanded them to serve the Lord with all their hearts, and cultivate peace and love, and hearken to the whisperings of the Holy Spirit and pray much; and inasmuch as they would do this they should have power over disease and death, and we should all meet again in the due time of the Lord (*Journal of Erastus Snow*, April 6, 1847; as printed in *Utah Humanities Review* 2 [April 1948], 2:107).

Sylvester Henry Earl

It was hard for me to leave my little family sick among howling wolves and the roaming savages of the West, but the servants of the Lord said go and I felt as ever to leave all for the benefit of the Gospel or the salvation of the people (Sylvester Henry Earl, *Autobiographical*

Sketch, microfilm of typescript, April 10, 1847 [LDS Church Archives, The Church of Jesus Christ of Latter-day Saints, Salt Lake City], n.p.).

Eliza Maria Partridge Lyman

(April 8, 1847)

The wagons of the Pioneers started this afternoon. They are going west to look for a location for the Latter Day Saints and have no idea where that is but trust the Lord will lead them to the place (Eliza Maria Partridge Lyman, *Journal of Eliza Maria Partridge Lyman, 1846 February–1885 December* [LDS Church Archives, The Church of Jesus Christ of Latter-day Saints, Salt Lake City], n.p.).

EMIGRATION CAMP

Brigham Young had planned for the main body of Saints to remain at Winter Quarters until the following year, when the members of the Vanguard Company would have a definite location for the Saints and could return to help the main body cross the plains. However, the winter had been hard on the Saints at Winter Quarters; diseases were rampant and the exhausted Saints were anxious to join their leaders in the West. The second and much larger company, named Emigration Camp, was led by Elders Parley P. Pratt and John Taylor. In the end, they waited only two months after the departure of the Vanguard Company to begin their journey west.

George Whitaker

(George Whitaker was employed by Parley P. Pratt to assist the Pratt family in their journey west. Whitaker accompanied the second group of pioneers to travel west, led by Elders Pratt and Taylor.)

We left our Winter Quarters, [and] traveled about ten miles on to a large open plain. There we remained two or three days to be organized into companies. Brothers Pratt and Taylor were with us. They took a prominent part in the organization. Before President Young had left he had appointed some of the captains of hundreds. We were organized into companies of hundreds, fifties and tens. To each of those divisions was a captain. Bishop Edward Hunter was the captain of our hundred. Brother Joseph Horn was the captain of our fifty and Brother Abraham Hoagland was the captain of our team ("Life of George Whitaker, A Utah Pioneer, as written by himself," typescript, 31, Utah State Historical Society, Salt Lake City).

John Taylor

(John Taylor wrote the following in a letter to Brigham Young, dated August 18, 1847.)

Our numbers far exceed what we anticipated, for instead of numbering one hundred wagons we have near six hundred; the cattle were generally weak in coming off the rushes; we had to recruit our cattle and send to Missouri for bread stuffs. You know, brethren, that it takes a little time and labor to start a large wheel, it has, however, commenced rolling and will, we trust, not stop until it reaches the valley of the Salt Lake (John

John Taylor

(Courtesy of the Church Archives, The Church of Jesus Christ of Latter-day Saints)

Taylor, *Journal History of The Church of Jesus Christ of Latter-day Saints*, August 18, 1847 [LDS Church Archives, The Church of Jesus Christ of Latter-day Saints, Salt Lake City], n.p.).

Fanny Young Murray

(Fanny Murray was a sister of Brigham Young.)

The wagons went four abreast, and you can hardly imagine their appearance. Some that were there declared it the grandest sight their eyes were ever blest with. Their wagons were all neatly prepared with everything for their comfort that could be obtained, but yet they will suffer enough (Fanny Young Murray to Gould and Laura Murray, Winter Quarters, July 5, 1847, in *Helen Mar Whitney Papers* [LDS Church Archives, The Church of Jesus Christ of Latter-day Saints, Salt Lake City], n.p.).

George W. Hill

There was only one thing that made [us] venture to start from the Missouri River in 1847, and that was the health of my wife. She had taken the scurvy in the winter superinduced by our living as we did without vegetables. And as soon as the weather began to get warmer in the spring, she got worse instead of better and came very near dying. In fact, I had no hopes for her but to get on the road traveling as soon as possible, thinking a change of scenery, a change of air, and a change of water might be beneficial to her. I was determined to try it, let the consequences be what they might. I knew that we did not have money enough to get a decent outfit to go with, but I would have preferred to have started with my gun only and to have taken my chance [living off the land] rather than to have remained in that inhospitable region with the scurvy taking the people off by the hundreds as it was doing. . . .

You may think this was a very hazardous undertaking; well, we thought so too, but the stakes were terrible we had to play. . . .

We now hastened our departure from winter quarters, glad to get away from that inhospitable place with life even, for we did not think we should have had even that if we had remained much longer ("Incidents in the Life of George Washington Hill," unpublished, *Joel E, Ricks Collection*, "Cache Valley Historical Material, Spring 1847" [LDS Church Archives, The Church of Jesus Christ of Latter-day Saints, Salt Lake City], 17–31).

Levi Jackman

Where [we were going], we could not tell or what we should have to contend with. We only knew that we must go and the Lord would attend to the bringing out the result (Levi Jackman, *Autobiography of Levi Jackman*, typescript, 35, Utah State Historical Society, Salt Lake City).

M. J. Thompson

Soon after parting from our kindred on the banks of the Missouri and while grieving over the separation, I was gently chided by my mother who rehearsed to me the story of Lot's wife, and exhorted me never to "look back." This made a deep impression upon my mind. . . . I

[was] more or less in dread all the way over the plains, for my rebellious thoughts, in spite of me, would often go back to the loved ones we had left behind (M. J. Thompson, "Early Church Recollections," *Juvenile Instructor*, July 15, 1897, 431).

8

LIFE IN THE WILDERNESS

Thousands of years before the pioneer trek west, the prophet Jeremiah foresaw the pioneers' journey in the wilderness. He wrote, "For there shall be a day, that the watchmen upon the mount Ephraim shall cry, Arise ye, and let us go up to Zion unto the Lord our God. . . . I will cause them to walk by the rivers of waters in a straight way, wherein they shall not stumble" (Jeremiah 31:6, 9). For many of the Saints, the prospect of life on the prairie was a terrifying one; for others, it was an adventure. For all, however, it was something very new. Many of those who were about to make a journey of over a thousand miles had never driven a team of oxen. People who had lived their entire lives in urbane societies were now called upon to hunt for their food, cook over a burning buffalo chip, and wash their clothing in streams. Rolling wagons were a difficult replacement for the homes they had left, bringing new challenges and hazards. A buffalo stampede could easily set a team of oxen running, often destroying all the property a family owned. The slow but steadily moving wagon wheels were merciless to children and adults who fell into their path, as the oxen were not easily stopped. Battling the elements, confronting wild animals, and getting lost all proved to be dangers along the trail. However, despite the hazards and hardships, the accounts left of life on the trail are filled with the writer's feelings of gratitude to the Lord for deliverance from their enemies.

WAGON TRAVEL

Ruth May Fox

Imagine if you can these would-be drivers, who had, perhaps, never seen a Texas steer before, go through the procedure for the first time of yoking their cattle. Truly no rodeo could match the scene. The men had to be instructed in this art, and some did not learn very quickly. The same was true of the use of firearms. Every man was supposed to have his own gun and ammunition, though he had never fired a shot in his life (Ruth May Fox, "From England to Salt Lake Valley in 1867," *Improvement Era*, July 1935, 38:408).

Hannah Cornaby

Imagine, if you can, the operation of starting over one hundred ox teams, chiefly by men who had never done anything of the kind before. . . . The oxen were wild, and getting them yoked was the most laughable sight I had ever witnessed; everybody giving orders, and nobody knowing how to carry them out. If the men had not been saints, there would doubtless have been much profane language used; but the oxen, not understanding "English," did just as well without it. But it did seem so truly comical to witness the bewildered look of some innocent brother, who, after having labored an hour or more to get "Bright" secured to one end of the yoke, would hold the other end aloft, trying to persuade "Buck" to come under, only to see "Bright" careering across the country, the yoke lashing the air, and he not even giving a hint as to when he intended to stop (Hannah Cornaby, *Autobiography and Poems* [Salt Lake City: J. C. Graham Co., 1881], 32).

George Whitaker

I had never driven a team in my life before, but I thought I could drive as [the oxen] did not seem to be very spirited. Brother Pratt got into the wagon to show me how to drive as he knew by this time that I was an Englishman and had never been used to handling the lines. . . . I thought I could drive as well as he could. He told me not to whip the horses and let them take their time. I got along very well until I began to think they were not going fast enough. I gave them a little whip which made them start up in a hurry, and the first thing I knew they were on the full gallop. I thought they were going to get away with me, but I held on to them with all my might until finally I brought them to. This was one of my first lessons in driving a team. . . . I told him I thought I had done first-rate. I did not tell him of the runaway. I got along very well after that ("Life of George Whitaker, A Utah Pioneer, as written by himself," typescript, 10, Utah State Historical Society, Salt Lake City).

Ann Agatha Walker Pratt

Our family being numerous and help scarce, two of we women rather thought we could manage . . . to drive our own team, which consisted of a yoke of cattle, for, though just coming from a large city, and not being used to this kind of a life—never having seen cattle yoked together still I thought, well, what any other woman can do, I can, so, shouldering my whip, I drove out of Winter Quarters, and soon learned to manage my team first class (Ann Agatha Walker Pratt, "Personal Reminiscences," *Woman's Exponent* [March 15, 1893], 21:139).

Duckworth Grimshaw

(Grimshaw, who did not know how to drive a team of oxen, received his first lesson from John W. Young.)

[Young] took the whip and brought it down on the ox leader then gave the nigh leader a prod in the ribs with the whip stock and this brought the cows up in good style. I thought, well they seem to understand that sort of driving, but when I tried it I found the lash around my own neck and decided [that] to become efficient in driving required practice like everything else (Kate B. Carter, comp., *Our Pioneer Heritage*, 20 vols.Kate B. Carter, comp. [Salt Lake City: Daughters of Utah Pioneers, 1958–77], 11:231–42).

Joseph F. Smith

My team leaders' names were Thom and Joe—we raised them from calves, and they were both white. Thom was trim built, active, young, and more intelligent than many a man. Many times while traveling sandy or rough roads, on long, thirsty drives, my oxen were lowing with the heat and fatigue. I would put my arms around Thom's neck and cry bitter tears! That was all I could do. Thom was my favorite and best and most willing and obedient servant and friend. He was choice! (Joseph F. Smith, *Reminiscent account,*

Joseph F. Smith
(Courtesy of the Church Archives, The Church of Jesus Christ of Latter-day Saints)

holograph, in *Joseph F. Smith Papers* [LDS Church Archives, The Church of Jesus Christ of Latter-day Saints, Salt Lake City], n.p.).

Ann Agatha Walker Pratt

At night, when we drove into camp the wagons formed in the shape of a horseshoe, the first two with the front ends pretty close together, the next drove close enough for the tongue to lie outside of the wheels of the first one, and so on until the fifty were in place. The enclosure forming a corral for the cattle through the night. Each driver unyoked his cattle (I frequently unyoked mine) then those whose turn it was, herded them till dark. The rest of the men would gather material for fires, often nothing but dried grass or Buffalo chips as they were called (Pratt, "Personal Reminiscences," *Woman's Exponent* [March 15, 1893], 21:139).

William Henry Jackson

The Mormon corral presents a lively, interesting scene, three hundred men, women, and children grouped within the space occupied by the encircled wagons very naturally making it so. A few of the families have small tents that are put up both inside and outside the corral; the rest sleeping either in their wagons or under them. The whole outfit is divided into messes of convenient size, and, as soon as camp is located, the first thing to do is to start the fires; those whose duty it is to provide fuel foraging around in every direction for "chips," sage brush, or any other material available, and soon forty or fifty bright little fires are twinkling inside and outside the corral, with coffee pots, frying pans, and bake ovens filling the air with appetizing incense. From a little distance one of these encampments, at night resembles an illuminated city in miniature, and as one approaches near there is usually the sound of revelry. In every Mormon train there are usually some musicians, for they seem to be very fond of song and dance, and as soon as the camp work is done the younger element gather in groups and "trip the light fantastic tow" with as much vim as if they had not had a twenty mile march that day (*The Diaries of William Henry Jackson*, ed. LeRoy R. Hafen and Ann W. Hafen [Glendale: The Arthur H. Clark Company, 1959], 64–65).

Louisa Palmer

At eight [the wagons] were on their way. At noon camp was made for lunch and at night camp was made for the night by water if possible. A corral was made of the wagons. The cattle were herded if there were no Indians in the vicinity. After supper there was usually a dance; the fiddle music was furnished by the teamsters. After the dance a meeting was held which was opened by song and prayer and the subject spoken upon was about the travel for the next day. The roll was called twice each day. At nine-thirty all were supposed to be in bed ("Louisa Harriett Mills Palmer," in *Our Pioneer Heritage*, 13:456).

Peter Neilson Sr.

[I], as well as other brethren, have quietly gone between our oxen and blessed them and immediately they moved on, showing us that the Spirit of the Lord can subdue and make biddable the ox as well as man ("Biographical Sketch of Peter Neilson Sr.," typescript copy, 10, in author's possession, compliments of his descendant, Reed Neilson; as cited in Carol Cornwall Madsen, *Journey to Zion* [Salt Lake City: Deseret Book, 1997], 325).

Ezra T. Benson

(Burdened by the weight of his wagon, Ezra T. Benson sought the advice of Brigham Young as to whether he should remain and wait or continue with the company.)

The road being so bad I went to Bro. Brigham and told him I could not proceed further on account of the heaviness of my load and weakness of my teams, I told him I was willing to tarry there till I could get on further, to which he replied, that I must not stop, but to go with him and the camp. He asked, what I had for loading, I replied six hundred pounds of flour and a few bushels of meal, etc. He said, "Bring your flour and meal to my camp, and I will lighten you up"; I accordingly complied and to my surprise he requested John D. Lee to weigh it out and divide it among the camps, leaving about fifty pounds of flour and a half bushel of meal to support myself and family going into a wilderness country. When we started, I found my wagons rolled comfortably along, while many of the companies' wagons would sink to their axletrees in the mud, and I would say to them, "Go to Bro. Brigham, and he will lighten your loads" ("Ezra T. Benson, Autobiography," *Instructor* [1945], 80:216, in *Writings of Early Latter-day Saints and Their Contemporaries, A Database Collection,* comp. Milton V. Backman [Provo, Utah: BYU Religious Studies Center, 1996], 216.)

James Bryant

There was always one of the men ready to ride his saddle horse into the river; if his horse had to swim he would return as soon as possible, but if man and horse could wade all of the way across, the company was allowed to march on through. If he had to swim we then made camp, sometimes for ten days making rafts or floats to enable everything to be taken over to the opposite side (James Bryant, "John Murdock Company," in *Our Pioneer Heritage,* 6:61).

George Whitaker

The way we bridged the streams was my putting strong poles across the brush and dirt upon that. It would not take us more than two or three hours to bridge a small stream ("Life of George Whitaker," 18).

Sarah Burbank

When fording streams we could just see the oxen's backs and horns and thought our wagons would go under, but we got out alive by the help of the Lord (Sarah Burbank, "Memories of Nauvoo and Crossing the Plains," in *Voices From the Past: Diaries, Journals, and Autobiographies,* comp. Campus Education Week Program [Provo, Utah: Brigham Young University Press, 1980], 29).

Eliza Maria Partridge Lyman

[August] 21st Crossed the Platte river. The rocks in the bottom are so large that it seemed sometimes as if they would tip the wagon over. I held fast the baby and Sister Caroline held fast to me so that I was not thrown quite out of bed (*Journal of Eliza Maria Partridge Lyman, 1846 February–1885 December,* microfilm [LDS Church Archives, The Church of Jesus Christ of Latter-day Saints, Salt Lake City], 44).

Eliza Maria Partridge Lyman

We had to sleep as best we could which was anything but comfortable, some lying on boxes, some on chairs, and others in wet beds. I laid across a box in Father Huntington's wagon, with my head on his and Mother's bed with my feet on the front end board and my clothes wet about a quarter of a yard deep about my ankles. I do not know why I did not freeze, for I had no bed and very little covering. It must be that there was not room in the wagon for the frost to get in, it was so full of folks (*Journal of Eliza Maria Partridge Lyman*, n.p.).

Levi Jackman

A little after noon [we] crossed Beaver Fork, a stream about three rods [forty-nine and a half feet] wide, 2 ½ feet deep. The banks were high and steep. We had to attach ropes to the tongues of the wagons and men to the ropes to help the teams up (Levi Jackman, *Autobiography of Levi Jackman*, typescript, 37, Utah State Historical Society, Salt Lake City).

Henry Roberts

(Henry was later known as B. H. Roberts.)

I was decidedly tired, nearly unto exhaustion. Fearing that my riding, which was "agin" the law, would be discovered, I slipped the broad board from the barrel head and conceived the idea of dropping down in the barrel, secure from the eyes of those who might oust me from my seat in the wagon if I were found. To my surprise, if not amazement, I discovered when I let myself down in the barrel that my feet went into about three or four inches of a sticky liquid substance which turned out to be molasses. The smarting of my chapped feet almost made me scream with pain, but I stifled it. Too tired to attempt to climb out, I remained and gradually slipped down and went to sleep doubled up in the bottom of the barrel, with such results as can well be imagined. It was daylight when I woke up, and there began to be the usual camp noises of teamsters shouting to each other to be prepared to receive the incoming teams driven from the prairie by night herdsmen. As I crawled out of the uncomfortable position, and with molasses dripping from my trousers, I was greeted by some of the teamsters and emigrants who caught sight of me with yells and laughter. I crept away as fast as I could to scrape off the syrup, which added to the weight and thickness of shirt and trousers, for there was no change of clothing for me, and so bedaubed I had to pass on until dusk and drying somewhat obliterated the discomfort (B. H. Roberts, *The Autobiography of B. H. Roberts*, ed. Gary James Bergera [Salt Lake City: Signature, 1990], 31–32).

Sarah Mousley

[The prairie by the Platte River is] the beautifulest scenery my eye's ever rested upon. The bluffs on each side the wild flowers beautiful to behold; the air redolent with odor; the calm, still waters of beautiful lakes all, all serving alike to invoke an adoration to the God [by] whose word we have left the happy scene of childhood years to repair to the mountains with the saints of light (*Diary of Sarah Mousley*, July 24, 1857, Utah State Historical Society, Salt Lake City).

Sarah DeArmon Pea Rich

It was a grand sight to see those herds of wild animals [buffalo], thousands in a gang, racing across the prairies; for the sight of our wagons seemed to frighten them, and it caused us to fear they might attack us in their flight. Well, after we got through with the buffalos, we came into a land alive with what is called prairie dogs—the whole country was alive with them. They lived in holes in the ground, and would make the hills sound with their barking all night long. They are about the size of small puppies, and as cunning as they can be. . . . If we could have caught them alive we would have tried to tame them just because they were so small and pretty. . . . From Mr. Rich's journal, he says he believes he saw at one time ten thousand head of buffalo feeding together while passing through the buffalo country (*Reminiscences of Sarah DeArmon Pea Rich [1885–1893]*, holograph [LDS Church Archives, The Church of Jesus Christ of Latter-day Saints, Salt Lake City], n.p.).

Sara Alexander

I shall always be glad I have seen the Indians in their primitive grandeur, in their own country where they were kings and where they dominated so royally. I pity their humiliation in compelling them to become civilized. So much has to be crushed in the march of improvement and in the making of a nation ("A Little Story of the Experiences of Sara Alexander When Crossing the Plains in 1859," typescript, n.p., Utah State Historical Society, Salt Lake City).

Mary Pugh Scott

Some of the children, while walking, wore a bag and picked up buffalo chips and sticks to make fires for the evening meals. As soon as we camped everyone tried to share in the labors. Some carried water and gathered wood for fires. Big high sagebrush was used and in timber country we burned wood. But all was not desolation on the long journey.

We enjoyed the smell of the pretty wild roses. At some places beautiful wild flowers of all hues could be seen and we enjoyed the singing of the birds. Young girls tended weary babies until they could be fed and put to sleep. After prayers the camp retired for the night, with camp fires burning and the lights of lanterns in the wagons. The lowing of the cattle [and] bleating of the sheep mingled with the neighing of the horses in the corrals of the wagons.

The howling of coyotes and wolves on distant hills and prairies mingled with the Half Hour Cry of the faithful guards, "All is well. All is Well" (LaRee Barson McCauley, *Life Story of Mary Pugh*, typescript, 5, Utah State Historical Society, Salt Lake City).

DAY-TO-DAY CHORES

Eliza Maria Partridge Lyman

Wednesday 4th Stayed in camp all day. Washed, ironed, baked (*Journal of Eliza Maria Partridge Lyman*, n.p.).

Oliver B. Huntington

As soon as we had struck our wagon in the corral, unyoked the cattle, gathered wood, or buffalo chips for cooking, and usually to save fuel, dig a hole in the ground about three feet long, one wide and six inches deep. This prevented the wind from blowing the heat away. . . .

The next thing was to get the cows (they were drove all together clean behind all the company) and milk, then drive stakes to. . .

These were regular and sometimes as many more, according to camping ground, sometimes have to go a mile and a half for water and sometimes had to dig wells. Each ten herded their cattle and every man and boy able to do it took their regular turn according to the number of the ten. In the ten I was in, there was an increase until the number of wagons amounted to twenty-four and twenty-five persons to herd, and it came each ones turn once in five days taking five to each day's company.

The guarding of the camp fell on each man proportionally once in seven and sometimes six nights, and then half the night, only. The herding and guarding together with my daily tasks kept me beat down and wore out all the time. The women were as well drove beat down as the men.

Sundays were scarcely a day of rest nor could it be if we traveled Monday (Wallace Stegner, *The Gathering of Zion, The Story of the Mormon Trail* [New York: McGraw-Hill, 1964], 203).

Mary Pugh Scott

Here we . . . who have been raised in luxury, are bravely trying to drive a mule team across the plains, holding our babies. We take turns driving. You can just imagine [us] women climbing in and out over wagon wheels to cook on the camp fire and wash clothes.

We sleep in our camp wagons or on the ground along the swampy river bottoms. . . . I am now 27 years old and trying hard to be a good wife. We cook in a camp kettle, it is an iron pot with three legs.

It had a heavy lid and could be set right on the beds of coals and biscuits, corn bread or cake could be put in, then a shovel full of coals was put on top to bake them. Some who had no kettles cooked on hot rocks to do their baking. Some of our meals were just broiled meat and bread. Other times all we had to eat was water gruel (a very thin mush). . . . Milk and cream could be placed in a churn in the morning and by night you could have a pat of butter by the jolting wagon over rough trails (McCauley, *Life Story of Mary Pugh*, 4–5).

Sarah Burbank

When we came to a stream, we would wash our clothes and dry them on the grass, for we might not get a place again for fifty or one hundred miles. We gathered dried dung and buffalo chips to make a fire to cook our food, dug a hole in the ground, put the skillet in the hole with a tight lid on it, put the buffalo chip on the lid, and set it afire. It baked the bread fine. That was the way we did our baking until we got where there was wood again (Burbank, "Memories of Nauvoo and Crossing the Plains," in *Voices from the Past*, 28).

C. C. A. Christensen

Our costumes would look fine at one of our so-called "Hard Times Balls." Our harts . . . assumed the most grotesque shapes. . . . Ladies' skirts and the men's trousers hung in irregular trimmings. . . . The ladies [were not] particular about whether their skirts could hide their poor footwear, if indeed they were well enough off to own a pair of shoes ("By Handcart to Utah: The Account of C.C.A. Christensen," Richard L. Jensen, trans., *Nebraska History* [Winter 1985], 66:342).

Richard Warburton

No one knows, unless they had had the same experience, what a trial it was to drive [a] team all day and guard at night. The loss of sleep was something fearful ("British Immigrants," *An Enduring Legacy* [Salt Lake City: Daughters of Utah Pioneers, 1987], 10:117–18).

George Whitaker

We never traveled on Sunday. We always rested on that day. We would put on our Sunday clothes and have a meeting. We always tried to camp by a grove of trees on a Saturday night so that we could meet in the shade on Sunday. We enjoyed our meetings just as well as though we were in a fine meeting house ("Life of George Whitaker," 20).

George Washington Hill

I was appointed hunter for the company. This increased my labors a great deal, for whenever we were in camp I was off with my gun trying to obtain meat for the fifty. And sometimes while traveling I would leave my wife, although she was hardly able to set up, to drive the team of four yoke of cattle, and take my gun and travel for miles away from the track to procure meat. In this way I have killed deer and hung them on my shoulders and carried them for as much as four miles without laying them down. And always, as soon as camp was formed in the evening, in the place of resting myself from the labors of the day, I would take my gun and go and try for meat. In this way I managed to keep meat for the family all the way and for the company the most of the time (George Washington Hill, *Incidents in the Life of George Washington Hill [1878]* [LDS Church Archives, The Church of Jesus Christ of Latter-day Saints, Salt Lake City], n.p.).

BATTLING THE ELEMENTS

William Clayton

The rain beat through the wagon covers and drenched the families and effects. It was the most severe storm we have experienced and with such wind it seems impossible to preserve our little clothing and provisions from being spoiled. But in the midst of all, the camp seems cheerful and happy and there are but few sick (William Clayton, *William Clayton's Journal: A Daily Record of the Journey of the Original Company of Mormon Pioneers from Nauvoo, Illinois, to the Valley of the Great Salt Lake* [New York: Arno Press, 1973], 14–15).

Lucy Meserve Smith

When I would wash a dish and raise it out of the water, there would be ice on it before I could get it wiped (Lucy Meserve Smith, "Original Historical Narrative of Lucy Meserve Smith" [1888–1890] [LDS Church Archives, The Church of Jesus Christ of Latter-day Saints, Salt Lake City], n.p.).

Eliza Maria Partridge Lyman

It continued to rain all day. It was almost impossible to get any thing to eat as we had to cook it out doors in the rain, over shoe in mud (*Journal of Eliza Maria Partridge Lyman*, 25).

Eliza Maria Partridge Lyman

Monday 27th A'woke in the morning and found it raining, it rained all day.

Tuesday 28th It has rained all night and is raining yet.

Wednesday 29th The weather cloudy with some rain.

Thursday 30th Still raining (*Journal of Eliza Maria Partridge Lyman*, 28).

Ruth May Fox

One night we pitched our tent in this sand when lo the wind blew and the rain descended and beat upon that tent and great was the fall thereof. Mother was hurried to the wagon of a friend and we girls held up the tent while father tried to drive in the pins, which was an almost hopeless task. . . . However, as we trudged along the next day we sang lustily:

> We may get wet a little when we have a
> shower of rain,
> The heat may skin our noses, but they'll
> soon get well again.
> And when we think of Zion's land, we'll
> forget the wet and pain
> So, Gee up! my lads. Gee whoa!
> Push on my lads, Heigh Ho!
> For there's none can lead a life like we
> merry Mormons do.
> (Ruth May Fox, "From England to Salt Lake Valley in
>   1867," *Improvement Era*, July 1935, 38:409)

Nancy Naomi Alexander Tracy

We had to cross over one fork of the Platte River. It was one quarter of a mile wide. We had to pile everything as high as we could in the wagon and then sit on top. The water was shallow at first but grew deeper as we got into the stream. Of course the men had to go in the water to guide the teams and hold on to the ox bows. The water came up to their shoulders and was very chilly. But we got across safely and unloaded the fifty wagons and crossed back to bring a herd of sheep over. That means that the men had to cross the ugly stream three different times. Then we had to stop over one day in order to dry the things. I was glad we saw the last of the river ("Life History of Nancy Naomi Alexander Tracy Written by Herself," [1895], typescript copy [L. Tom Perry Special Collections, Harold B. Lee Library, Brigham Young University, Provo, Utah], n.p.).

Eliza R. Snow

(Sister Snow described the harsh conditions for giving birth on the trail.)

[As I] journeyed onward, mothers gave birth to offspring under almost every variety of circumstances imaginable, except those to which they had been accustomed; some in tents, others in wagons—in rainstorms and in snowstorms. [I] heard of one birth which occurred under the rude shelter of a hut, the sides of which were formed of blankets fastened to poles stuck in the ground, with a bark roof through which the rain was dripping. Kind sisters stood holding dishes to catch the water. . . thus protecting the [little one] and its mother from a showerbath [on its entrance to] the stage of human life (B. H. Roberts, *A Comprehensive History of The Church of Jesus Christ of Latter-day Saints*, 7 vols. [Salt Lake City: Deseret News Press, 1930], 3:45).

ACCIDENTS AND HAZARDS

Sarah DeArmon Pea Rich

We were Several days traveling through the buffalo country Some days we could See herds of thousands together and Several times they would come in large herds crossing just ahead of our teams as hard as they could go and in Such large numbers that the roaring of them would frighten our teams So that the drivers had all they could do to prevent a Stampede among our cattle (Sarah DeArmon Pea Rich, *Autobiography, 1885–1893*, microfilm [LDS Church Archives, The Church of Jesus Christ of Latter-day Saints, Salt Lake City], 36).

Diana Eldredge

(Diana remembered the strategy those in her company used to save their lives and property during a buffalo stampede.)

The men of the company crowded all the wagons of the train into as close a bunch as possible and all the women and children into the wagons. They crowded the cattle into a line with their heads turned from the buffalo, and then stationed themselves at the head of their oxen with whips and no other weapons. . . . As the herd crowded closer to us, pawing the earth and tossing their heads, the men kept up an incessant shout and cracking of whips. Suddenly when they were just about upon us, the herd separated and one part went to one side of our camp and the other half circled the other side of our camp. Not one head of cattle was lost, nor one person injured ("History of Diana Eldredge Smoot," typescript copy in author's possession; as cited in Madsen, *Journey to Zion*, 319).

George Whitaker

On arriving home we found my sister Harriet very sick. She had been chopping some wood and had broken a blood vessel which caused her to come very near dying, but by the administration of the elders and the goodness of God, she got well very fast ("Life of George Whitaker," 31).

Karen Nielsen Jensen

(Jensen described a stampede, the cause of which still remains a mystery.)

The frenzied animals broke into a wild run . . . simultaneously rushing across the plains at utmost speed. Women and children were leaping from the flying wagons, men were applying whips or using reins in a vain attempt to check the terrified animals. Scattered and broken vehicles only added to the fright of the animals (Karen Nielsen Jensen, in *An Enduring Legacy*, 6:168).

Ann Agatha Walker Pratt

On one occasion I was jumping out while the cattle were going, and my skirt caught on the tongue bolt, and threw me down, and before I could extricate myself the nigh front wheel passed over my leg just above the ankle. I scrambled into the wagon the best way I could, I turned down my stocking expecting to see a bad bruise for it was very painful, but lo and behold there was no bruise there. I was much astonished but very thankful. The pain soon passed away and I drove my team as usual. I must relate another remarkable incident that happened. While toiling through the quick-sand of the Black hills . . . one of our dear little ones, a boy fifteen months old, being asleep was left in the wagon. It being a hot day, the sides of the cover had been tied up. The child on awaking, finding himself alone, looked out at the side and fell right between the wheels, the hind one passing over his limbs before he could be rescued. His father picked him up—I durst not look up for I expected to see his tender limbs severed from his body, but strange to say—owing to the soft sand, and the great mercy of God, all the hurt was a red mark made by the iron tire across his limbs. His father administered to him, and in a little while he was holding the whip apparently as well as ever (Pratt, "Personal Reminiscences," 21:139).

ENCOUNTERS WITH NATIVE AMERICANS

George Humpherys

I was talking to the assistant wagon master and driving the lead team, when we heard a terrible yell. We looked up the road and saw a large band of Indians coming towards us.

They were very modest in their request, for they demanded 10 yoke of oxen, 1,000 lbs. of flour, 300 lbs. sugar, 100 lbs. coffee, and 100 lbs. bacon. If we wouldn't give it to them, we would have to fight and they would take what they wanted. There was between three and four hundred Indians. Some of the men wanted to fight it out with them, but our wagon master, Mr. James Clayton, would not hear of that if there was any other way to get along with them. He told us to prepare for the worst, for we may have to fight, but he would do all he could to avoid it.

After talking to them for some time, he thought of the man in our group with smallpox. He told the chief to go with him to the wagon where the sick man lay. A number of the Indians followed their chief, thinking they were going to get all they asked for.

But when they got within twenty-five yards of the wagon, Mr. Clayton called to the sick man to look out of the wagon for he wanted to see him. He arose and looked out. The scales were just falling off his face. The chief gave a look and said, "Smallpox!" He turned his horse and yelled for his men to follow, and they did so. It was almost two miles to the Platte River, and they rode as fast as they could till they got there. Then they crossed and looked around for a few minutes, then rode off again. Mr. Clayton was watching them through a large glass.

We could not get sight of an Indian for three weeks after that. We had to conclude that smallpox was a very good thing to have close by (George Humpherys, *Autobiographical sketch*, holograph [LDS Church Archives, The Church of Jesus Christ of Latter-day Saints, Salt Lake City], n.p.).

Mary Pugh Scott

One day, due to a delay, our family wagons got separated from the main body of the Saints. Suddenly we were completely surrounded by a big band of wild Indians (who enjoyed scalping people just for the fun of it). We sat terrified and motionless with fear, praying silently that we would some way be spared a tragic end. Yelling and shouting wildly they rode around us. We shook with fear not daring to move or speak. They came closer and closer then gathered in a big group.

They held a big "Pow-Wow." Minutes seemed like hours as we tried to keep our children quiet. They gestured and yelled louder and we grew more frightened as our fate seemed so hopeless. Again I breathed a prayer, Father I am so young, will I have to die here on the plains with my family, now we are so near the end of our journey? Will I never see Zion after I have given my all for my religion? Then some of the Indians slid off their ponies and as they came nearer we saw a young white man.

He had been captured by them and forced to live with them—but he had recognized John Scott as a boy he had gone to school with in Canada. He begged and pleaded with the Indians to spare our lives and he finally persuaded them to go away. It was a miracle from God we always thought after, and today we owe all of our lives to that brave young man's pleadings and to our kind Heavenly Father (McCauley, *Life Story of Mary Pugh*, 6).

Emma James

One day as we were skipping along beside the carts and singing, for we were always happy as I remember it, a group of Indians on horse back rode up and followed along with us for a while. . . . One of the Indians seemed fascinated by the contraptions being pulled along by people. Finally his curiosity got the best of him. He leaped off his horse, ran over to one of the carts which was being pulled by a woman and her daughter and gave it such a hard push that it nearly ran over them. The woman and girl screamed and got out of the shafts as fast as they could. The Indians pushed the cart off a little ways, and then, apparently satisfied, he jumped on his horse and rode off. He, with some of his friends came back later to beg for food. We gave it to them because we were told that the Indians were our brethren and that we should treat them so. We never did have any trouble with them except that they never seemed to learn that it was stealing to take something which didn't belong to them (Laleta Dixon, "History of My Ancestor, William James of the Willey [sic] Handcart Co., 1856," typescript copy [LDS Church Archives, The Church of Jesus Christ of Latter-day Saints, Salt Lake City], n.p.).

Harry Roberts

(Brother Roberts was picking currant berries and got separated from the main camp, when he encountered three Native Americans.)

Coming to the summit of a swale in which the wagon road passed, we saw to our horror three Indians on horseback just beginning to come up out of the swale and along the road. Our contact with the Indians around the Wyoming encampment had not been sufficient to do away with the fear in which the red men were held by us, and it could be well imagined that the hair on our heads raised as we saw an inevitable meeting with these savages. . . .

I approached my savage knowing not what to do, but as I reached about the head of the horse, I gave one wild yell, the Scotch cap full of currants was dropped, and I made a wild dash to get by—and did— whereupon there was a peal of laughter from the three Indians. They say Indians never laugh, but I learned differently. As the race for the train continued with an occasional glance over the shoulder to see what the Indians were doing, I saw they were bending double over their horses with their screams of laughter (*The Autobiography of B. H. Roberts*, 26–27).

Priscilla Merriman Evans

My husband in a joking way told an Indian, who admired me, that he would trade me for a pony. He thought no more about it, but the next day here came the Indian with a pony and it was no joke to him. Never was I so frightened in all my life. . . . There was no place to hide and we did not know what to do. The captain was called and they had some difficulty in settling with the Indian without trouble ("Priscilla Merriman Evans," in *Heart Throbs of the West*, comp. Kate B. Carter [Salt Lake City: Daughters of Utah Pioneers, 1948], 9:9).

Levi Jackman

Monday, May 3. . . . We saw smoke ahead and found that what little feed there was would soon be destroyed by fire, which would be hard for us.

Tuesday, May 4. . . . We started on but had not gone far before we found that our fears were too true. The Indians had set fire to the old grass which was among the new and all had been burned together, excepting here and there a small spot. The sight was gloomy indeed (*Autobiography of Levi Jackman*, 41).

Peter Howard McBride

We saw a great many buffalo as we traveled up the Platte River. The people were forbidden to kill them, as it made the Indians angry. So they hired the Indians to kill what they [the pioneers] needed to eat. An Indian sold a man a whole buffalo for five cents' worth of tobacco. Both parties were satisfied. Sometimes a herd of fifty thousand buffalo would cross the plains, and one time our company met three thousand Sioux Indians, all warriors all in war paint. Our people were much frightened, fear held the whole camp in its grip as they all expected to be annihilated. But their fears were groundless. They told our interpreters they were going to fight the Pawnee tribes. They wouldn't hurt us because we were mostly squaws and papooses. It would be cowardly to fight us, so they gave us the road (Peter Howard McBride, *Life Sketch*, typescript, in possession of Ella Cochran Madsen, Placerville, California. Original writings in private possession of descendants; as cited in Susan Arrington Madsen, *I Walked to Zion* [Salt Lake City: Deseret Book, 1994], 44).

Diana Eldredge

There were about one hundred braves in war paint and feathers headed by a chief. They thought we had come to take their land away from them, but when they were finally convinced that we did not want to molest them, they seemed quite friendly. We cooked them a dinner after which the "peace pipe" was smoked by all men in both bands. A large fire was built and the pipe was passed around the circle. As we moved on they followed us for two or three days, but they offered no opposition to us ("History of Diana Eldredge Smoot," typescript copy in author's possession; as cited in Madsen, *Journey to Zion*, 318).

Gustave Louis Henroid

Upon one occasion, having lost track of the road, I traveled for miles alone until late in the shades of evening, approaching a small stream running into a deep ravine surrounded by a beautiful cluster of lovely shady trees. Suddenly descending the banks of the creek, what was my terrible surprise in stumbling in the midst of a band of Sioux Indians who were busily engaged in jerking buffalo meat, they having just concluded a big hunt. What could I do? Hungry and tired, lost and alone, a youth sixteen years old, standing before about one hundred stalwart, ferocious, powerful somber kings of the prairies . . .

[I] had the cowardice of unmounting my pony and making of the poor frightened steed a fortress, such as it was, to protect the also frightened rider from a shower of arrows. They never came. . . . I carelessly fastened my horse to a young sapling then quietly stepped in the midst of the tepees and singling out one of the big Tycoons offered to shake hands with the great warrior who in return gave me a very unmusical grunt; having had a fair musical education my ear was not slow to catch the vibration of his dissatisfied growl. I pointed with a smile to the tempting broiling buffalo steaks, having a fear in my heart that I might be an unwelcome and uninvited guest, intruding among the Royal blood of princes and princesses of the forest.

No signs of approval from anyone. I helped myself to a good size chunk of half fried meat, this must have been a settler for my dark friends, they interpreted it as an act of great courage and bravery on my part and no one interfered with me while I partook of one of those lunches that would perhaps have caused Delmonico's chef de cuisine to blush as well as to my epicurean proclivities. They were all amazed. I managed by gestures and signs to make my red friends understand that I had lost my way. They pointed to me where to find the wagon road, and starting out in that direction about twilight, I reached our camp just before the break of day ("Gustave Louis Henroid," in *Our Pioneer Heritage*, 11:316–32).

HARD WORK

Mary Jane Mount Tanner

(The boy that Mary's mother hired to drive the family's team to Salt Lake left the family when they were only about halfway to the valley. When he left, Mary's mother took the reigns into her own hands.)

Mother drove the team the rest of the way, yoking and unyoking in addition to her other duties. One of her oxen would never learn to hold back, and when going downhill she had to hold his horn with one hand and pound his nose with the other to keep him from running into the wagon ahead of him, a feat which would astonish some of our belles of the present day, and yet she was reared as tenderly and as little accustomed to hardship as any of them. Many times the bushes caught her dress, and she had no choice but to rush on, leaving it in pieces behind her. I wonder if those coming after her knew what those tattered rags meant (Mary Jane Mount Tanner, *Autobiography, Reminiscences and Diary* [LDS Church Archives, The Church of Jesus Christ of Latter-day Saints, Salt Lake City]; as cited in Madsen, *I Walked to Zion*, 113).

Nancy Naomi Alexander Tracy

We were now on the last half of our journey and began to feel anxious to get to our final stopping place. My husband was beginning to feel the wear of the trip severely.

Memory fails to think of anything worthy of note as we traveled on, although there was one place I remember well. The wagons had to be let down an embankment into a stream and had to travel on some distance in the stream before they could climb the bank to the road again. The men in letting the wagons down the bank into the stream had to tie strong ropes to the back of the wagons and several of them had to pull back on the ropes so as to let the wagons down easily. It took some time and was slow work but was accomplished. . . .

The travel became slower and more fatiguing. At last we got to the crossing of the Green River. The river ran on very swift and looked angry and deep. The first ten drove in. There was one Brother Gifford who held on to his ox bows till he lost his hold and went down. He could not swim but one of the brethren went to his rescue and brought him out more dead than alive but he was brought around after a while. The rest got across safely and moved on toward the mountains that we were now approaching ("Life History of Nancy Naomi Alexander Tracy," n.p.).

Andrew Christian Nielson

For five miles all around the plains you could see oxen, wagons, teamsters, and a dozen horsemen going at breakneck speed, and it was a miracle that no one was hurt, nor anything broken, but under these conditions I have seen strong men cry ("Andrew Christian Nielson, Pioneer," in *Our Pioneer Heritage*, 11:277).

AMUSEMENTS

Sarah DeArmon Pea Rich

While passing through the buffalo country we did not travel very fast for all the men folks Seemed to want to kill a buffalo So they would travel a few miles and camp and go hunting for that was new Sport for them (Rich, *Autobiography, 1885–1893*, 35).

Mary Pugh Scott

An English emigrant, whose sense of smell had left him due to age, was one day hungrily out looking for food, [when he] found a strange animal and killed it. (It was furry and black and white.) He skinned it and proudly brought it to camp, a skunk. And to his amazement everyone fled as he approached and for some days he was an outcast (McCauley, *Life Story of Mary Pugh*, 5).

C. C. A. Christensen

A very old man, who had completely lost his sense of smell, came into camp one day, after the rest of us had things somewhat in order, with a skunk which he counted on cooking for soup. This almost made the rest of us leave. He had killed it with his cane and knew nothing about its peculiar means of defense ("By Handcart to Utah: The Account of C.C.A. Christensen," *Nebraska History*, 66:342).

Mary Jane Lyttle

Young lovers strayed in the moonlight not far from camp, and I suppose repeated the old, old, but ever new story (Caroline Hopkins Clark, in *Our Pioneer Heritage*, 10:47).

Clarissa Young Spencer

One of father's [Brigham Young] most outstanding qualities as a leader was the manner in which he looked after the temporal and social welfare of his people along with guiding them in their spiritual needs. On the great trek across the plains when everyone but the most feeble walked the greater part of the way, the Saints would be gathered around the campfire for evening entertainment, if the weather was at all favorable. Then songs would be sung, music played by the fiddlers, and the men and women would forget the weariness of walking fifteen miles or so over a trackless desert while they joined in dancing the quadrille. It was his way of keeping up "morale" before such a word was ever coined (Clarissa Young Spencer, *One Who Was Valiant* [Caldwell, Idaho: Caxon Printers, 1940], 162).

Catherine Adams

We had many good times. . . . In the evenings after the horses were tethered the men would light a big bonfire, clear off a level piece of ground, dampen it down to pack it a bit, and have a dance. There were some fine musicians along who played the fiddle, mouth organ, and accordion, and we used to enjoy sitting around the fire listening to them or having a sing-song (G. A. Skov, "From Handcart to Airplane," *Deseret News* [April 4, 1931], 7).

Louisa Pratt

When we camped near a level spot of earth where water had been standing and dried away, the young men would propose a dance. The older ones, feeling the absolute need of diversion, would accede as it would cost nothing and would cheer and enliven us on our wearisome journey. In the midst of our amusements, we did not forget our prayers. We have large campfires around which we all gather, sing songs, both spiritual and comic, then all unite in prayer ("Louisa Pratt autobiography," in *Heart Throbs of the West*, 8:239).

～9～

A TRIED PEOPLE

The nature of the journey west varied along the trail and among the different companies that traveled. However, one of the few experiences that every company underwent at any given point along the trail was that of hardship. Whether in a wagon train or handcart company, enduring the rain and mud of Iowa or the snow and ice of Wyoming, no company was exempt from the hardships and trials that were part of the very nature of making a journey across a continent on foot. Numerous Saints wrote accounts of the hardships they endured; these accounts varying as much in time and place as in the nature of the hardship.

Nancy Naomi Alexander Tracy

May the Lord have mercy on our enemies' souls for their cruelty and wickedness to an innocent and law abiding people. But we are to be a tried people and to be made perfect through suffering ("Life History of Nancy Naomi Alexander Tracy Written by Herself," [1895], typescript copy [L. Tom Perry Special Collections, Harold B. Lee Library, Brigham Young University, Provo, Utah], n.p.).

Eliza Cheney

(In a letter to her family back in the States, Eliza Cheney wrote of her determination to endure all things for the Kingdom of God.)

I am willing to endure anything my sisters of the Church have to endure to help to build up this great and [latter-day] kingdom that the way may be prepared for the judgment of God upon the earth (Eliza Cheney to Parents, Brothers, and Sisters, January 1848, in *Historical*

Letters and Sketches, 1841–1919, Eliza Jane Rawson Collection [LDS Church Archives, The Church of Jesus Christ of Latter-day Saints, Salt Lake City], n.p.).

ROUGH TERRAIN

Hosea Stout
(Courtesy of the Church Archives, The Church of Jesus Christ of Latter-day Saints)

Hosea Stout

This day capped the climax of all days for traveling. The road was the worst that I had yet witnessed up hill and down through sloughs on spouty oak ridges and deep marshes, raining hard, the creek rising. The horses would sometimes sink to their bellies (*The Diary of Hosea Stout*, 3 vols. [Provo, Utah: Brigham Young University Harold B. Lee Library, 1941–43], 2:202).

Helen Mar Whitney

The road lay over a prairie, and the earth being soft and inundated with the previous rains, all that could were obliged to walk to favor the poor animals. Our feet would sink into the deep mud at every step, and some of us came near being minus of shoes (Helen Mar Whitney, *A Woman's View: Helen Mar Whitney's Reminiscences of Early Church History*, ed. Jeni Broberg Holzapfel and Richard Neitzel Holzapfel [Provo, Utah: BYU Religious Studies Center, 1997], 352–53).

Erastus Snow

(March 24, 1846)

When we wished to go to our neighbors to see our teams, we forded the seas of mud and congratulated each other on the prospects before us (Andrew Karl Larson, *Erastus Snow: The Life of a Missionary and Pioneer for the Early Mormon Church* [Salt Lake City: University of Utah Press, 1971], 107).

George Whitaker

(March 1846)

Some were heavily loaded and had very poor teams and seemed to be in the way of others that had good teams. We had to travel in line one after another. Very often the wagons that had the poor teams would get stuck in a mud hole and would have to be helped out, as no one was allowed to pass another thus situated. Therefore it became very trying to a good many. We all needed a great deal of patience. Things did not go along as pleasantly as some had expected. It was a new thing to most of us, and we found many things to contend with. It seemed very pleasant to me. I was young and strong and always willing to put my shoulder to the wheel and help my brethren ("Life of George Whitaker, A Utah Pioneer, as written by himself," typescript, 15, Utah State Historical Society, Salt Lake City).

EXHAUSTION

Elizabeth White

(October 1856)

We finally reached the last crossing of the Platte River. We were then about five hundred miles from Salt Lake. Our company camped on the east side, and the handcart company passed over that night. All our able-bodied men turned out to help them carry women and children over the river. Some of our men went through the river seventy-five times. The snow fell six inches during that night; there were thirteen deaths during the night. They were so worn out ("Autobiography of Elizabeth White Stewart," typescript, in *Ancestors of Isaac Mitton Steward and Elizabeth White*, comp. Mary Ellen B. Workman, privately printed, 1978; as cited in Susan Arrington Madsen, *I Walked to Zion* [Salt Lake City: Deseret Book, 1994], 61).

Lucina Mecham

(1853)

My sister Sarah and I stopped to rest one day, and the wagons passed us. Sarah said she was not going any farther. I begged her to come with me, but she said she would rather be eaten by wolves than go on. She tried to get me to go and catch the wagons, but I told her I would not leave her. Then she said, "I will not see the wolves get you, so come on, let us go to camp" ("Journal of Lucina Mecham Boren," in *Treasures of Pioneer History*, comp. Kate B. Carter, 7 vols. [Salt Lake City : The Daughters of Utah Pioneers, 1952-1957], 6:301–48).

Exposure to the Elements

George Whitaker
(February 9, 1845)

I did not sleep very warm as my bed was by the tent door and the wind blew in very cold. I did not say anything as I thought I would get used to it in time. We all got up about daylight next morning. Brother Pratt was up and around the first. He asked us how we had slept. I did not hear any complaints. I did not make any myself. We made a fire and got our breakfast. We all felt to rejoice and felt first-rate. Bro. Pratt had very recently built him a large and commodious brick house. It seemed as though there was something more than human nature which caused them to feel so joyful and happy to leave their comfortable homes and to go out in the dead of winter with so many young children to face the cold and the storms, and not even knowing where they were going. It seemed to me that we must be in possession of some power besides the power of man ("Life of George Whitaker," 11).

Harriet Decker Hanks
(Summer of 1847)

I had never heard of a cloud burst, but I was called to witness one that nearly cost myself and baby our lives. We had camped in Emigration canyon for noon lunch. I started with my little boy for a walk. I had not got far from the wagon when I heard a very unusual sound, and looking back across the canyon, the mountain seemed to be coming down into the road, and the roar was deafening. In less time than it takes to describe it, the water was upon me. I started for my wagon, but the water came to my waist. I had my babe in my arms. I found my strength leaving me. I could not stand. I was near a stump. I placed my baby on the stump and held him and myself from being swept away in the current, until an old gentleman seeing my danger came to me. I took [the] baby in my arms and he took us both to our wagon. By this time the water was running into my wagon box and logs, stones and other debris were hurled in every direction, but the blessed mill irons [that had been loaded in the wagon for transport to Utah] saved the day. They anchored the wagon and kept it from oversetting ("A Sketch of My Pioneer Life Written for My Dear Grand Daughter Madie E. Hatch," in *Descendants of Ephraim Knowlton Hanks and his Wives*, comp. Golden Leon and Teton Hanks Jackman [Provo, Utah: n.p.], LDS Family and Church History Department Archives, Salt Lake City).

George Washington Hill
(Winter 1846, Winter Quarters)

We had a very hard-winter and were very poorly prepared for it; we had a very hard time. I built a small log house with a chimney, made of sods cut out with a spade. We were very poorly clad, poorly fed, poorly housed, and I think [that was] the most severe winter I ever experienced. It seemed as if the adversary was determined to leave no stone unturned that would discourage me or that would hinder me in the prosecution of the journey or the accomplishing of the purpose for which I had set out, but I had endeavored to count the cost before starting and I had determined to go through if I had to go alone and on foot with nothing, realizing that the Savior's words were just as true when he said, "He that will not leave father and mother, houses and lands, wives and children, is not worthy of me" [Matthew 10:37], and also, "He that putteth his hand to the plow and looketh back is not worthy of me" [Luke 9:62], as when he said, "He that believeth and is baptized shall be saved" [Mark 16:16]. So that the exertions of the adversary were all wasted on me; they never served to discourage me in the least. They had but one effect on me, and that was to make me weep when alone that circumstances were so hard with me and that I could not provide any better for those that were dependent on me during this winter (George Washington Hill, *Incidents in the Life of George Washington Hill* [1878] [LDS Church Archives, The Church of Jesus Christ of Latter-day Saints, Salt Lake City], n.p.).

DISEASE AND DEATH

Caroline Hopkins Clark

(September 23, 1866)

Today we had more trouble on account of the death of our dear little Frank. He [kept getting] worse everyday . . . and died on September 23. He suffered a lot with pain. He has never been well since he had the measles. His little body just wasted away. He was very merry on the journey and was often singing until the last two days (Caroline Hopkins Clark, "Gathering to Zion," in *Voices From the Past: Diaries, Journals, and Autobiographies,* comp. Campus Education Week Program [Provo, Utah: Brigham Young University Press, 1980], 73).

Eliza Maria Partridge Lyman

(April 2, 1846)

At the river we came across Henry Jacobs' wagon in the mud, his wife Zina sick in bed on the top of the load, so near the wet cover that she could hardly raise her head, a babe in her arms but a few days old, and no other wagon near or friend to do any thing for her except her husband (Eliza Maria Partridge Lyman, *Journal of Eliza Maria Partridge Lyman, 1846 February–1885 December,* microfilm [LDS Church Archives, The Church of Jesus Christ of Latter-day Saints, Salt Lake City], 24).

Levi Jackman

On Monday last [July 5, 1847] I was taken violently sick with the mountain fever. I do not know as I ever experienced such excruciating pain before in my life as I did through the night Monday. It was mostly in my back and hips. I am now getting better. There are more or less several taken sick almost every day. The stony ground that we have to travel on makes it very hard for those who have to ride in the wagons. . . .

Monday, July 12. . . . My health remains quite poor so that I am hardly able to walk (Levi Jackman, *Autobiography of Levi Jackman,* typescript, 56, Utah State Historical Society, Salt Lake City).

Julia Sophia McKee

You never knew when you got up in the morning whether you would live to see the sun go down or not ("Incidents of the Life of Julia Sophia McKee, written by Herself from Memory, November 30, 1892," 4, typescript copy in author's possession; as cited in Carol Cornwall Madsen, *Journey to Zion* [Salt Lake City: Deseret Book, 1997], 328).

Sarah Burbank

Then we went along the Platte River where we had cholera. Five died with it in our company. . . . Abby died with cholera and was buried without a coffin by the Platte River along with others. We had to go on in the morning, never to see their graves again. The night that Abby was buried the wolves were howling. It was awful to hear the dirt thrown on their bodies. A young lady and I were the only ones to wash and dress her with what we could find—her underclothes and nightgown. We sewed her up in a sheet and quilt. That was all that could be done for her burial. All the women in the camp were afraid to prepare the body for burial for fear they would catch the cholera from her (Sarah Burbank, "Memories of Nauvoo and Crossing the Plains," in *Voices from the Past*, 28–29).

Caroline Hopkins Clark

I have no doubt that when my sisters know that I have lost the baby, they will say, that it would not have died if I had stayed home. There is the same good here as there. She died with the same complaint as the other children. She was so well the beginning of the journey, but we know she is safe and that if we prove true to the gospel that we have embraced, that we shall have her again with the others at the resurrection (Clark, "Gathering to Zion," in *Voices from the Past*, 73).

Nancy Naomi Alexander Tracy

(August 1846)

Our second son [Laconius Moroni Tracy], eleven years old, took his fish hook and line as he always did when we camped on a stream and went to the creek. He caught quite a string of fish and came up to the wagon and gave them to his older brother. Then he came to me and said,

"Oh, mother, my head aches so it seems all on fire." It was about the middle of July and whether it was a sun stroke or brain fever, we could not tell. Of course, we could not travel on. We did everything we could under the circumstances, but he died on the third of August [1846]. This was indeed a trying ordeal to have to bury our dear boy here in the wilderness. There were four families who stayed with us. It was night when the boy died, and we were alone in the wagon except my husband's cousin, Orlin Colvin. I happened to have some fine bleached cloth, and I made his clothes and dressed him. Brother Blodget took the side boards of our wagon and made him a decent coffin. We had funeral services, and he was laid in the silent grave on a little hill not far from where he caught his last fish. There was one other little grave there where someone had buried a child but the grave was not marked ("Life History of Nancy Naomi Alexander Tracy," n.p.).

Eliza Maria Partridge Lyman

(1846)

Sunday [July] 14th My first child was born here, in a wagon. I have named him Don Carlos. I am very uncomfortably situated for a sick woman. The scorching sun shining upon the wagon through the day and the cool air at night, is almost too much of a change to be healthy.

Wednesday 15th Brother Lyman went over the river. It was about this time that the Mormon Battalion was called for.

August 9th Since I last wrote I have been very sick with child bed fever. For many days my life seemed near its end. I am now like a skeleton so much so that those who have not been with me do not know me till told who I am. It is a fearful place to be sick with fever in a wagon with no shade over except the [wagon] cover and a July sun shining every day. All the comfort I had was the pure cold water from a spring near by. But the Lord preserved my life for some purpose for which I thank Him. My babe in consequence of my sickness is very poor but as I get better I hope to see him improve. Left the spring and went up the river about 12 miles. . . .

Nov 14th Don Carlos weighs 13 lbs, having gained 2 lbs during the last month. He is a great comfort to me.

Dec 6th My Baby sick and getting worse. Has cried all day but I cannot see what ails him.

[December] 12th The baby is dead and I mourn his loss. We have done the best we knew how for him, but nothing has done any good, he continued to fail from the time he was taken sick. My sister Caroline and I sat up every night with him and tried to save him from death for we could not bear to part with him, but we were powerless. The Lord took him and I will try to be reconciled and think that all is for the best. He was my greatest comfort and was nearly always in my arms. But he is gone and I cannot recall him, so I must prepare to meet him in another and I hope a happier world than this. I still have friends who are dear to me, if I had not I should wish to bid this world farewell, for it is full of disappointments and sorrow, but I believe that there is a power that watches over us and does all things right.

He was buried on the west side of the Missouri on the second ridge back, the eleventh grave on the second row counting from right to left, the first row being farthest from the river. This will be no guide as the place cannot be found in a few years (Lyman, *Journal of Eliza Maria Partridge Lyman*, 32–35).

Jane Snyder Richards

An instance of inhumanity should be recorded. While on our travels we passed a house with some farming about it. This was the last of civilized life until we reached Cutlers Park. A few days previously, [my daughter] had asked for some potato soup, the first thing she had shown any desire for for weeks, and as we were then traveling, we came in sight of a potato-field. One of the sisters eagerly asked for a single potato. A rough woman impatiently heard her story through, and putting her hands on her shoulders, marched her out of the house, saying, "I won't give or sell a thing to one of you damned Mormons." I turned on my bed and wept, as I heard them trying to comfort my little one in her disappointment. When she was taken from me, I only lived because I could not die (*Reminiscences of Jane Snyder Richards*, [1880], holograph [LDS Church Archives, The Church of Jesus Christ of Latter-day Saints, Salt Lake City], n.p.).

Jane Richards
(Courtesy of the Church Archives, The Church of Jesus Christ of Latter-day Saints)

Nancy Naomi Alexander Tracy

Charley Jonson, the widow Lamb's teamster, who, when he came in was so thirsty and hungry that he could not wait for supper, and so cut a piece of raw buffalo meat and ate it. The poor fellow, that night he was taken with cholera and died next morning. The brethren worked all night with him but could not save him. His groans were heart-rending to hear. They dug a deep grave, rolled him up in blankets, and carried him there. They could do no better under the circumstances ("Life History of Nancy Naomi Alexander Tracy," n.p.).

Hosea Stout

(May 9, 1846)

I returned immediately home and found the poor little afflicted child in the last agonies of death. He died in my arms about four o'clock. This was the second child which I had lost, both dying in my arms. He died with the whooping cough and black canker. He had worn down ever since he first took it . . . My wife is yet unable to go about and little Hosea, my only son now, is wearing down with the same complaint and what will be the end thereof. I have fearful foreboding of coming evil on my family yet. We are truly desolate and afflicted and entirely destitute of anything even to eat, much less to nourish the sick (*The Diary of Hosea Stout*, 2:226).

Harriet Decker Hanks

(February 12, 1846)

My Husband, in helping to get the wagon from the river, got very wet and took a violent cold that settled on his lungs from which he never recovered. He died six weeks later and was buried by the roadside between two large trees to mark his resting place. I was then twenty years old—a widow [with] a baby boy a few months old—left to get along the best I could. I had been tenderly cared for four years of my married life, but was inexperienced in this and many things I was called to go through; and you that have lost a kind, loving husband and protector, even when surrounded with home comforts know the sorrow and loneliness of heart. But homeless and traveling I knew not where, I felt desolate indeed ("A Sketch of My Pioneer Life Written for My Dear

Grand Daughter Madie E. Hatch," in *Descendants of Ephraim Knowlton Hanks and his Wives*, n.p.).

Mary Dart

There is a feeling, a loneliness connected with burying our dead a long distance from human habitation ("Sketch of the Life of Mary Dart Judd," typescript [LDS Church Archives, The Church of Jesus Christ of Latter-day Saints, Salt Lake City], 16).

Faith in the Face of Adversity

George Whitaker

(February 1846)

There was nothing said in regard to our homes and our pleasant places we had left in Nauvoo. We had given them up never to see them again. We felt we were going to a better country where we could live in peace, free from mobs and strife, where we could worship God according to our own conscience, none to molest or make us afraid ("Life of George Whitaker," 11).

Nancy Naomi Alexander Tracy

My life, ever since I became a Mormon, has been made up of moving about, of persecutions, sacrifices, poverty, sickness, and death. Through all my sufferings I never doubted but felt to cling to the gospel ("Life History of Nancy Naomi Alexander Tracy," n.p.).

Alma Ash

(Alma traveled to Zion years after the first pioneer companies arrived in Salt Lake City. Sailing from England in 1885, he then traveled by train across the long prairies. In speaking of the journey, he recalled feeling a deep appreciation for those who had walked the long, arduous miles to the valley.)

We took great interest in everything we saw and especially that which pertained to the history and travels of our people. I well remember how we regarded Omaha and Council Bluffs. We looked upon these places as almost sacred. Many times we would imagine we saw the old ox teams and the handcarts as they wended their way along the prairies or waded through the streams and rivers and then struggled up the rugged hills. Oh, what a journey, we would say. No wonder that many grew sick and weary and laid them down to die. Yes, in our mind's eye we saw them in all conditions: burying their dead by the wayside; in the corral at the shade of the evening; at prayer and at the dance; and we instinctively thanked God for the faith which these Saints had, to do this work (Alma Ash, *Autobiography of Alma Ash*, typescript [LDS Church Archives, The Church of Jesus Christ of Latter-day Saints, Salt Lake City], 30).

A Legacy of Faith

Sarah DeArmon Pea Rich

It truly was a dangerous trip and had we not been convinced by the power of the Lord to know that we were preparing to help lay the foundation for the building up of the Kingdom of our Heavenly Father on this earth according to His Holy Commandment to his Prophet Joseph Smith, we never could have undertaken such a journey.

It was our faith and our knowledge that the Lord had set His hand the second time to establish His work on the earth in order to prepare a people to be worthy to receive Him at His Second Coming, which we as a people know is near at hand, and that this work of the Latter days, will never stop, nor be stopped until He makes His appearance the second time to redeem His chosen people.

The day is now near at hand, and the rising generation that will read this book will many of them live to see that day. So, my dear children and grandchildren and great-grandchildren, and many others of my young readers, let me beg of you to lay aside all folly and foolishness, and humble yourselves before the Lord, and seek a knowledge of this the work of the Lord in this the Latter day, and be prepared to help in this Great work. For, as sure as you live and read my testimony to the truth of this work of the Lord in this the Latter days. . . it is true (Sarah DeArmon Pea Rich, *Autobiography*, in *Writings of Early Latter-day Saints and Their Contemporaries, A Database Collection*, comp. Milton V. Backman [Provo, Utah: BYU Religious Studies Center, 1996], 73–74).

J. Reuben Clark

(In the general conference of October 1947, the centennial of the arrival of the Saints in the Salt Lake Valley, President J. Reuben Clark gave the following remarks in commemoration and honor of those who traveled across the plains.)

I would like to say something about the last wagon in each of the long wagon trains that toiled slowly over the plains, up mountain defiles, down steep, narrow canyons, and out into the valley floor that was to be home—this last wagon: last, because the ox team that pulled it was the smallest and leanest and weakest, and had the tenderest feet of any in the train; it was slow starting, and slow moving; last, because, worn and creaking, it took more time to fix and to grease, for young Jimmy generally had trouble in getting the wagon jack under the "ex" [the point where a shaft called the "reach" crosses the axle]; last, because its wind-rent cover was old and patched and took hours to mend and tie up to keep out the storm; last, because the wife, heavy with child, must rest till the very moment of starting; last, because sickly little Bill, the last born, poorly nourished, must be washed and coaxed to eat the rough food, all they had; last, because it's with all his tasks—helping little Bill, cooking and cleaning up the breakfast (Mother was not able to help much)—Father took a little longer to yoke his cattle and to gird himself for the day's labor; last, because his morning prayers took a few more minutes than the others spent—he had so many blessings to thank the Lord for and some special blessings to ask the Lord to grant, blessings of health and strength, especially for his wife, and for little Bill, and for the rest, and then the blessings for himself that his own courage would not fail, but most of all for the blessing of faith, faith in God and in the Brethren who sometimes seemed so far away. For they were out in front where the air was clear and clean and where they had unbroken vision of the blue vault of heaven. The Brethren had really visioned the glory of the Lord, who walked near them, put his thoughts into their minds; his Spirit guided and directed them . . .

But back in the last wagon, not always could they see the Brethren way out in front, and the blue heaven was often shut out from their sight by heavy, dense clouds of the dust of the earth. Yet day after day, they of the last wagon pressed forward, worn and tired, footsore, sometimes almost disheartened, borne up by their faith that God loved them, that the restored gospel was true, and that the Lord led and directed the

Brethren out in front. Sometimes, they in the last wagon glimpsed, for an instant, when faith surged strongest, the glories of a celestial world, but it seemed so far away and the vision so quickly vanished because want and weariness and heartache and sometimes discouragement were always pressing so near. . . .

When the train moved forward in the early morning sun and the oxen with a swinging pull that almost broke the tongue got the last wagon on the move, the dust in the still morning air hung heavy over the road. Each wagon from the first stirred up its own cloud, till when the last wagon swung into line, the dust was dense and suffocating. It covered that last wagon and all that was in it; it clung to clothes; it blackened faces; it filled eyes already sore, and ears. The wife, soon to be a mother, could hardly catch her breath in the heavy, choking dust, for even in the pure air she breathed hard from her burden. Each jolt of the wagon, for those ahead had made wagon ruts almost "ex" deep, wrung from her clenched lips a half-groan she did her best to keep from the ears of the anxious, solicitous husband plodding slowly along, guiding and goading the poor, dumb cattle, themselves weary from the long trek. So through the long day of jolting and discomfort and sometimes pain, and sometimes panting for breath, the mother, anxious only that the unborn babe should not be injured, rode, for she could not walk; and the children walked, for the load was too heavy and big for them to ride; and the father walked sturdily alongside and prayed. . . .

So through dust and dirt, dirt and dust, during the long hours, the longer days—that grew into weeks and then into months, they crept along till, passing down through its portals, the valley welcomed them to rest and home. . . .

That evening was the last of the great trek, the mightiest trek that history records since Israel's flight from Egypt, and as the sun sank below the mountain peaks of the west . . . they of the last wagon, and of the wagon before them, and of the one before that, and so to the very front wagon of the train, these all sank to their knees in the joy of their souls, thanking God that at last they were in Zion—"Zion, Zion, lovely Zion; Beautiful Zion; Zion, city of our God!" ["Beautiful Zion, Built Above," *Hymns*, no. 44]. They knew there was a God, for only he could have brought them, triumphant (J. Reuben Clark Jr., "To Them of the Last Wagon," *Ensign*, July 1997, 36–38).

☙ 10 ❧

From Wyoming to Utah

As the Saints continued their journey through the seemingly endless expanse of wilderness, the natural landmarks that dotted the trail west began to provide the pioneers with a sense of progression and familiarity. For many, structures such as Chimney Rock, Independence Rock, and Devil's Gate not only provided beautiful and interesting scenery but also added a sense of chronology and progression to their trek.

Chimney Rock

Richard Ballantyne

Camped opposite Chimney Rock . . . Here the scenery is remarkably, interesting and romantic. It produces an impression as if we were bordering on a large and antiquated city (Richard Ballantyne, *Journal, 1848 May–August* [LDS Church Archives, The Church of Jesus Christ of Latter-day Saints, Salt Lake City], 15).

Chimney Rock
(Courtesy of the Church Archives, The Church of Jesus Christ of Latter-day Saints)

Sophia Goodridge

(Sophia described the view she enjoyed from the top of Chimney Rock.)

The Sweetwater flows southwest at the base of the rock and winds around the foot of the mountains (*Diary of Sophia Lois Goodridge*, September 8, 1850, Utah State Historical Society, Salt Lake City).

Wilford Woodruff

(Wilford Woodruff and John Brown went ahead of the rest of the camp and climbed Chimney Rock to offer a prayer to the Lord.)

We offered up our prayers according to the order of the priesthood. We prayed earnestly for the blessing of God to r[est] upon President Young and his brethren, the Twelve and all of the Pioneer Camp and the whole Camp of Israel and House of Israel, our wives and children, and relatives [in the] Mormon Battalion, all the Church Abroad . . . And that the Lord would hasten the time . . . [for] the building up of Zion in the last days. . . . And while offering up our prayers the spirit of the Lord descended upon us and we truly felt to rejoice (Wilford Woodruff, *Wilford Woodruff's Journal, 1833–1898*, ed. Scott G. Kenney, 9 vols. [Midvale, Utah: Signature Books, 1983], 3:211).

Sarah DeArmon Pea Rich

On the 29th of July we camped in sight of what is called Chimney Rock and on August first, we camped at the foot of Chimney Rock. This is a large mound with a rock sticking up in the center like a chimney about two hundred and fifty feet high. Here many of our camp went on to the top of the mound and found the names of some of the pioneers that were ahead of us for they had [passed] there some time before. Here my husband wrote his name on the rock with red keel, also my name, and the names of his other wives that were with us, and our children's names. We left and traveled on and came in sight of Laramie peak. We then began to cheer up thinking we were getting nearer our journey's end, for we had word from President Young and Kimball telling us to cheer up, and it would not be long before we would find a resting place (Sarah DeArmon Pea Rich, *Autobiography, 1885–1893*, microfilm [LDS Church Archives, The Church of Jesus Christ of Latter-day Saints, Salt Lake City], 38).

SCOTT'S BLUFF

While the Camp of Israel was stationed at Scott's Bluff, Brigham Young took the opportunity to reprove the members of his company for overindulgence in cardplaying and dancing, and other forms of laziness.

He also called them to repentance for the spirit of contention that they had allowed to enter the Camp of Israel, saying that he would not travel with them any longer unless they repented and committed to walking more uprightly before God.

Wilford Woodruff

Traveled to Scott's Bluffs and Alexander Bediam and myself explored Scott's Bluffs from top to bottom for about ten miles; they had many grand formations of nature in some places. We rolled off large rocks of near a ton's weight that would go thundering down the mountain and into the vale beneath, leveling the cedars to the earth and starting the wolves from their hiding places as it bounded on its way for half a mile from its starting place. After spending several hours of hard labor, though pleasant, among those grand ruins or bluffs we left them and returned to camp. We passed Burdoe's trading post.... Brother Corrier turned his wagon bottom side upwards; broke [the] thing up. The Indians tried to raise a stampede among us, but did not do it. Traveled 20 miles and camped (*Wilford Woodruff Journals*, August 14, 1850 [LDS Church Archives, The Church of Jesus Christ of Latter-day Saints, Salt Lake City], n.p.).

Levi Jackman

Saturday, [May] 29. Cold, wet morning. Did not start early. For some time past some of the brethren had indulged in many things that were leading them astray, such as dancing too much and playing card, dice, etc., and using bad language. Br. Young, seeing the situation of the camp, improved an opportunity this morning after the rain had stopped to call the camp together. He reproved them sharply for their conduct and warned them of the distress that would come to them unless they repented and reformed. After much good instruction and admonition, he called on them to know whether they would reform. They covenanted that they would. He then appointed the next day for a day of fasting and prayer, and for [the] breaking of bread. After noon we traveled eight and one-half miles. It rained smartly before we camped, but stopped before sunset.

Sunday, [May 30]. We attended to the duties of the day. A good spirit prevailed and many expressed their determination to do better

(Levi Jackman, *Autobiography of Levi Jackman*, typescript, 47–48, Utah State Historical Society, Salt Lake City).

Brigham Young

I remarked last Sunday that I had not felt much like preaching to the brethren on this mission. This morning I feel like preaching a little, and shall take for my text, "That as to pursuing our journey with this company with the spirit they possess, I am about to revolt against it." This is the text I feel like preaching on this morning, consequently I am in no hurry. In the first place, before we left Winter Quarters, it was told to the brethren and many knew it by experience, that we had to leave our homes, our houses, our land and our all because we believed in the Gospel as revealed to the Saints in these last days. The rise of the persecutions against the Church was in consequence of the doctrines of eternal truth taught by Joseph. Many knew this by experience. Some lost their husbands, some lost their wives, and some their children through persecution, and yet we have not been disposed to forsake the truth and turn and mingle with the gentiles, except a few who have turned aside and gone away from us, and we have learned in a measure, the difference between a professor of religion and a possessor of religion. Before we left Winter Quarters it was told to the brethren that we were going to look out a home for the Saints where they would be free from persecution by the gentiles, where we could dwell in peace and serve God according to the Holy Priesthood, where we could build up the kingdom so that the nations would begin to flock to our standard. I have said many things to the brethren about the strictness of their walk and conduct when we left the gentiles, and told them that we would have to walk upright or the law would be put in force, etc. Many have left and turned aside through fear, but no good upright, honest man will fear. The Gospel does not bind a good man down and deprive him of his rights and privileges. It does not prevent him from enjoying the fruits of his labors. . . . You can see the fruits of the spirit, but you cannot see the spirit itself with the natural eye, you behold it not. You can see the result of yielding to the evil spirit and what it will lead you to, but you do not see the spirit itself nor its operations, only by the spirit that's in you. Nobody has told me what has been going on in camp, but I have known it all the while. I have been watching its movements, its influence, its effects, and I know the result if it is not put a stop to. I want you to understand that inasmuch as we are beyond the power of the gentiles where the devil has tabernacles in the priests and the people, we are beyond their reach, we are beyond their power, we are beyond their grasp, and what has the devil now to work upon? Upon the spirits of men in this camp, and if you do not open your hearts so that the Spirit of God can enter your hearts and teach you the right way, I know that you are a ruined people and will be destroyed and that without remedy, and unless there is a change and a different course of conduct, a different spirit to what is now in this camp, I go no farther. I am in no hurry. Give me the man of prayers, give me the man of faith, give me the man of meditation, a sober-minded man, and I would far rather go amongst the savages with six or eight such men than to trust myself with the whole of this camp with the spirit they now possess. Here is an opportunity for every man to prove himself, to know whether he will pray and remember his God without being asked to do it every day; to know whether he will have confidence enough to ask of God that he may receive without my telling him to do it. If this camp was composed of men who had newly received the Gospel, men who had not received the priesthood, men who had not been through the ordinances in the temple and who had not had years of experience, enough to have learned the influence of the spirits and the difference between a good and an evil spirit, I should feel like preaching to them and watching over them and telling them all the time, day by day. But here are the Elders of Israel, men who have had years of experience, men who have had the priesthood for years, and have they got faith enough to rise up and stop a mean, low, groveling, covetous, quarrelsome sprit? No, they have not, nor would they try to stop it, unless I rise up in the power of God and put it down. I do not mean to bow down to the spirit that is in this camp, and which is rankling in the bosoms of the brethren, and which will lead to knock downs and perhaps to the use of the knife to cut each other's throats if it is not put a stop to. I do not mean to bow down to the spirit which causes the brethren to quarrel. When I wake up in the morning, the first thing I hear is some of the brethren jawing each other and quarreling because a horse has got loose in the night. I have let the brethren dance and fiddle and act the [fool] night after night to see what they will do, and what extremes they would go to, if suffered to go as far as they would. I do not love to see it. The brethren say they want a little exercise to pass away time in the evenings, but if you can't tire yourselves bad enough with a day's journey without dancing every night, carry your guns on your shoulders and walk, carry your wood to camp instead of lounging and lying asleep in your wagons, increasing the load until your teams are tired to death and ready to drop to the earth. Help your teams over mud holes and bad places instead of lounging in your wagons and that will give you exercise enough without dancing. Well, they will play cards, they will play checkers, they will play dominoes, and if they had the privilege and were where they could get whiskey, they would be drunk half their time, and in one week they would quarrel, get to high words and draw their knives to kill each other. This is what such a course of things would lead to. Don't you know it? Yes. Well, then, why don't you try to put it down? I have played cards once in my life since I became a Mormon to see what kind of spirit would attend it, and I was so well satisfied, that I would rather see in your hands the dirtiest thing you could find on the earth, than a pack of cards. You never read of gambling, playing cards, checkers, dominoes, etc., in the scriptures, but you do read of men praising the Lord in the dance, but whoever read of praising the Lord in a game at cards? If any man had sense enough to play a game at cards, or dance a little without wanting to keep it up all the time, but exercise a little and then quit it and think no more of it, it would do well enough, but you want to keep it up till midnight and every night, and all the time. You don't know how to control your senses. Last winter when we had our seasons of recreation in the council house, I went forth in the dance frequently, but did my mind run on it? No! To be sure, when I was dancing, my mind was on the dance, but the moment I stopped in the middle or the end of a tune, my mind was engaged in prayer and praise to my Heavenly Father and whatever I engage in, my mind is on it while engaged in it, but the moment I am done with it, my mind is drawn up to my God. The devils which inhabit the gentiles' priests are here. . . . Do we suppose that we are going to look out a home for the Saints, a resting place, a place of peace where they can build up the kingdom and bid the nations welcome, with a low, mean, dirty, trifling, covetous, wicked spirit dwelling in our bosoms? It is vain! . . . Joking, nonsense, profane language, trifling conversation and loud laughter do not belong to us. Suppose the angels were witnessing the hoe down the other evening, and listening to the haw haws the other evening, would they not be ashamed of it? I am ashamed of it. . . . Now let every man repent of his weakness, of his follies, of his meanness, and every kind of wickedness, and stop your searing and profane language, for it is in this camp and I know it, and have known it. I have said nothing about it, but I now tell you, if you don't stop it you shall be cursed by the Almighty and shall dwindle away and be damned. Such things shall not be suffered in this camp. . . . I am one of the last to ask my brethren to enter into solemn covenants, but if they will not enter into a covenant to put away their iniquity and turn to the Lord and serve Him and acknowledge and honor His name, I want them to take their wagons and retreat back, for I shall go no farther under such a state of things. If we don't repent and quit our wickedness we will have more hindrances than we have had, and worse storms to encounter, I want the brethren to be ready for meeting tomorrow at the time appointed, instead of rambling off, and hiding in their wagons to play cards, etc. I think it will be good for us to have a fast meeting tomorrow and a prayer meeting to humble ourselves and turn to the Lord and he will forgive us (William Clayton, *William Clayton's Journal: A Daily Record of the Journey of the Original Company of Mormon Pioneers from Nauvoo, Illinois, to the Valley of the Great Salt Lake* [New York: Arno Press, 1973], 189).

Horace K. Whitney

Saturday the 29th [May 29, 1847].—The clouds dark and loring with a drizzly rain, similar to that of yesterday morning. The horn was blown about half past 10 a.m. for the brethren to get up their cattle and horses as it had somewhat the appearance of clearing off fair. Some of them had wandered a considerable distance so that as much as an hour elapsed before they could be brought to the camp and put before the wagons. After which the brethren in the camp were called together and President Young arose and first told the captains of tens to call their respective companies around them which was done and Thomas Bullock, the clerk, proceeded to call the roll. And two were absent who had gone out hunting this morning, viz.—Joseph Hancock and Andrew Gibbons. The president then said, "I will take this for my text: I shall make a revolt at the idea of going with this company any farther with the spirit that they now possess. From this I shall make my discourse." He then proceeded to say that the practice some of the members of this camp had indulged in for a few days past, would ultimately lead them to ruin and death, viz.: playing at cards, dominoes, checkers, dancing, levity, etc. That these situations were no harm within and of themselves, if the people just knew when to stop and break off immediately, and when they retired to their beds, not to forget to bow before the Lord and thank him for the privilege of dancing. That by and by, they would get to playing at cards, one would accuse the other of cheating, and then the next thing would be a knock down and from thence would draw weapons on each other and shed blood. Such, he said, were the inevitable consequences of such a course, if not checked in the bud. That the Devil knew better than to go so far as to make a man deny the Priesthood in this camp, but was content to make him commit these lesser offences, that would make him forget God, and finally lead to that result. He then called for a division of the camp, that is, for the Quorums of the Twelve, High Priests, Seventies, Elders and members, to form in a body by themselves. He then exhorted them separately to the observance of their duties, and called upon them all to covenant to desist from trivial and bad practices, and to serve faithfully the Lord with their whole hearts, which they did unanimously by raising their right hands. He then moved that tomorrow be a day devoted to fasting and prayer to be conducted by the Bishops, as himself with his brethren, the Twelve, and some others wished to retire apart by themselves. After he had ended, Heber [C. Kimball], Brothers O[rson] Pratt, W[ilford] Woodruff, and Colonel Markham each spoke a few minutes in confirmation of what had been said, and the meeting was dismissed. There were present of the Quorum of the Twelve, 8; High Priests, 18; Seventies, 78; Elders, 8; besides the members. The meeting lasted near two hours (Horace K. Whitney *Journals, 1843; 1846–47*, typescript [LDS Church Archives, The Church of Jesus Christ of Latter-day Saints, Salt Lake City], 65–6).

FORT LARAMIE

Wilford Woodruff

We next visited Fort Laramie, now occupied by thirty-eight persons, French mostly, who have married the Sioux. Mr. Burdow is the superintender. This fort is 168 by 116 outside. There are six rooms upon two sides, and three rooms upon the north and three upon the south occupied by stores, blacksmith and dwellings. It is quite a pleasant situation for a fort (*Wilford Woodruff's Journal*, 3:192–93).

William I. Appleby

Traveled about fifteen miles. Passed some traders' encampment, stopped a short time at noon, set three wagon tires, and encamped about two miles beyond Fort Laramie. During the day we passed the graves of three gold diggers, all from the State of Missouri, we believe. The wolves had disinterred one. Stoves, broken ploughs, pieces of wagons, iron, etc., lie strewn along the roads [likely from gold diggers that found these items too cumbersome to travel with]. I visited the Fort and the following morning, purchased twenty-eight pounds of bacon at ten cents per pound and carried the same on my back to camp, some two miles (William I. Appleby, *Journal*, September 5, 1849, as printed in the *Journal History of The Church of Jesus Christ of Latter-day Saints*, October 27, 1849 [LDS Church Archives, The Church of Jesus Christ of Latter-day Saints, Salt Lake City]).

SWEETWATER RIVER

Abner Blackburn

The Sweetwater River rippled along in its course from the lofty summit of Fremonts Peaks [in] the Rocky Mountains. . . . All the companies lay over to rest a few days in this lovely place [with] the hunters after game and sight seers on the mountains. Continued our journey up this stream with a gradual ascent until we reached the summit of the South Pass (*Frontiersman: Abner Blackburn's Narrative*, ed. Will Bagley [Salt Lake City: University of Utah Press, 1992], 60).

Samuel Gifford

The horror that reigned in camps ahead of us cannot be described. Sometimes for miles could be seen, feather beds, blankets, quilts, and clothing of every kind strewed over the plains, also wagon tires and irons of every description, gun barrels, stoves, etc. etc. The bottom of the Sweetwater was also lined with wagon tires, chains and other irons. And fresh graves could be seen in every direction. We met some missionaries going east who said they met companies of the gold emigration that were driving twelve abreast, hurrying to get away from the Cholera (Samuel Kendall Gifford,

Reminiscences, 1864, typescript [LDS Church Archives, The Church of Jesus Christ of Latter-day Saints, Salt Lake City], n.p.).

INDEPENDENCE ROCK

Samuel Harrison Bailey Smith

Independence Rock
(Courtesy of the Church Archives, The Church of Jesus Christ of Latter-day Saints)

We moved on until we arrived at Independence Rock. The evening of our arrival I went up to the top of the Rock to hear the band play, and also to sing several hymns. While here, one of the company's cows was poisoned by drinking below where two snakes were fighting (Samuel Harrison Bailey Smith, *Reminiscences and Diary*, April 1856–July 1863 [LDS Church Archives, The Church of Jesus Christ of Latter-day Saints, Salt Lake City], n.p.).

Curtis Edwin Bolton

Near Independence Rock I gathered about 50 lbs. saleratus [alkali soda]. The evening we camped there, the band played most beautifully till late. Some danced up on top of the rock where the band were. It was a clear night and full moon. My team became so weak here that I left Brother Brigham's company and stopped on good feed one week to recruit [rest and recuperate], and killed and dried some buffalo meat (*Curtis Edwin Bolton, Pioneer Missionary: History, Descendants and Ancestors*, comp. Cleo H. Evans [Fairfax, VA.: Mrs. Cleo H. Evans, 1968], 21).

Rachel Emma Wooley Simmons

(Rachel Simmons left in a company that departed from Winter Quarters in May 1848. She told of passing Independence Rock after hearing about it from companies that traveled west before hers.)

We heard so much of Independence Rock before we got there. They said we should have a dance on top of it, as we had many a dance while on the plains. We thought it would be so nice, but when we got there, the company was so small it was given up. We nooned at this place, but Father stayed long enough for us children to go all over it. I went with the boys and with Catherine. It is an immense rock with holes and crevices where the water is dripping cool and sparkling. We saw a great many names of persons that had been cut in the rock, but we were so disappointed in not having a dance. Our company was so small, and we had not a note of music or a musician. I was told afterwards, by some of the girls that we had traveled with, that they had a party there; but President Young had all the Music with him ("Journal of Rachel Emma Wooley Simmons," in *Heart Throbs of the West*, ed. Kate B. Carter, 8 vols. [Salt Lake City: Daughters of Utah Pioneers, 1950], 162).

Wilford Woodruff

We examined the many names and lists of names of the trappers, traders, travelers, and emigrants which are painted upon these rocks. Nearly all the names were put on with red, black, and yellow paint. Some had washed out and defaced. The greatest number was put on within a few years. Some of them were quite plain of about thirty years standing (*Wilford Woodruff's Journal*, 3:211).

DEVIL'S GATE

Devil's Gate provided an impressive sight for the Saints. A pass worn through rock by the Sweetwater River, the rock to each side rose three hundred and seventy feet in the air.

Parley P. Pratt

June 22nd: . . . The morning is calm and clear. Early this morning I visited the top of "Devil's Gate Rock," having with me my barometer and thermometer. By a barometrical measurement, the perpendicular walls were about 400 feet high about the river, where here cuts through a granite rock, forming a chasm about 900 or 1000 feet in length, and 130 feet in breadth. The rock upon the

Parley P. Pratt

(Public Domain, Courtesy of BYU Online Collection)

right bank runs back from the river about a quarter of a mile, and consists of alternated and perpendicular strata of gray granite and scoriated trap rock. I observed five alternate strata of trap rock trending to the northeast and southwest: these varied in breadth from one to five rods. The bed of the river in this chasm is nearly choked up by massive fragments of rock, which have been precipitated from above. About a quarter of a mile from the river, near the point of this granite hill, appeared some sandstone and conglomerate formation (cited in B. H. Roberts, *A Comprehensive History of The Church of Jesus Christ of Latter-day Saints*, 7 vols. [Salt Lake City: Deseret News Press, 1930], 3:179).

Erastus Snow

From the ford [at the Sweetwater River], we gradually ascended about five miles, passed through an opening in the chain of rocks, descended to the river bottom again, and camped about a mile above what is commonly called the Devil's Gate (having traveled about fifteen miles today), which is an aperture in the mountains or chasm through which the river forces itself: It is about one hundred feet wide with perpendicular rocks on either side, the barometrical height of which was ascertained by Prof. Pratt to be four hundred feet. From the lower end of this aperture I followed a foot path on the brink of the river, about half a mile until I was directly under the highest point of the rocks where the river, roaring furiously among the huge rocks, filled its narrow channel, and compelled me to retreat by the way I came ("From Nauvoo to Salt Lake in the Van of the Pioneers. The Original Diary of Erastus Snow," ed. Moroni Snow, *Improvement Era*, December 1911, 15:167–68).

Nelson W. Whipple

After we passed the South Pass, as it is called, the captain told his company that if they felt like dancing to dance and enjoy themselves, as he felt as though we were delivered from under the hands of our [enemies] who would not have the power to abuse us as they had before done (Nelson Wheeler Whipple, *Autobiography and Journal*, August 1850 [LDS Church Archives, The Church of Jesus Christ of Latter-day Saints, Salt Lake City], n.p.).

Green River Crossing

Horace K. Whitney

During this afternoon (at the Green River) we were all much surprised by the unexpected arrival of Elder Samuel Brannan who was at the head of the company of the brethren that went round by sea last year from New York city to California—He was accompanied by three men, two of whom had come through with him from the latter country—with one of them I was well acquainted. This man is [Charles C.] Smith and is, I believe, some distant relation of our prophet Joseph. He left Nauvoo (where I made his acquaintance) some two years since for Oregon. One of the other two men was one of the individuals seen with Mr. Bridger the other day—the other man I did not know. Elder Brannan gives a very favorable account of climate, soil, etc. of California and appears quite anxious that we should immediately go there to take possession of the country, before it becomes occupied by others. He had left Yerba Buena April 13th—This place is situated on the bay of San Francisco and from all accounts bids fair to become in time a flourishing city. . . . Mr. Smith informed us that in Oregon they had two seasons, rain and dry (Horace Kimball Whitney, *Journal*, cited in *Frontiersman: Abner Blackburn's Narrative*, 53).

Charles Darwin

(Darwin encountered the Latter-day Saint ferrymen that ran the ferry crossing the Green River.)

Four dollars is the charge for wagons and fifty cents for packs and men, though they do not hesitate to carry any one for nothing who is poor. Perfect gentlemen are they, in conversation and conduct and entire bearing. They had been several of them in the mines and got gold and now lived at Salt Lake. . . . Quite a comedy was enacted in my presence by a crowd who had a boat with them and thought to scare [the Saints running the ferry] by vulgarity and show of crossing themselves the owner of the ferry with their terms. He manfully and kindly resisted. I was glad to see the rascals foiled. I say rascals and their conduct justified the term (cited in Dale L. Morgan "The Ferries of the Forty-Niners," *Annals of Wyoming* [April 1960], 63).

FORT BRIDGER

Wilford Woodruff

The calculation was to spend the day at the fort . . . As soon as I got my breakfast I rigged up my trout rod that I had brought with me from Liverpool, fixed my reel, line, and artificial fly and went to one of the brooks close by camp to try my luck catching trout. The man at the fort said there were but very few trout in the streams. And a good many of the brethren were already at the creeks with their rods and lines trying their skill baiting with fresh meat and grasshoppers, but no one seemed to catch any. I went and flung my fly . . . it being the first time that I ever tried the artificial fly in America, or ever saw it tried. I watched it as it floated upon the water with as much intense interest as [Benjamin] Franklin did his kite. . . . And as Franklin received great joy when he saw electricity or lightning descend on his kite string, in like manner was I highly gratified when I saw the nimble trout dart my fly, hook himself, and run away with the line (*Journal of Wilford Woodruff*, July 8, 1847, 3:225).

ASCENDING THE MOUNTAINS

Ann Agatha Walker Pratt

As we neared our destination, our journey became wearisome and full of toil. Grass became scarce, cattle began to give out. Often, when an ox gave out, a cow was put in its place. The roads were rough, wagons had to be pitched up, till sometimes you would wonder how they could go at all. One of my calamities was my lock-chain giving out, and in going down a hill I had to hold the nigh ox by the horn and tap the off one over the face and keep saying, "Whoa, Back; Whoa, Back," and nearly hold my breath till I got down to the bottom, then stop, draw a breath of relief, see that all was right, then on again, for others were right on our heels and we had to get out of their way (You can just imagine what a condition our skirts were in.) (Ann Agatha Walker Pratt, "Personal Reminiscences," *Woman's Exponent* [March 15, 1893], 21:139).

Thomas Bullock

(Thomas Bullock describes trying to steer a wagon down one of the mountain ridges.)

[It is] like jumping off the roof of a house (Thomas Bullock, *Journal of Thomas Bullock*, July 22, 1847, typescript [LDS Church Archives, The Church of Jesus Christ of Latter-day Saints, Salt Lake City], n.p.).

Sarah DeArmon Pea Rich

(Years after she crossed the plains, Sarah told of her sentiments about making the journey on foot.)

O, what a time we all had crossing the plains from Nauvoo to Salt Lake City! When I now see those brethren and sisters come to these valleys riding in [train] cars in the shade, and that too, in one third shorter time than we were coming, and when they get here have something nice to eat and plenty in the land, and then hear them complain of hard times! I think they ought to have at least 2 weeks experience such as the brothers and sisters had when we came, then perhaps they would feel more thankful, and would not feel to complain, as I have heard many do. When we came there was no one to welcome us with potatoes, fat beef, honey, butter, and all the good things that this country could produce. No, we could have nothing of the kind, but yet we felt to thank the Lord for protecting us to where we could rest in peace (Rich, *Autobiography, 1885–1893*, 39).

11

"This Is the Right Place"

After traveling thousands of miles, Erastus Snow and Orson Pratt were the first pioneers to enter the Salt Lake Valley. Three days later, on July 24, 1847, Brigham Young arrived and recognized the valley as the "right place" from a vision he had received previously. Many, excited at the prospect of finally finding their home, described the valley as beautiful and glistening. Others reported the valley's barrenness and were prepared to walk another thousand miles to find a place with more foliage. Regardless, the Saints trusted in their leaders and made preparations to stay.

Entering the Valley

Because of the mountainous terrain and having to forge new trails across sagebrush-covered hills, many in the Vanguard Company, including Brigham Young, contracted Rocky Mountain spotted fever from tick bites. Not wanting to be detained further, Brigham Young divided the company into two and deployed an advance group to blaze a trail and to begin planting. This advance group consisted of forty-two men and twenty-three wagons and was led by Orson Pratt.

Orson Pratt

(Orson Pratt and Erastus Snow were sent ahead to blaze a trail for those following behind.)

No frost this morning, but a heavy dew. . . . Brother Erastus Snow . . . and myself proceeded in advance of the camp down Last

Creek four and a half miles, to where it passes through a canyon and issues into the broad, open valley below. . . . Mr. Snow and myself ascended this hill, from the top of which a broad, open valley about 20 miles wide and 30 miles long, lay stretched out before us, at the north end of which the broad waters of the Great Salt Lake glistened in the sunbeams, containing high mountainous islands from 25 to 30 miles in extent.

After issuing from the mountains among which we had been shut up for many days, and beholding in a moment such an extensive open scenery before us, we could not refrain from a shout of joy which almost involuntarily escaped from our lips the moment this grand and lovely scenery was within our view. . . .

July 22—This morning George A. Smith and myself, accompanied by seven others rode into the valley to explore, leaving the camp to follow on and work the road, which here required considerable labor. . . . After going down into the valley about five miles, we turned our course to the north, down towards the Salt Lake. For three or four miles from the mountains the springs were very abundant, the water excellent, and generally with gravel bottoms ("Over the Pioneer Trail: The Original Record of Prof. Orson Pratt," *Improvement Era*, August 1912, 15:944–46).

Thomas Bullock

Thomas Bullock

(Courtesy of the Church Archives, The Church of Jesus Christ of Latter-day Saints)

(Thomas was part of the advance company and reached the valley July 22, 1847.)

When we turned round the hill to the right and came in full view of the Salt Lake in the distance, with its blue hills on its islands towering up in bold relief behind the silvery lake, a very exclusive valley burst forth upon our view, dotted three or four places with timber—I should expect the valley to be about thirty miles long and twenty miles wide—I could not help shouting, "Hurra, hurra, hurra, there's my home at last" (*Diary of Thomas Bullock*, July 22, 1847, holograph [LDS Church Archives, The Church of Jesus Christ of Latter-day Saints, Salt Lake City], n.p.).

William Clayton

(William was a member of the advance company.)

There is an extensive, beautiful, level-looking valley from here to the lake which I should judge, from the number of deep green patches, must be fertile and rich.

The intervening valley appears to be well supplied with streams, creeks, and lakes . . . There is but little timber in sight anywhere, and that is mostly on the banks of creeks and streams of water which is about the only objection which could be raised in my estimation to this being one of the most beautiful valleys and pleasant places for a home for the Saints which could be found. Timber is evidently lacking but we have not expected to find a timbered country. There may be timber on the mountains which the long distance would render impossible to be seen with the naked eye, but the mountains through which we have passed have very little on them. In some places may be seen a grove of small fir or cedar or pine and in the valleys some cottonwood and other small timber. There is doubtless timber in all passes and ravines where streams descend from the mountains. There is no prospect for building log houses without spending a vast amount of time and labor, but we can make Spanish brick and dry them in the sun; or we can build lodges as the Pawnee Indians do in their villages. For my own part I am happily disappointed in the appearance of the valley of the Salt Lake, but if the land be as rich as it has the appearance of being, I have no fears but the Saints can live here and do well while we will do right (William Clayton, *William Clayton's Journal: A Daily Record of the Journey of the Original Company of Mormon Pioneers from Nauvoo, Illinois, to the Valley of the Great Salt Lake* [New York: Arno Press, 1973], 308).

Wilford Woodruff

(Wilford arrived with the main body of the Vanguard Company.)

This, the 24th day of July 1847, was an important day in the history of my life, and in the history of The Church of Jesus Christ of Latter-day Saints. After traveling from our encampment . . . we came in full view of the valley of the Great Salt Lake, or the Great Basin—the Land of Promise, held in reserve by the hand of God as a resting place for the Saints.

We gazed with wonder and admiration upon the vast fertile valley spread out before us for about twenty-five miles in length and sixteen miles in width, clothed with a heavy garment of vegetation, and in the midst of which glistened the waters of the Great Salt Lake, with mountains all around towering to the skies, and streams, rivulets and creeks of pure water running through the beautiful valley.

After a hard journey from Winter Quarters of more than one thousand miles . . . to gaze upon a valley of such vast extent surrounded with a perfect chain of everlasting mountains covered with eternal snow with their innumerable peaks like pyramids towering towards heaven, presented at one view to us the grandest scenery and prospect that we could have obtained on earth. Thoughts of pleasant meditation ran in rapid succession through our minds at the anticipation that not many years hence the House of God would be established in the mountains and exalted above the hills, while the valleys would be converted into orchards, vineyards, fields, etc., planted with cities, and the standard of Zion be unfurled, unto which the nations would gather (Matthias F. Cowley, *Wilford Woodruff* [Salt Lake City: Bookcraft, 1964], 313).

Wilford Woodruff

(Courtesy of the Church Archives, The Church of Jesus Christ of Latter-day Saints)

Wilford Woodruff

(Decades after arriving in the valley, Wilford recorded his experience of entering the valley with Brigham Young, who was sick with Rocky Mountain fever.)

I drove my carriage, with President Young lying on a bed in it, into the open valley, the rest of the company following; When we came out of the canyon into full view of the valley, I turned the side of my carriage around, open to the west, and President Young arose from his bed and took a survey of the country. While gazing on the scene before us, he was enwrapped in vision for several minutes. He had seen the valley before in vision, and upon this occasion he saw the future glory of Zion and of Israel, as they would be, planted in the valleys of these mountains. When the vision had passed, he said: "It is enough. This is the right place. Drive on." So I drove to the encampment already formed by those who had come along in advance of us ("The Pioneers," *Contributor* [August 1880], 1:253).

Lake. But still, the excitement of the journey and the unspeakable [joy] at being in Zion, and [being] delivered in such a marvelous manner from Babylon, crowded out from my mind the thoughts of the barrenness of the place (Alma Ash, *Autobiography of Alma Ash*, typescript [LDS Church Archives, The Church of Jesus Christ of Latter-day Saints, Salt Lake City], 30).

Clara Decker

I have come 1, 200 miles to reach this valley and walked much of the way, but I am willing to walk 1,000 miles farther rather than remain here (cited in Susan Arrington Madsen, *I Walked to Zion: True Stories of Young Pioneers on the Mormon Trail* [Salt Lake City: Deseret Book, 1994], 9).

Levi Jackman

July 28th. This evening Br. Young called the camp together and the men that had been exploring made their report. They had found no place that looks so well as this place. Many of the brethren expressed their feelings and all seem to feel that this was the place to stop. Br. Young then said that he wanted to know how the brethren felt in regard to it. But he knew that this was the place for the city, for he had seen it before, and that we were now standing on the southeast corner of the temple block. A vote was then taken on the subject and all voted that this be the place to stop (Levi Jackman, *Autobiography of Levi Jackman*, typescript, 60, Utah State Historical Society, Salt Lake City).

ENSIGN PEAK

Prophets since the days of Isaiah foretold of Ensign Peak, which would signal the gathering of Zion. When Brigham Young arrived at the valley, he and some of the brethren climbed a hill just north of Salt Lake and symbolically raised an ensign to the nations to commence the gathering of Zion. Thus, they named the hill Ensign Peak. Before the temple was completed, the brethren used the hill to administer temple endowments.

Ann Agatha Walker Pratt

I never shall forget the last day we traveled, and arrived in the Valley. It happened to be my turn to drive that day Sept. 28th. The reach of our wagon was broken and tied together after a fashion, and the way the front wheels wobbled about was a sight to behold. I kept expecting every minute to see the poor old concern draw apart and come to grief, but it held together and when my eyes rested on the beautiful entrancing sight—the Valley; Oh! how my heart swelled within me, I could have laughed and cried, such a commingling of emotions I cannot describe. My soul was filled with thankfulness to God for bringing us to a place of rest and safety—a home. No doubt our valley looks astonishingly beautiful to the strangers who come here now, but it cannot evoke the same emotions as it did to us, poor weary tired, worn out, ragged travelers. When I drove into camp, unyoked my cattle, and sat down on the wagon tongue, and began to realize that, in the morning I would not have to hitch up and toil through another day, such a feeling of rest—blessed rest permeated my whole being that is impossible to describe, and cannot be realized except by those who have passed through similar scenes.

After a day or two my husband with others began to explore Emigration and other canyons, made a road to the timber and in a very short time a log room was up, a rough fireplace was built, what few chairs we had brought with us, our trunks and boxes were brought in, and a few rough seats were improvised, enough for us to assemble around the fire with a semblance of a roof over our heads (we did not wait for it to be finished) that was an evening never to be forgotten. The first one of the kind in more than three months.

We spent the evening in singing, prayer, and praise to that kind Being who had brought and guided us to this haven of peace and safety (Ann Agatha Walker Pratt, "Personal Reminiscences," *Woman's Exponent* [March 15, 1893], 21:139).

George A. Smith

The question is frequently asked, "How did you ever find this place?" I answer, we were led to it by the inspiration of God. After the death of Joseph Smith, when it seemed as if every trouble and calamity had come upon the Saints, Brigham Young, who was President of the Twelve, then the presiding Quorum of the Church, sought the Lord to know what they should do, and where they should lead the people for safety, and while they were fasting and praying daily on this subject, President Young had a vision of Joseph Smith, who showed him the mountain that we now call Ensign Peak, immediately north of Salt Lake City, and there was an ensign fell upon that peak, and Joseph said, "Build under the point where the colors fall and you will prosper and have peace." The Pioneers had no pilot or guide, none among then had ever been in the country or knew anything about it. However, they traveled under the direction of President Young until they reached this valley.

When they entered [the valley] President Young pointed to that peak. "I want to go there." He went up to the point and said, "This is Ensign Peak. Now, brethren, organize your exploring parties, so as to be safe from Indians; go and explore where you will, and you will come back every time and say this is the best place." They accordingly started out exploring companies and visited what we now call Cache, Malad, Tooele, and Utah valleys, and other parts of the country in various directions, but all came back and declared this was the best spot.

I have traveled somewhat extensively in the Territory, and I bear my testimony this day, that this is the spot, and I feel confident that the God of Heaven by His inspiration led our Prophet right here. And it is the blessing of God upon the untiring energy and industry of the people that has made this once barren and sterile spot what it is to-day (*Journal of Discourses*, 26 vols. [London: Latter-day Saints' Book Depot, 1854–86], 13:85–86).

THIS IS THE PLACE?

While many pioneers saw a beautiful valley, some expressed disappointment at having to settle such a barren land. They had traveled from some of the lushest places in England and were hoping that Zion would look similar to their native land. Nevertheless, when the time came to vote on whether they would stay, the Saints decided that it was indeed the right place.

Eliza Maria Partridge Lyman

October 17th Reached the place of our destination in the valley of the Great Salt Lake. . . . We are now at our journey's end for the present. The weather is beautiful. The country barren and desolate. I do not think our enemies need envy us this locality or ever come here to disturb us (*Journal of Eliza Maria Partridge Lyman, 1846 February–1885 December* [LDS Church Archives, The Church of Jesus Christ of Latter-day Saints, Salt Lake City], n.p.).

Ruth May Fox

Our last pull was through Parley's Canyon and up to the top of the hill. This was accomplished at twilight, and here we got our first glimpse of the little city of Salt Lake.

I have to admit some disappointment as I exclaimed: "Oh, have we come all this way for that?" We continued on to the campground that night (Ruth May Fox, "From England to Salt Lake Valley in 1867," *Improvement Era*, July 1935, 38:450).

Alma Ash

Everything seemed pleasant enough to us until we approached the Rocky Mountains sometime before we arrived at Evanston, and then we saw a country which wore a different dress, and the sight made us homesick. . . . This was the first tinge of homesickness which I had felt. It seemed so rugged and barren and the whole country looked as if it had leprosy, being covered with white alkali and nothing visible but a few huts here and there. The train could not travel fast enough for us and we longed to gaze on verdure and smiling fields once more.

Early Sunday morning we arrived at Evanston, and at noon sometime at Ogden. . . . Late in the afternoon we were on our way to Salt Lake City and how we rejoiced and talked and wondered, and yet withal there seemed in my heart a feeling of unrest with a little disappointment at the kind of country we had to live in. I had heard the elders from Utah talk about it and my father had often said to his children that they would never see such a tame and lovely country as old England. I did not understand this until I saw the chains of everlasting and interminable hills of the great West. I remember well how dreary and forsaken the country looked west of the Jordan River in the direction of the Great

Isaiah 11:11–12; 18:3

And it shall come to pass in the last days that the mountain of the Lord's house shall be established in the tops of the mountains, and all nations shall flow unto it. And many people shall go and say, Come ye, and let us go to the mountain of the Lord, to the house of the God of Jacob; and he will teach us of his ways, and we will walk in his paths; for out of Zion shall go forth the law, and the word of the Lord from Jerusalem. . . .

And it shall come to pass in that day that the Lord shall set his hand the second time to recover the remnant of his people. . . . And he shall set up an Ensign for the nations, and shall assemble the outcasts of Israel, and gather together the dispersed of Judah from the four corners of the earth. . . .

All ye inhabitants of the world, and dwellers on the earth, see ye, when he lifteth up an Ensign on the mountains; and when he bloweth a trumpet, hear ye.

John D. Lee

Pres. Brigham Young said that the saying of the Prophets would never be verified unless the House of the Lord be reared in the Tops of the Mountains and the Proud Banner of Liberty wave over the valleys that are within the Mountains and I know where the spot is and I know how to make this Flag. Joseph sent the colors and Said where the colors settled there would be the spot (John D. Lee, *Diary*, January 13, 1846, typescript [LDS Church Archives, The Church of Jesus Christ of Latter-day Saints, Salt Lake City], n.p.).

B. H. Roberts

Several miles north of their encampment [some of the brethren] ascended a peculiarly shaped, mound-like mountain for the purpose of getting a view of the valley that might reveal more of the general character of it than several days of exploring journeys might give. . . . Before leaving the mound-like summit of the mountain on which they stood, someone suggested that here would be a good place "to raise an ensign to the nations," whereupon Brigham Young named the mountain "Ensign Peak" (B. H. Roberts, *A Comprehensive History of The Church of Jesus Christ of Latter-day Saints*, 7 vols. [Salt Lake City:

Deseret News Press, 1930], 170–71; see *History of Brigham Young*, Ms., book 3, July 26, 1847.)

Wilford Woodruff

We . . . went north of the camp about five miles, and we all went on to the top of a high peak in the edge of the mountain, which we considered a good place to raise an ensign. So we named it "Ensign Peak", or "Hill." I was the first person that ascended this hill, which we had thus named. Brother Young was very weary in climbing to the peak, he being feeble (had not yet recovered from effects of mountain fever) (Wilford Woodruff, *Wilford Woodruff's Journal, 1833–1898*, ed. Scott G. Kenney, 9 vols. [Midvale, Utah: Signature Books, 1983], July 26, 1847).

B. H. Roberts

(The ensign that was raised was not the physical raising of a banner or a flag but the symbolic raising of a flag for the "Empire of Christ.")

The "Ensign" that these Latter-day Saint Pioneers had in mind, and of which they had frequently spoke en route, was something larger and greater than any national flag whatsoever; and what it was meant to represent was greater than any earthly kingdom's interest, and I speak not slightingly of earthly kingdoms either; but this "Ensign" in the minds of the "Mormon" Pioneers concerned not one nation, but all nations; not one epoch or age, but all epochs and all ages; not nationality, but humanity. It was to be the sign and ensign of the Empire of Christ; it was a prophecy of the time to come when "the kingdoms of this world would become the kingdoms of our Lord and of his Christ; and when he shall reign forever and forever" (B. H. Roberts, "The 'Mormons' and the United States Flag," *Improvement Era*, November 1921, 25:5–6).

Brigham Young

(During the October general conference of 1849, Addison Pratt was sustained as a missionary to the Society Islands. Prior to this conference, Brother Pratt had served several missions in the South Pacific Islands. Due to his absence, he had never received

his endowment. Thus, before leaving for the Society Islands, he received his endowments on Ensign Peak. He was the first to receive the endowment in the Salt Lake Valley.)

Addison Pratt received his endowments on Ensign Hill on the 21st, the place being consecrated for the purpose. Myself and Elders Isaac Morley, P. P. Pratt, L. Snow, E. Snow, C. C. Rich and F. D. Richards, Levi W. Hancock, Henry Harriman and J. M. Grant being present. President H. C. Kimball, Bishop N. K. Whitney and Elder John Taylor came after the ordinances were attended to. Elders C. C. Rich and Addison Pratt were blessed by all, President Kimball being mouth (*History of Brigham Young*, Ms., 1849, 107).

Joel Hills Johnson

(Five years after the brethren visited Ensign Peak, Joel Johnson penned the song "Deseret," which later became known as "High on the Mountain Top." He felt an overwhelming impulse like fire in his bones to describe the symbolic significance of Ensign Peak.)

> High on the mountain top a banner is unfurled.
> Ye nations now look up; it waves to all the world.
> In Deseret's sweet, peaceful land,
> On Zion's mount behold it stand!
> For God remembers still his promise made of old
> That he on Zion's hill Truth's standard would unfold!
> Her light should there attract the gaze
> Of all the world in latter days.
> ("High on a Mountain Top," *Hymns*, no. 5)

President Gordon B. Hinckley

(In the October general conference of 2000, President Hinckley declared that the construction of the Conference Center fulfilled one of Isaiah's prophecies.)

An now today, as another significant accomplishment of this millennial year, we dedicate this great Conference Center. It is a unique and remarkable building. . . . Today we shall dedicate it as a house in which to worship God the Eternal Father and His Only Begotten Son, the Lord Jesus Christ. We hope and we pray that there will continue to go forth to the world from this pulpit declarations of testimony and doctrine, of faith in the Living God, and of gratitude for the great atoning sacrifice of our Redeemer.

As I contemplate this marvelous structure, adjacent to the temple, there comes to mind the great prophetic utterance of Isaiah:

"And it shall come to pass in the last days, that the mountain of the Lord's house shall be established in the top of the mountains, and shall be exalted above the hills; and all nations shall flow unto it.

"And many people shall go and say, Come ye, and let us go up to the mountain of the Lord, to the house of the God of Jacob; and he will teach us of his ways, and we will walk in his paths: for out of Zion shall go forth the law, and the word of the Lord from Jerusalem. . . .

"O house of Jacob, come ye, and let us walk in the light of the Lord" (Isaiah 2:2–3, 5).

I believe that prophecy applies to the historic and wonderful Salt Lake Temple. But I believe also that it is related to this magnificent hall. For it is from this pulpit that the law of God shall go forth, together with the word and testimony of the Lord (Gordon B. Hinckley, "This Millennial Year," *Ensign*, November 2000, 67).

~~ 12 ~~

SETTLING THE SALT LAKE VALLEY

The Saints plotted the temple as the city's nucleus and laid out the rest of the city blocks from there. They worked quickly, knowing that thirteen companies were en route to the valley that year. Mice, bears, wolves, and other forms of wildlife made their stay uncomfortable, but they quickly adapted. Their first winter in Utah was mild, but their first spring was harsh. Stormy weather destroyed their crops, and the Saints resorted to eating sego lilies for survival. Then crickets swarmed what crops remained and consumed them. The Lord, however, remembered His people and sent seagulls to devour the insects and preserve the remaining crops. As a result, the sego lily became Utah's state flower, and the seagull, Utah's state bird.

GETTING SETTLED

When the advance company first arrived in the Salt Lake Valley, they immediately began irrigating the land and preparing it for planting. When Brigham Young arrived, he and the brethren selected the temple site as the center of what would become Salt Lake City, and they meticulously plotted out the city. They constructed a fort known as the Old Fort for protection and also a bowery for religious services until they could complete the temple.

Gordon B. Hinckley

Two hours after the arrival of the main body of pioneers the first plowing in the Salt Lake Valley was undertaken. But the ground was so dry and hard that the plows were broken: Then one of the canyon streams was diverted, the soil was soaked, and the plowing thereafter was easier. On July 24 potatoes were planted and the ground watered. This was the beginning of irrigation by Anglo-Saxon people. In fact, it marked the beginning of modern irrigation practice.

Other seed also was planted. There was small chance that a crop of any consequence might mature, but it was hoped that at least enough to reproduce the seed would develop, and thus they would have seed for the following spring.

Brigham Young arrived on Saturday. On the following day the people met for worship, and in addition they received a statement of the policies that were to prevail in the new colony. President Young declared:

"No work shall be done on Sunday. If you do, you will lose five times as much as you will gain. None must hunt on that day . . . No man who has come here should try to buy land, as there is none for sale. But every man shall have his land measured out to him for city and farming purposes. He may till it as he pleases, but he must be industrious and take care of it. There is to be no private ownership of streams of water; and wood and timber for fuel, in order to save the live timber for future use. Walk faithfully in the light of these laws and you will be a prosperous people" (Gordon B. Hinckley, *What of the Mormons?* [Salt Lake City: Deseret Book Co., 1947], 173–74).

Wilford Woodruff

(Brigham Young originally planned on using forty acres for the Salt Lake Temple, but it was later reduced to ten acres. The other thirty acres were used for three different public squares throughout the city.)

We walked from the north camp to about the center between the two creeks [forks of City Creek], when President Young waved his hands and said, "Here is the forty acres for the temple (we had conversed upon the subject of the location of the temple previous to this), and the city can be laid out perfectly square north and south, east and west" (*Wilford Woodruff's Journal*, July 28, 1847).

B. H. Roberts

The apostles at the same time decided to lay out the city in blocks of ten acres with streets eight rods wide running at right angles; with twenty feet on each side given to sidewalks. The blocks were to be divided into lots containing one and one quarter acres in each. It was decided also to build but one house on a block, and that twenty feet back from the line and in the center of the lot—"That there might be uniformity throughout the city." One of the advantages of this plan, it was urged, would be the security of the city from fire in the event of fire breaking out at any one point. It was further determined that "upon every alternate block four houses were to be built on the east, and four on the west sides of the square, but none on the north and south sides. But the blocks intervening were to have four houses on the north and four on the south, but none on the east and west sides. In this plan there will be no houses fronting each other on the opposite sides of streets, while those on the same side will be about eight rods apart having gardens running back twenty rods to the center of the block" (B. H. Roberts, *A Comprehensive History of The Church of Jesus Christ of Latter-day Saints*, 7 vols. [Salt Lake City: Deseret News Press, 1930], 3:280).

Brigham Young

Let every man cultivate his own lot and set out every kind of fruit and shade trees and beautify the city (*Wilford Woodruff's Journal*, July 28, 1847).

B. H. Roberts

The city was first named, *"City of the Great Salt Lake."* Temple square was the initial center for naming the streets, and the streets around the temple block were called, respectively, North, South, East and West Temple Streets; the others to be named as required, First North, Second North, First West, Second West, and so following on all sides. . . .

Subsequently blocks of land for farming and pasturing purposes were laid off outside the city limits in five, ten and twenty acre plots respectively, the smaller plots lying nearest the city boundaries, the others following in the order of their size. All this, of course, to prevent monopoly, and possible attempts at speculations in town lots or near by farming lands (*Comprehensive History of the Church*, 3: 281–82).

THE OLD FORT

Utah's First Fort

(When organizing the city, the pioneers decided to allocate four ten-acre blocks for public use. On one of these blocks the fort was constructed.)

On this ten-acre square during the years 1847–1849 stood the first fort, historic Mormon Bastion, sometimes called the "Plymouth Rock of the West." Homes were erected of logs or adobe side by side, with the rear walls forming a protective barrier, enclosed by a nine foot mud wall. By December 1847, over 2,000 people were living in the fort which was extended one block north and one block south. The first school convened here in October 1847. A bowery, built in the center, served as a meeting place. Within its walls Anglo-Saxon civilization was first brought to the Great Basin and the Ensign of our republic raised over this domain, then Mexican territory. Here on December 9, 1848, the first petition to establish self-government in the Rocky Mountain West was signed. It became a public park July 24, 1898 (statement on a monument marker, Pioneer Park, 300 South, 300 West, Salt Lake City).

Maria Dilworth Nebeker

I attended the first school in Utah taught by my sister, Mary Jane [Dilworth], in a small round tent seated with logs. The school was opened just three weeks after our arrival in the valley. The first morning we gathered before the door of the tent, and in the midst of our play, my sister called us and said, "Come children, come; we will begin now." There were just a few of us, I think only nine or ten. One of the brethren came in, and opened the school with prayer. I remember one thing he said. It was to the effect that "we be good children and he asked God that the school would be so blessed that we all should have his holy light to guide us into all truth." The first day, Mary Jane taught us the twenty-third Psalm, and we sang much, and played more (Levi Edgar Young, "Education in Utah," *Improvement Era*, July 1913, 16:882).

RAIN

John Taylor

(The brethren heard that the valley received minimal precipitation. Thus, they constructed the houses with flat roofs. However, heavy rain and snow descended upon the valley in the spring of 1848 and caused the roofs to leak.)

We have had a great quantity of rain this spring. . . . Indeed, some people began to pray for rain before they ascertained that their houses were not waterproof, and almost wished that they had deferred their supplications a little longer (Samuel W. and Raymond W. Taylor, *The John Taylor Papers: Records of the Last Utah Pioneer,* 2 vols. [Redwood City, CA: Taylor Trust, 1984], 1:138).

M. Isabella Horne

It was no uncommon thing to see a woman holding an umbrella over her while attending to her household duties. The Fort presented quite a ludicrous appearance when the weather cleared up. In whatever direction one looked, bedding and clothing of all descriptions were hanging out to dry (M. Isabella Horne, "Pioneer Reminiscences," *Young Woman's Journal,* July 1902, 294).

Mary Isabella Horne

(Courtesy of the Church Archives, The Church of Jesus Christ of Latter-day Saints)

Eliza R. Snow

A long storm of snow, sleet and rain occurred, and for several days the sun did not make its appearance. The roof of our dwelling was covered deeper with earth than the adjoining ones, consequently it did not leak so soon, and some of my neighbors huddled in for shelter; but one evening, when several were socially sitting around, the water commenced dripping in one place, and then in another; they dodged it for a while, but it increased so rapidly that they finally concluded they might as well go to their own wet houses. After they had gone I spread my umbrella over my head and shoulders as I ensconced myself in bed, the lower part of which, not shielded by the umbrella, was wet enough before morning. The earth overhead was thoroughly saturated, and after it commenced to drip the storm was much worse indoors than out (Levi Edgar Young, "Sociological Aspects of 'Mormonism,'" *Improvement Era*, September 1920, 23:954).

M. Isabella Horne

In the beginning of March we had a severe storm of rain and sleet, completely saturating the roofs, so that it rained as fast in the house as it did outside. The first consideration was to secure our provisions, for they were our salvation. Buffalo robes and all available covering were brought into use for protection. We were in a bad situation. Mr. Horne tacked wagon covers to the roof and at the foot of the bed to let the water run off on to the floor. We had an oilcloth table cover which he tacked over our head where we ate, emptying the water into buckets every little while. Wraps and umbrellas were used while doing our cooking and housework (M. Isabella Horne, "Home Life in the Pioneer Fort," *Juvenile Instructor*, March 15, 1894, 29:182).

WILDLIFE IN THE SETTLEMENT

As part of settling the valley, the Saints had to learn to adapt to the new forms of wildlife. Aside from insects and rodents, the valley also housed snakes, hogs, bears, wolves, coyotes, and wildcats, all of which either threatened the safety of the Saints, or terrified them.

M. Isabella Horne

As spring opened there were other difficulties to meet and overcome. Snakes came crawling out of the ground around our houses, terrifying the children. These were soon killed or frightened away. Mice also came out of the ground by thousands, and were a terrible scourge. Before we were aware of it they had got into our trunks and boxes, eating our clothing and making sad havoc of everything they could destroy. Falling down on us from the roof, running over us by night, crawling into our coats and wraps hanging on the walls, and running up the sleeves and backs when we put them on to go out. As "necessity is the mother of invention," a variety of traps were soon made, the most effectual one being very simple, and which I will describe. A piece of thin board about a foot and a half long and six inches wide was whittled off round at each end, leaving the middle four inches long. A little grease was put on the edges of the wide part, which was then laid over a pail of water. When the mice ran to get the grease the board turned and tipped them into the water. Dozens were killed in an evening.

Sister Haight brought a cat with her. I gave fifty cents for one of her kittens when it was three weeks old, and she proved very useful. From her I supplied several of my neighbor's with cats, which, with the traps, soon began to diminish the troublesome little pests. Then we had an awful time with bedbugs. The timber of which our houses were built was full of them, and it was years before they were entirely subdued (Horne, "Home Life in the Pioneer Fort," 29:182–83).

George Q. Cannon

The big gray wolves came down from the mountains in March 1848, and chased the cattle which were feeding on the east bench in sight of the fort. They succeeded in killing several head. . . .

The people of Great Salt Lake City suffered so much annoyance from the wolves howling at night, and from the depredations of foxes, catamounts, and other animals that it was thought advisable to organize two companies of one hundred men each, John D. Lee and John Pack to be captains, to destroy these wild animals (Claude T. Barnes, "Wild Animals of Utah Pioneer Days," *Improvement Era*, March 1955, 58:161, 190).

Emily Stewart Barnes

We still slept in the wagon box outside and, say, how the wolves would howl! It was not one but many. They were hungry and came close to the box and howled (Claude T. Barnes, *The Grim Years – The Story of Emily Steward Barnes* [1949]; cited in Claude T. Barnes, "Wild Animals of Utah Pioneer Days," *Improvement Era*, March 1955, 58:190).

Lorenzo Young

One night soon after our arrival I spread some strychnine about, and in the morning found fourteen white wolves dead. . . .

I doubt that a wild gray wolf exists in Utah, although I do get a rumor now and again from San Juan County. Coyotes, mountain lions, and wildcats are still common, sometimes still appearing within the Salt Lake City limits (Barnes, "Wild Animals of Utah Pioneer Days," 58:190).

MIRACLE OF THE SEAGULLS

After a mild but cold winter, the Saints looked forward to replenishing their meager provisions through the harvesting of spring wheat. Unfortunately, late frosts damaged a great portion of their crops. Food had to be rationed, and in order to supplement their meals, the Saints resorted to eating thistle, sego lilies, and wolf meat. Weeks later, hordes of crickets moved into the valley and depleted the remaining crops. The Saints tirelessly tried to kill the vicious predators, but to no avail. Finally, on the Sabbath, during Charles C. Rich's address, seagulls swarmed the valley and devoured the crickets.

Priddy Meeks

(That first spring found the Saints close to starving, with little food that had to be rationed. In an effort to overcome his hunger, Priddy resorted to eating wolf meat, sego lilies, and thistle roots.)

My family went several months without a satisfying meal of victuals. I went sometimes a mile up Jordan to a patch of wild roses to get the berries to eat which I would eat as rapidly as a hog, stems and all. I shot hawks and crows and they ate well. I would go and search the mire holes and find cattle dead and fleece off what meat I could and eat it. We used wolf meat, which I thought was good. I made some wooden spades to dig seagoes [sego lily] with, but we could not supply our wants.

Sego lily
(Courtesy of the Church Archives, The Church of Jesus Christ of Latter-day Saints)

We had to exert ourselves to get something to eat. I would take a grubbing-hoe and a sack and start by sunrise in the morning and go, I thought six miles before coming to where the thistle roots grew, and in time to get home I would have a bushel and sometimes more thistle roots. And we would eat them raw. I would dig until I grew weak and faint and sit down and eat a root, and then begin again. I continued this until roots began to fail ("Journal of Priddy Meeks," ed. J. Cecil Alter, *Utah Historical Quarterly* [Salt Lake City: Utah State University, 1942], 10:163).

James E. Talmage

The spring saw everybody busy, and soon there were many flourishing gardens, containing a good variety of vegetables. In the early part of March plowing commenced. The spring was mild and rain plentiful, and all expected an abundant harvest. But in the latter part of May, when the fields had put on their brightest green, there appeared a visitation in the form of vast swarms of crickets, black and baleful as the locust of the Dead Sea. In their track they left behind them not a blade or leaf, the appearance of the country which they traversed in countless and desolating myriads, being that of a land scorched by fire. They came in solid phalanx, from the direction of Arsenal Hill, darkening the earth in their passage. Men, women and children turned out en masse to combat this pest, driving them into ditches or on to piles of reeds, which they would set on fire, striving in every way, until strength was exhausted, to beat back the devouring host. But in vain they toiled, in vain they prayed; the work of destruction ceased not, and the havoc threatened to be as complete as was that which overtook the land of Egypt in the last days of Israel's bondage. "Think of their condition," says Mr. Cannon, "the food they brought with them almost exhausted, their grain and other seeds all planted, they themselves twelve hundred miles from a settlement or place where they could get food on the east, and eight hundred miles from California, and the crickets eating up every green thing, and every day destroying their sole means of subsistence for the months and winter ahead" (Hubert Howe Bancroft, *History of Utah* [San Fransisco: The Historical Company, 1889], 279–81; as cited in James E. Talmage, "Were They Crickets or Locusts, and When Did They Come?" *Improvement Era*, November 1909, 13:98).

John R. Young

As the summer crept on, and the scant harvest drew nigh, the fight with the crickets commenced. Oh, how we fought and prayed, and prayed and fought the myriads of black, loathsome insects that flowed down like a flood of filthy water from the mountainside. And we should surely have been inundated, and swept into oblivion, save for the merciful Father's sending of the blessed sea gulls to our deliverance.

The first I knew of the gulls, I heard their sharp cry. Upon looking up, I beheld what appeared like a vast flock of pigeons coming from the northwest. It was about three o'clock in the afternoon. My brother Franklin and I were trying to save an acre of wheat of father's, growing not far from where the Salt Lake Theatre now stands. The wheat was just beginning to turn yellow. The crickets would climb the stalk, cut off the head, then come down and eat it. To prevent this, my brother and I each took an end of a long rope, stretched it full length, then walked through the grain holding the rope so as to hit the heads and thus knock the crickets off. From sunrise till sunset we kept at this labor; for as darkness came the crickets sought shelter, but with the rising of the sun they commence their ravages again.

I have been asked "how numerous were the gulls?"

There must have been thousands of them. Their coming was like a great cloud; and when they passed between us and the sun, a shadow covered the field. I could see the gulls settling for more than a mile around us. They were very tame, coming within four or five rods of us.

At first we thought that they, also, were after the wheat, and this thought added to our terror; but we soon discovered that they devoured only the crickets. Needless to say, we quit drawing the rope, and gave our gentle visitors the possession of the field. As I remember it, the gulls came every morning for about three weeks, when their mission was apparently ended, and they ceased coming. The precious crops were saved (John R. Young, *Memoirs of John R. Young, Utah Pioneer, 1857* [Salt Lake City: Deseret News, 1920], 64–66).

Priddy Meeks

Finally, the crickets came so thick it made the earth black in place, and it did look like they would take what little we had growing, which looked nice and flourishing. . . . Now everything did look gloomy. Our provisions giving out, and the crickets eating up what little we had growing, and we a thousand miles away from supplies. . . .

When Sunday come [June 4], we had a meeting. Apostle [Charles C.] Rich stood in a open wagon and preached out of doors. It was a beautiful day, and a very solemn one too.

While preaching, he says, "Brethren, we do not want you to part with your wagons and teams, for we might need them." Intimating that he did not know, but we might have to leave. That increased my solemnity. At that instant, I heard the voice of fowls flying overhead, that I was not acquainted with. I looked up and saw a flock of seven gulls. In a few minutes there was another larger flock passed over. They came fast and more of them until the heavens were darkened with them, and lit down in the valley till the earth was black with them, and they would eat crickets and throw them up again and fill themselves again and right away throw them up again. A little before sundown, they left for Salt Lake, for they roosted on a sand bar. A little after sunrise in the morning, they came back again and continued that course until they had devoured the crickets.

I guess this circumstance changed our feeling considerable for the better (Priddy Meeks, *Journal of Priddy Meeks* [Provo, Utah: Brigham Young University, 1938], 17–18).

George Q. Cannon

Then the miraculous happened. I say it deliberately, the miraculous happened, as men commonly view the miraculous. There was heard the shrill, half scream, half plaintive cry of some sea gulls hovering over the wheat fields. Presently they light and begin devouring the crickets. Others come—thousands of them—from over the lake. The upper feathers of the gull's wings are tinted with a delicate grey, and some of the flight feathers, primaries, to be exact, are marked with black, but the prevailing color is white; and as they came upon the new wheat fields, stretched upward and then gracefully folded their wings and began devouring the devourers, to the cricket-vexed colonists they seemed like white-winged angels of deliverance—these gulls. They were tireless in their destructive—nay, their *saving* work. It was noted that when they were glutted with crickets they would go to the streams, drink, vomit and return again to the slaughter. And so it continued, day after day, until the plague was stayed, and the crops of the Pioneers saved.

At the time when the prospects began to appear most gloomy, and all human power seemed useless, the sea gulls came in flocks, visited the fields, pounced upon the crickets and devoured them. . . . On Sunday the fields were deserted by the people, who devoted the day to worship. This was a feast for the gulls—they devoured without let or hindrance.

On Monday morning, on visiting the fields, the people found on the edges of the water ditches, the place where the crickets were always the most numerous, pile after pile of dead crickets which had been eaten by the gulls, and then vomited when they were full ("History of the Church," *Juvenile Instructor*, 19:100).

Aroet Lucious Hale

(Because the Saints were so grateful for what the seagulls had done, they made it illegal to kill them.)

A fine of five dollars was placed upon the head of anyone that killed a seagull. One thing singular, the oldest mountaineers and trappers said that they never saw a seagull until after the Mormons settled this country (Aroet Hale, *Autobiography*, typescript, in *Writings of Early Latter-day Saints and Their Contemporaries, A Database Collection*, comp. Milton V. Backman [Provo, Utah: BYU Religious Studies Center, 1996], 19).

THANKSGIVING

Parley P. Pratt

On the 10th of August [1848] we held a public feast under a bowery in the center of our fort. This was called a harvest feast; we partook freely of a rich variety of bread, beef, butter, cheese, cakes, pastry, green corn, melons, and almost every variety of vegetable. Large sheaves of wheat, rye, barley, oats and other productions were hoisted on poles for public exhibition, and there was prayer and thanksgiving, congratulations, songs, speeches, music, dancing, smiling faces and merry hearts. In short, it was a great day with the people of these valleys, and long to be remembered by those who had suffered and waited anxiously for the results of a first effort to redeem the interior deserts of America, and to make her hitherto unknown solitudes "blossom as the rose" (Parley P. Pratt, *Autobiography of Parley P. Pratt*, ed. Scot Facer Proctor and Maurine Jensen Proctor [Salt Lake City: Deseret Book, 2000], 461).

13

THE GATHERING

Brigham Young and most of those in the Vanguard Company remained in the Salt Lake Valley only thirty-three days before beginning the trek back to Winter Quarters to assist their families, and others, in coming west the following year. They left their hard-won home on August 16, 1847. During this return trip, they encountered the 1,553 Saints who were traveling west in the Emigration Camp Company, led by Elders Parley P. Pratt and John Taylor. President Young and those traveling with him were reunited with their families in Winter Quarters on October 31, 1847. There they would remain for the winter and then travel back across the trail, arriving in the Salt Lake Valley in September 1848.

Wilford Woodruff

We as a pioneer company have accomplished more this season than can be found on record concerning any set of men since the days of Adam. [We have] traveled with heavy loaded wagons over one thousand miles, having made our road more than one half of the way over and through the rough mountains and canyons, and searched out a glorious land as a resting place for the Saints. And in one month after our arrival [we] laid out a city two miles square and built a fort and fortification of hewn timber drawn seven miles from the mountains and of unburnt brick, surrounding ten acres of ground, forty rods of which was covered with block houses, besides planting about one hundred acres of corn, potatoes, buckwheat, turnips, and gardens (*Wilford Woodruff's Journal, 1833–1898*, ed. Scott G. Kenney, 9 vols. [Midvale, Utah: Signature Books, 1983], August 25, 1847).

Heber C. Kimball

I wish to God we had not got to return. If I had my family here, I would give everything I have [to stay here in the Salt Lake Valley]. This is a Paradise to me. It is one of the most lovely places I ever beheld (*Journal of Horace K. Whitney*, August 22, 1847, LDS Family and Church History Department Archives, Salt Lake City).

Brigham Young

(Only a mile outside of Winter Quarters, on October 31, 1847, Brigham Young addressed the nine members of the Twelve, after having traveled back across the plains with them.)

Brethren, I will just say to the Pioneers, I want you to receive my thanks for your kind service and willingness to obey orders. I am satisfied with you as you have [labored] with me and the Twelve. The boys have done first rate. We've accomplished more than we expected. Out of 143 men, all of them are well. Not a man died; we have not lost a horse, mule, or ox, but through carelessness; the blessings of the Lord have been with us. If the brethren are satisfied with me and the Twelve, please signify it, (which was unanimously done). I feel to bless you all in the name of the Lord God of Israel. You are dismissed to go to your own homes.

We drove into the town in order, about an hour before sunset. The streets were crowded with people to shake hands as we passed through the lines; we were truly rejoiced to once more behold our wives, children and friends after an absence of over six months, having traveled over 2000 miles, sought out a location for the saints to dwell in peace, and accomplished the most interesting mission in this last dispensation. Not a soul of our camp died, and no serious accident happened to any, for which we praise the Lord (*General Church Minutes*, October 31, 1847, 3 p.m.; see also Joseph Smith, *History of The Church of Jesus Christ of Latter-day Saints*, ed. B. H. Roberts, 7 vols. [Salt Lake City: Deseret Book, 1964], 7:617).

Wilford Woodruff

Each one drove to his own home [in Winter Quarters]. I drove up to my own door and was truly rejoiced to once more behold the face of my wife and children again after being absent over six months and having traveled with the Twelve and the pioneers near 2,500 miles and sought out a location for the Saints and accomplished one of the most interesting missions ever accomplished at the last days (*Journal of Wilford Woodruff*, October 31, 1847 [LDS Church Archives, The Church of Jesus Christ of Latter-day Saints, Salt Lake City], n.p.).

THE NEW PROPHET SUSTAINED

When the Prophet Joseph was martyred, the Quorum of the Twelve had assumed the responsibility of leading the Church. Although Brigham Young was the senior Apostle and therefore the leader of the Church, the need to formally reorganize the First Presidency had weighed heavily on his mind. Finally, on December 5, 1847, Brigham Young met with the nine members of the Quorum of the Twelve who were in Winter Quarters to discuss the need to reorganize the First Presidency. After Brigham Young and his chosen counselors were unanimously sustained by those in attendance, the reorganization of the First Presidency was proposed to the members of the Church for their sustaining vote on December 27, 1847; thus the precedent for the succession of prophets had been set.

Orson Pratt

(As long as the Twelve were leading the Church, they were confined to stay near the main body of Saints to provide leadership. Orson Pratt emphasized that a First Presidency was needed so that members of the Quorum of the Twelve would be able to travel to foreign missions.)

We have been able to overcome apostates and the powers of darkness with the highest quorum taken away out of our midst. How much more shall we be able to overcome them when we have all the quorums flourishing. . . . The time has come when the Twelve must have their hands liberated to go to the ends of the earth (minutes of meeting, December

Orson Pratt
(Courtesy of the Church Archives, The Church of Jesus Christ of Latter-day Saints)

24–27, 1847, *Brigham Young Papers*, Utah State Historical Society, Salt Lake City).

Amasa Lyman

The interests of the [Church] can't be served any longer without a President. The work is faltering for want of the servants of the Lord being set free. He who furnishes the materials is the man. He is at the head already. He has been acknowledged for years (minutes of meeting, December 24–27, 1847, *Brigham Young Papers*).

Ezra T. Benson

(At the meeting of the Twelve on December 5, 1847, Ezra T. Benson made the following remarks expressing his determination to support Brigham Young as the new prophet.)

I have not exchanged a word with Brigham on the matter. I feel now . . . that everything is right and it is hard to get it wrong. . . . I have a testimony that he is called of God. My conscience is perfectly clear and my feelings the same as they ever have been, I am willing to lift him up a peg. That's my private and public feelings. The arguments that have been used are gone. The time has come and it may as well be done now as any other. I can act tonight [December 5, 1847] as well as any time. As the revelation says "It is of necessity." . . .

It is plain to me as the nose on my face. . . . I am not concerned but that the Lord will carry on the work and that all will be right. I could not get it into my mind that God would send an angel, call one of his servants, and then suffer one ignoramus to lead away the people to the Devil. I would not worship such a God and I believe God would remove our head out of its place. I am here and I am willing to act. . . . I want to keep with the quorum of the Twelve and I mean to stick with Brother Brigham (minutes of a meeting with the Twelve, December 5, 1847, *Brigham Young Papers*).

Wilford Woodruff

Many interesting remarks were made by the various individuals who spoke, and we were followed by President Young. After which Orson Hyde moved that Brigham Young be the President of The Church of Jesus Christ of Latter-day Saints and that he nominate his two

A CALL TO SAINTS EVERYWHERE

President Young was not only concerned with gathering the Saints in the United States to Zion, but his thoughts also extended to those converts across the ocean. However, the call to come to Zion was not proclaimed by President Young alone. Many people left records testifying that the Spirit impressed them with a feeling of urgency to gather with the Saints.

Brigham Young

(President Young wrote the following directive in a letter to Nathaniel Felt on November 24, 1847.)

The whisperings of the Spirit is now to all saints, "gather yourselves together, to the place which has been pointed out, for a place of rest and salvation; a place for the building of the House of the Lord, a place 'sought out,' and a city which need not be forsaken [if] the inhabitants thereof will work righteousness" (letter to Nathaniel Felt, November 24, 1847, *Brigham Young Papers*).

Brigham Young

To all Saints in any country bordering upon the Atlantic, we would say . . . come immediately and prepare to go West—bringing with you all kinds of choice seeds, of grain, vegetables, fruits, shrubbery, trees, and vines—every thing that will please the eye, gladden the heart, or cheer the soul of man, that grows upon the face of the whole earth; also the best stock of beast, bird, and fowl of every kind; also, the best tools of every description, and machinery for spinning, or weaving, and dressing cotton, wool, flax, and silk, etc. . . . So far as it can be consistently done, bring models and drafts, and let the machinery be built where it is used, which will save great expense in transportation, particularly in heavy machinery, and tools and implements generally (Brigham Young, "General Epistle from the Council of the Twelve Apostles to The Church of Jesus Christ of Latter-day Saints Abroad," *Millennial Star* [March 15, 1848], 10: 85).

counselors, and they three form the First Presidency. Seconded by Wilford Woodruff and carried unanimously. President Young nominated Heber C. Kimball as his first counselor; seconded, and carried unanimously. President Young nominated Willard Richards as his second counselor; seconded, and carried unanimously (*Wilford Woodruff's Journal*, December 5, 1847).

Brigham Young

(On December 27, 1847, the last day of a four-day general conference of the Church, the decision was brought before the congregation, and the members were asked for their sustaining vote. After being sustained as the prophet of the Church, Brigham Young made the following statement.)

This is one of the happiest days of my life. . . . Is not the bliss of heaven and the breezes of Zion wafted here? Who feels hatred, malice, or evil? If you come to the door with a bad spirit, it would not come in with you; no, it could not mingle here: but when you enter, your feelings become as calm and gentle as the zephyrs of paradise; and I feel glory, Hallelujah!

We have been driven from Nauvoo here, but the hand of the Lord is in it—visible as the sun shining this morning; it is visible to my natural eyes; it's all right.

As the Lord's will is my will all the time, as He dictates so I will perform. If He doesn't guide the ship, we'll go down in the whirlpool (B. H. Roberts, *A Comprehensive History of The Church of Jesus Christ of Latter-day Saints* [Salt Lake City: Deseret News Press, 1930], 3:315–17).

Orson Hyde

(On October 7, 1860, Orson Hyde recalled a meeting that took place at his home, in February 1848, wherein the Twelve heard the voice of the Lord, verbally confirming that Brigham Young was the prophet of God.)

In the month of February, 1848, the Twelve Apostles met at Hyde Park, Pottawattamie County, Iowa, where a small Branch of the Church was established; and I must say that I feel not a little proud of the circumstance, and also very thankful, on account of its happening in my own little retired and sequestered hamlet, bearing my own name. We were in prayer and council, communing together; and what took place on that occasion? The voice of God came from on high, and spake to the Council. Every latent feeling was aroused, and every heart melted. What did it say unto us? "Let my servant Brigham step forth and receive the full power of the presiding Priesthood in my Church and kingdom." This was the voice of the Almighty unto us at Council Bluffs . . . I am one that was present, and there are others here that were also present on that occasion, and did hear and feel the voice from heaven, and we were filled with the power of God. This is my testimony (*Journal of Discourses*, 26 vols. [London: Latter-day Saints' Book Depot, 1854–86], 8:233–34).

EVACUATION OF WINTER QUARTERS

The Saints settled Winter Quarters under an agreement with the Omaha and Otoe Native American tribes who owned the land, upon the condition that they would vacate the area after two years, leaving any improvements to the land to the Native Americans. When the Church leaders returned to Winter Quarters in the fall of 1847, the matter of what to do with the city's four thousand inhabitants became an increasing concern. The brethren quickly decided that moving the Saints east, across the Missouri River, to the lands that had recently been vacated by the Pottawatamie Indians, was the best possible action. After determining that, rather than settle in one main location, it would be easier to sell their lands at a profit if they were more spread out. By the spring of 1848, Winter Quarters was abandoned.

Brigham Young

I am in favor of vacating this place and the brethren draw their houses over the river (meeting of the Twelve and others, November 8–9, 1847, *Brigham Young Papers*).

Orson Pratt

I motion that every man and family who cannot go West, go into the state of Iowa and settle where they may until they can fit themselves

out for the mountains (meeting of the Twelve and others, November 8–9, 1847, *Brigham Young Papers*).

George A. Smith

If the design is to sell improvements, it will be best to scatter all over the country for farms; then they may be sold (meeting of the Twelve, November 9, 1847, *Brigham Young Papers*).

A General Epistle to the Saints

(The following epistle was sent out to the Saints from the Twelve in December 1847.)

Gather yourselves together speedily, near to this place, on the east side of the Missouri River, and, if possible, be ready to start from hence by the first of May next, or as soon as grass is sufficient. . . . Let the Saints who have been driven and scattered from the east bank of the river . . . ; and let all the Saints in the United States and Canada gather to the same place, by the first spring navigation, or as soon as they can, bringing their money, goods, and effects with them. . . .

To the Saints in England, Scotland, Ireland, Wales, and adjacent islands and countries, we say, emigrate as speedily as possible to this vicinity, looking to and following the counsel of the Presidency at Liverpool; shipping to New Orleans, and from thence direct to Council Bluffs, which shall save much expense. . . . And to all Saints in any country bordering upon the Atlantic, we would say, pursue the same course. . . .

For the time has come for the Saints to go up to the mountains of the Lord's house, and help to establish it upon the tops of the mountains ("General Epistle from the Council of the Twelve Apostles to The Church of Jesus Christ of Latter-day Saints Abroad," December 23, 1847 [LDS Church Archives, The Church of Jesus Christ of Latter-day Saints, Salt Lake City], n.p.).

Brigham Young, Heber C. Kimball, Willard Richards

Let all who can procure a bit of bread, and one garment on their back, be assured there is water plenty and pure by the way, and doubt no longer, but come next year to the place of gathering, even in flocks, as doves fly to their windows before a storm ("Seventh General Epistle of the Presidency of The Church of Jesus-Christ of Latter-day Saints," *Millennial Star* [July 17, 1852], 14:325).

Ezra T. Benson

We filled the mission that we were sent to do and come home humble and like little children. The Lord God of Israel has been with us. Shall we not sit down and give up the ship? We have a good man at the helm. No, let us arise and have more perseverance then we ever did before. . . . That valley is a place reserved by the Almighty for this people. We have been tried in poverty and sickness. Now you are going to be tried in riches, in homes, farms and vineyards. . . . You may as well have it all. We have gold, warmth, salt, soil, tar and springs. We have been in the valley to set the big wheel to work and that sets all the little wheels whirling. . . . We have not laid the foundation for our coming day (minutes of an outdoor Sunday morning meeting at Winter Quarters, November 14, 1847; as cited in Richard E. Bennett, *We'll Find the Place: The Mormon Exodus 1846–1848* [Salt Lake City: Deseret Book Co, 1997], 283).

George Whitaker

I wanted to go with [the Saints]. I had no desire to go home. The camp of the Saints was my home. Where they went I wanted to go. I had the spirit of emigration and there was nothing in the world that would stop me excepting sickness or death ("Life of George Whitaker, A Utah Pioneer, as written by himself," typescript, 13, Utah State Historical Society, Salt Lake City).

Clara Durtschi Burgener

I went to Geneva, Switzerland, and got a job in a café, and while I was there, in one of the letters from mother, she mentioned that two

Mormon missionaries came to see them. This worried me very much because I knew how avoided and despised people were who became Mormons.

That night I wrote a letter home and pleaded with them not to listen to those missionaries. But I couldn't do it, because it seemed just like a hand was stopping me from writing those words. It was the same way every time I wrote a letter home, and it made me think and wonder.

I went home for Christmas. The first evening I was home one of those missionaries came, and I was really surprised to see such a handsome young man and without any horns. . . .

With the help of the Lord and through prayer and study, I soon received a testimony of the Gospel, that this was the only true church and that Joseph Smith was a true prophet of God. In all these fifty years of trials and sorrow, I have never doubted for one minute that this was the only true Gospel. The spirit of gathering with the Saints in Zion came over me. Never before had I wanted to go across the ocean (Clara Durtschi Burgener, "From Switzerland to Utah By the Power of Faith," in *Voices From the Past: Diaries, Journals, and Autobiographies*, comp. Campus Education Week Program [Provo, Utah: Brigham Young University Press, 1980], 125–26).

Valborg Rasmussen Wheelwright

(Valborg Wheelwright journeyed to Zion at the age of thirteen. He wrote about the intense desire he had at a young age to join the Saints in Utah.)

I begged Mother every day and tried to make her see how important it was that I go to Utah. I would listen to no argument from her. . . . I'd make her come and kneel down with me each morning before she went to work.

I had really never had anything so important to pray about before as this object now in view. Oh, I had had my small everyday wishes, but never a need so great that it required more than just a few minutes of prayer. This was different. I constantly asked my Heavenly Father to help Mother see the truthfulness of the gospel. It was the truth. I knew it was. It was a gift from God. I couldn't have been more convinced of anything in my life than I was of that. And God was calling me to Zion. I preached all summer to my mother, my schoolmates—anyone who would listen: "He who is not willing to leave father, mother, for my name's sake, is not worthy of me." This was the scripture I quoted to substantiate my point of view. So many children didn't have a chance to go, and I did. Somehow I knew that I would go and that Mother would know it was the right thing for me to do. . . .

After six weeks of prayer and meeting and talks with Elder Hansen, Mother gave her consent. After that, all the King's men couldn't have stopped me from going. . . .

The whole family thought Mother had lost her mind. [My older brother] Karl and his wife, a fine girl from Dresden, came from Copenhagen when they heard I was going to Utah. Aunt Amalie came down from Middlefort. Both of them offered me homes with them if I would not go with Elder Hansen. They could not understand. Had I been looking for a better home I'm sure I would have enjoyed Germany of the Danish isles, but I was about my Father's business (Valborg—An autobiography of Valborg Rasmussen Wheelwright, as told to his son Lorin F. Wheelwright; cited in Susan Arrington Madsen and Fred E. Woods, *I Sailed to Zion* [Salt Lake City: Deseret Book, 2000], 38).

Jane Charters Robinson Hindly

I believed in the principal of the gathering and felt it my duty to go although it was a severe trial to me in my feelings to leave my native land . . . but my heart was fixed. I knew in whom I had trusted, and with the fire of Israel's God burning in my bosom, I forsook my home (Jane Charters Robinson Hindly, "Jane C. Robinson Hindly Reminiscences and Diary" [LDS Church Archives, The Church of Jesus Christ of Latter-day Saints, Salt Lake City]; cited in Madsen and Woods, *I Sailed to Zion*, 157).

THE PERPETUAL EMIGRATION FUND

In 1849, in an effort to assist both the Saints that had been exiled from Illinois and those still overseas in their journey to Zion, Brigham Young announced the creation of the Perpetual Emigration Fund. Through this Church-funded program, money was loaned to those Saints who were desirous to come to the Salt Lake Valley but who were too impoverished to finance the trip. Upon arrival, the immigrants were then obligated to find employment and repay the debt, reimbursing the fund and providing for others to make the journey. Over time, this fund assisted approximately thirty thousand Saints to gather to Utah.

Brigham Young

(A precursor to the establishment of the Perpetual Emigration Fund, Brigham Young sent out this proclamation in December 1847, calling for financial help from those Saints who had means, in order to help others come to Zion.)

To the rich saints in the United States,

The Camp of Israel in the wilderness is in want; the hands of the servants of the Lord are stayed for lack of means; the operations of the Church are paralyzed with poverty, but the time for the Lord to favor Zion is at hand. . . . Send us of your substance, that the poor may be blessed, the sick relieved, the hungry fed, the naked clothed, and the camp may move forward to their destination. Send us of your substance . . . not by farthings, by pence and by shillings, but by hundreds and thousands and by tens of thousands. . . . The time has verily come to favor Zion and help must be had, for the Lord designs it. . . . If you refuse or neglect this our call . . . and prove not your faith by your works, . . . the spirit will take its departure from your souls; your light will be turned into darkness, and you will ere long be left to mourn that your money has perished with you (Brigham Young to "the rich saints in the United States," *Journal History of The Church of Jesus Christ of Latter-day Saints*, December 6, 1847).

Deseret News

(The Deseret News *reported on the celebrations that went on when the first company of Saints from Europe to come to Utah through the help of the Perpetual Emigration Fund arrived in the valley.)*

[The newly arrived Saints] danced for joy, and their hearts were made glad by a distribution of melons and cakes . . .

As the escort and the train passed the Temple Block they were saluted with nine rounds of artillery, which made the everlasting hills shake their sides with joy; while thousands of men, women, and children gathered from various parts of the city to unite in the glorious and joyful welcome (*Deseret News*, September 18, 1852; cited in "Church Emigrant," *The Contributor* [July 1892], 13:417).

Heber C. Kimball

Not only those who are indebted to the Perpetual Emigrating Fund, but all ought to throw in their mites and enlarge this Fund. The means can be paid in here, and the poor can be brought out from the nations. Hundreds have come on this year on the strength of this Fund. It is the duty of those who have been brought out by it to go and work forthwith for means to pay their indebtedness. It does not belong to you, but it belongs to those who have made the Fund: it belongs to that Company, and to every individual, if they have not placed in it any more than a picayune or a halfpenny.

Heber C. Kimball

(Public Domain, Courtesy of BYU Online Collection)

Look at the poor in old England. I have heard that some have feelings against me, because I have spoken of the poverty of the people in that country. I know more about its poverty than the natives of the country do. . . . In the last letter that came from my son William, he wrote that "I feel to weep and mourn and lament, when I behold the poverty of the people: they are starving to death, and there are scores and hundreds of my brethren in the poor-houses of the country: the husband is put in one poor-house, the wife in another, and the children in another."

That is the case with out brethren there; and while you are here in the midst of luxuries—while you are enjoying these blessings of the Lord, can you see your own brethren afflicted? It is not only so in England, but in Ireland, in Scotland, in Denmark, and in Sweden, and in all the nations of the earth (*Journal of Discourses*, 7:40).

Brigham Young

(In a letter to President Franklin D. Richards in Liverpool, President Young gave instructions for how funds from the Perpetual Emigration Fund were to be distributed.)

In your elections of the Saints who shall be aided by the Fund, those who have proven themselves by long continuance in the Church shall be helped first, whether they can raise any means of their own or not; . . . if they have not a sixpence in the world. But be wary of assisting any of those who come into the Church now, during these troublesome times for Britain, whose chief aim and intention may be to get to America (Brigham Young, *Millennial Star* [December 22, 1855], 17:814–15).

Editorial in the Millennial Star

The clouds of war have continued to gather thicker and darker over the horizon of the nations. . . . Famine has stared multitudes in the face during the past winter . . . The present is full of calamity and evil. At this moment thousands are anxiously inquiring in their hearts, "Is there no way of escape from these evils?" . . . There is beyond the sea a haven of peace, and a refuge from the impending storms . . . The Spirit whispers: "Get ye up out of these lands for the judgments of the Almighty are being poured out upon the nations, for they are ripening in transgression" ("Editorial," *Millennial Star* [April 21, 1855], 17:248–49).

Richard Smyth

(In response to the call to gather to Zion, Richard Smyth, of Dublin, Ireland, composed the following lines.)

Israel, Israel, God is calling—
Calling thee from lands of woe;
Babylon the Great is falling;
God shall all her towers o'erthrow.
Come to Zion
'Ere His floods of anger flow.
Israel, Israel, God is speaking:
Hear your great Deliverer's voice!
Now a glorious morn is breaking
For the people of His choice.

Come to Zion,
And within her walls rejoice.
Israel, angels are descending
From celestial worlds on high
And towards man their powers extending
That the Saints may homeward fly.
Come to Zion
For your coming Lord is nigh.
Israel, Israel, canst thou linger
Still in error's gloomy ways?
Mark how judgment's pointing finger
Justifies no vain delays.
Come to Zion
Zion's walls shall ring with praise.
("Israel, Israel, God is Calling," *Hymns*, no. 7)

John Taylor

We have expended millions upon millions in gathering the poor to this land, by what is known as the Perpetual Emigration Fund. We may ask, why did this people in these valleys expend such large sums? Was it because they were sending for relatives and friends? No, but because they were of the family of Christ, the sons and daughters of God, and desired to come to Zion (*Journal of Discourses*, 19:127).

George Albert Smith

(In April 1872, twenty-three years after the Perpetual Emigration Fund was established, President George A. Smith called attention to the blessings that had resulted from the fund.)

Look at the tens of thousands of families now in Utah in comfortable circumstances with houses, farms, wagons, cattle and horses of their own, many of them with carriages, and these families taken by the contributions of the Latter-day Saints from the most abject servitude and poverty from the bowels of the earth, from within the walls of factories, where but for this fund they must have remained for their lives; but now they are in comparative independence and enjoying the blessings of freemen (*Journal of Discourses*, 15:15).

⇜ 14 ⇝

SAINTS CROSSING THE SEAS

While the Saints in America worked to establish Zion in the midst of the Rocky Mountains, those converted to the gospel overseas had unique challenges of their own to overcome. The call to gather to Utah meant a long, and often dangerous, voyage over the ocean before even beginning the trek across the plains. It also meant putting an ocean between themselves, family, friends, and the culture they had known all their lives. Between 1840 and 1890, more than 85,000 Saints waved good-bye to their homeland and all that they knew to journey to America. The outstanding faith of these Saints was evidenced by their willingness to sacrifice everything to answer the call of a prophet to gather to Zion.

CONVERSIONS IN DISTANT LANDS

John Allen Sutton

(John Sutton was fifteen years old when he was converted to the gospel in England. Four and a half years later he sailed for America to join with the Saints.)

I was thoroughly convinced that the doctrine was true and according to scriptures. I then spoke to one of the elders, Henry Sanders, who told me if I believed, I could be baptized. I replied that I did.

This was on Sunday. There was a great commotion in the place. There were many enemies to this people already in the village who declared that if the [Elder] went to baptize me, they would drown him. Not being daunted, we started to the stream of water and I believe nearly one hundred people followed us. The Elder told the people that he was going to perform one of the ordinances of the gospel of Jesus Christ and if they would be quiet, he would show them how it was done. He then took me into the waters and baptized me, and not a word was said by any person. Thus I entered into a new life to me.

After receiving confirmation on the next Sabbath Day, I became very fervent in the performance of all the duties they required of me. My father and mother, brothers and sisters thought I was very foolish and that it would not last long, but finding that not to be the case and that many people were joining the Church in the little village, persecution began to rage and my greatest enemies were those of my own household.

I had now made up my mind to leave the land of my nativity and go to America, to Salt Lake City, it being a part of our religion to gather from the world. So strong was this feeling on me to gather, that nothing seemed to stay the progress (John Allen Sutton, *Autobiography* [LDS Church Archives, The Church of Jesus Christ of Latter-day Saints, Salt Lake City], 1–7, 9).

Gustave Louis Henroid

(Gustave Henroid was one of the first Saints to be baptized in the French mission. He told of his conversion to the Church during one of the groundbreaking missions in this dispensation.)

In June 1850, Mormon missionaries came to France from the United States. They were John Taylor, an apostle, Curtis E. Bolton and John D. Pack and others. Bolton came to Havre and directed his steps to my father's house, not knowing us from anyone else. They were traveling without purse or scrip. Father told Bolton that as he had no home, he might stay with us until he could do better. He lost no time in telling us of his mission to the world; that the gospel had been restored to the earth together with the authority and priesthood of God; . . .

The result was, in brief, that the family, one after another, were baptized, except Father, and joined The Church of Jesus Christ of Latter-day Saints. With few exceptions, I believe that we were the first Mormons of the French Mission. I was baptized on the second day of November, 1851, in a beautiful stream of clear water near Havre. It had been raining incessantly for several days, but as we were entering the stream for baptism, the sun came out brightly and a magnificent rainbow arched over our heads, lasting until the ceremony had terminated. It seemed that the heavens were smiling upon us and it occurred to those present that even the angels were rejoicing for the repentance and obedience manifested, and also for the establishment of the everlasting Gospel in a new country. . . .

My father having observed a great change in the every day deportment, the honest, sincere and moral life of his children and also their love and strong adherence to the Gospel of the ancient days as now again revealed, first favored and then advised us to gather to Utah with the Saints and devote our lives and abilities to the faith and church which had so regenerated and ameliorated the conduct and spiritual improvement of his children; being willing to admit to John Taylor that there must be something wonderful in Mormonism according to its influence and workings upon the heart and minds of the believers ("Gustave Louis Henroid" [1893] in *Our Pioneer Heritage*, comp. Kate B. Carter, 20 vols. [Salt Lake City: Daughters of Utah Pioneers, 1958–77], 11:316–32).

Alma Ash

(Alma Ash was born in Birmingham, England, in 1861, and traveled to the United States in 1885. He told of the strong desire he had to gather with the Saints.)

Whenever I saw [a Mormon] family emigrate to Zion, it used to cause very peculiar feelings to enter my heart. And oh, with what joy I [pondered] upon the gathering. . . . The possibility of [my family traveling to Zion in] the near future would give me the greatest joy. Indeed, I know of nothing which brought so much joy to my young heart as to talk about going to the [Salt Lake] Valley. . . . Many times we young Mormon exiles (children of Mormon neighbors) played "Going to the Valley" by constructing a train and a ship and the like, of chairs and tables. [We would] imagine we were traveling along. I remember also keeping marbles and tops which I intended [to give] as presents to my companions who had already gone to the valley, and whom I expected to soon follow. I also kept tools which I thought would assist in the building of a house when we got to Utah (Alma Ash, *Autobiography of Alma Ash*, typescript [LDS Church Archives, The Church of Jesus Christ of Latter-day Saints, Salt Lake City], 2–3).

Margaret Watson DeWitt

(Margaret DeWitt told of how she and her sister worked to pay for their journey to Zion.)

We worked in a factory, earning the money to pay our way to Utah. Having had experience in working in the factories in Glasgow, [Scotland] where there were five hundred steam looms on one floor, I felt at home in the work. They started me out with two looms; when my sister saw that I could handle them easily and still have plenty of spare time, she said to the manager, "My sister is an ambitious little girl and I'm sure she can handle more looms when you can give them to her."

They gave me four for awhile, but soon increased it to six, the most ever given to any experienced girls in the factory.

I made it a point always to be prompt; and the watchman would laugh as he held his lantern so that he could see my face as I sat at the big doors each morning waiting for him to open them and let me in. The minute the engine started I was at my loom. Some of the girls were always ten minutes or more late; when they remarked at my higher wages on pay-day, it was pointed out to them that ten minutes each day will soon amount to dollars and cents. . . . Our boarding house was managed by two old maid sisters who had rented a large house especially for factory girls. We paid them each month; and outside of our board, lodging, and clothes, we saved every cent for our journey across the plains (Margaret Watson DeWitt, "Autobiography of Margaret Miller Watson DeWitt," *Relief Society Magazine*, July 1929, 16:379–83).

LEAVING FAMILY AND HOMELAND

Augusta Dorius Stevens

(Augusta Stevens emigrated to the United States at age fourteen and wrote of the hardships of leaving her home and traveling to a foreign land.)

My thought would go back to my parents in Denmark feeling sure that I should never see them again because the journey into the wild west seemed so long and hard and uninviting that it seemed I could never hope to have them join me in the distant place some-where far in the west known as Zion. Surely my elderly parents—at least when I had left in the Old Country—could not endure the hardships of such a journey. I had my sobs and cries and pangs of sorrow. What comfort it would have been to me if I could even have been able to speak or understand the American language in this to me the New Land of America (Augusta Dorius Stevens, "Autobiog-raphy of Augusta Dorius Stevens [1922]," *Augusta Stevens Papers,* typescript [LDS Church Archives, The Church of Jesus Christ of Latter-day Saints, Salt Lake City], 4).

Ruth May Fox

When the time came for our departure [from England], I was in the seventh heaven. The lady who was to be my stepmother, and her daughter—who was about my own age—and myself left our home under cover of darkness to avoid the curiosity of the neighbors. Could anything be more thrilling?

After a walk of four or five miles under the stars, we boarded the train to Liverpool. Arriving there, some necessities . . . had to be pur-chased. . . . Then came the novelty of climbing into a great steamship. To stand on a floating city and gradually pull away from the wharf with hundreds of people waving their hats or handkerchiefs in a fond adieu and hearty "God-speed you" is an event never to be forgotten (Ruth May Fox, "From England to Salt Lake Valley in 1867," *Improvement Era,* July 1935, 38:406–7).

Margaret Watson DeWitt

(Margaret DeWitt was orphaned as a child and lived with her sister Belle. Unfortunately, Belle opposed the Church, forcing Margaret to run away from home in order to join the Saints.)

I left my sister Belle's home. We had eaten breakfast, and I left as if I were on my way to the factory. I saw the clothes spread on the green to bleach (she had washed the day before) and I picked up my night-cap and slipped it into my pocket. This was all I took with me except the clothes I stood up in.

I went directly to my friends, the McKays, who informed me that the next sailboat would not leave for two weeks. I couldn't go back home to Belle, so my kind Mormon friends, the McKays, hid me up for two weeks in the home of a widow who boarded me: the McKays paid her for her trouble. During this time the McKays outfitted me with clothes for my journey.

Bills had been posted and rewards offered for my capture, so, fearing detection, I disguised myself when I went to the sailboat. Just before boarding the ship I posted a letter to my sister Belle telling her not to continue her search for me as I was on my way to America. I crossed the gang-plank and entered the ship. Then I went below into the steerage until the ship had started.

I then went up on deck and took a last fond farewell of my native land. I was overcome with conflicting emotions as I saw it disappearing from my sight. For, though I was glad and eager to come to America, where I could learn more about Mormonism and join my sister Jane, yet I felt sad to leave forever my native land, my brothers and sisters and friends. I extended my arms and cried, "Good-bye forever, old home." The ship, the *Isaac Wright*, bore me off (DeWitt, "Autobiography of Margaret Miller Watson DeWitt," 16:379–83).

Priscilla Mogridge Staines

(At age twenty, Priscilla Stains sailed from England for the United States. She wrote of the hardship of leaving the land and people she loved.)

I was alone. It was a dreary winter day on which I went to Liverpool. The company with which I was to sail were all strangers to me. When I arrived at Liverpool and saw the ocean that would soon roll between me and all I loved, my heart almost failed me. But I had laid my idols all upon the altar. There was no turning back. I remembered the words of the Savior: "He that leaveth not father and mother, brother and sister, for my sake, is not worthy of me," and I believed his promise to those who forsook all for his sake; so I thus alone set out for the reward of everlasting life, trusting in God (cited in Edward W. Tullidge, *The Women of Mormondom* [New York: Tullidge and Drandall, 1877], 288).

Mary Haskin Parker Richards

(Mary Richards was given the opportunity to travel to Zion when a man named George Rhodes offered to pay her passage from New York to Nauvoo. After procuring her tickets across the ocean, and traveling to Liverpool, Mary was informed that Rhodes had been robbed and no longer had the means to finance her travel to Utah. Mary Richards recorded a conversation she had upon hearing the news.)

Now our hopes were lighted. Sister Bleasdale says "Mary, the ship will sail in the morning. What shall we do?" I replied, "Our passage is paid. Our provisions are on board. Let us go to [New York]. The Lord is just as able to sustain us there as he is if we should remain here. And so long as we walk uprightly before him we shall have no cause to fear, for he has promised that he will never forsake those who put their trust in him (Maurine Carr Ward, ed., *Winter Quarters: The 1846–1848 Life Writings of Mary Haskin Parker Richards* [Logan: Utah State University Press, 1996], 53–55, 58–61).

Valborg Rasmussen Wheelwright

I swung myself up the gangplank amidst the waving handkerchiefs of my schoolmates who were bidding me goodbye. I remember standing still, holding on to the railing as the boat glided out into the wide, soft darkness. I stood my ground without a tear until I saw a sweet, tear-stained face come into view. It was my mother. As she squeezed through the crowds, the heat and confusion almost overcame me. I remember whispering through the dark and the stillness, "Oh God, be with us that we may meet again in that land out West, as thou hast promised those who are faithful." It was a child's prayer, and through the whispering of the spirit I felt complete consolation. I was assured that I had done God's will (Valborg—An autobiography of Valborg Rasmussen Wheelwright, as told to his son Lorin F. Wheelwright [Salt Lake City: Pioneer Music Press, 1978], 20–33).

Frederick Zaugg

(Frederick Zaugg wrote of the opposition he and his family had to overcome due to the prejudice against the Church in Switzerland, at the time. He sailed for America in May 1884.)

Mother received no encouragement from her brother to let me go to America, especially to the Mormons. He told her she would not see me again. "Well I am sure I will see him again if not in this world then across the curtain for I am sure now that Jesus is the Christ and that he is alive and is the Father of our Salvation and will eventually bring us to God. I am trusting him with all I have, even my son." . . .

The month was spent in preparation for the great journey to Utah, and I spent some time working with father and mother helping them hoeing weeds. Father and mother both encouraged me to hope for the best that we may meet again in the due time of the Lord and in a more friendly world. I bid farewell to my school mates. It was hard, but we were prepared for it by the spirit of truth which we now enjoyed.

I bid farewell to my school mates, some of them were nice about it, sincere, and others sneered and had some funny remark to make; all wondered what would happen to me. One of my teachers gave me a good handshake and said, "Fred, I don't see that you could better yourself with the Mormons. They live in a city on the shores of a great salt sea. They have a wall 40 feet high around it and name their city Salt Lake City. They will keep you a slave." I answered, if the people are as good as the Mormon missionaries, I would not care if I never got out (Frederick Zaugg, *Autobiography*, typescript, 20–33, original in private possession; cited in Susan Arrington Madsen and Fred E. Woods, *I Sailed to Zion* [Salt Lake City: Deseret Book, 2000], 132–33).

Mary Powell Sabin

(Mary Sabin's account of Mrs. Deveraux, a fellow traveler, stands as a testament of the sacrifices the Saints were willing to make to obey the commandment to come to Zion.)

When we had been on the ocean three weeks, Mrs. Deveraux died. They sewed her up in a sheet and buried her in the sea. In the commencement of the voyage, she remarked to my mother, "I'll go on board the ship and start my husband to Utah. If I should die, he will journey on. If we do not commence the journey, perhaps my husband

and children will not reach Utah" (Mary Powell Sabin, *Autobiography*, 1926, microfilm [LDS Church Archives, The Church of Jesus Christ of Latter-day Saints, Salt Lake City], 7).

Ann L. West Neville

(Ann told of the sacrifice her mother made in sending her daughters off to join the Saints in America.)

Mother said that if she could of called the ship back, she surely would have done it. She had not realized what it meant until the big ship sailed way out of sight and maybe [she would] never see us again. But she remembered the promise made [to] them, so [she] went home and worked harder than ever making shirts and fancy boxes, which was her trade, to help get money to pay their passage to America ("Biography of Ann L. West Neville," written January 1929, in private possession of Marilyn H. Mecham, Salt Lake City; cited in Madsen and Woods, *I Sailed to Zion*, 49).

Stephen Forsdick

Our organization [on the ship] was then accomplished. Christopher Arthur from Newport was appointed president and John Lyons [Lyon] and Richard Waddington counselors and Elder [George] Sims as clerk. The bunks were divided into wards, with a president over each and others were appointed to see that the beds were made and everything kept clean and neat during the voyage.

A watch was appointed to see that all hands were in their bunks by ten o'clock at night. We had three London policemen on board and they were assigned to police duty. . . .

As soon as we were organized we commenced a routine which was about as follows: up at daylight and get breakfast. Then came morning prayers in all the wards, then it was sweep and clean up. After that we could promenade on deck, sing or do whatever we chose until time to get dinner (Stephen Forsdick, *Autobiography*, duplication of typescript [LDS Church Archives, The Church of Jesus Christ of Latter-day Saints, Salt Lake City], 11).

SEASICKNESS

Gibson Condie

The ship began to toss to and fro. The buckets or cans would tip over. The people then began to be sick, dizzy, [and] began to vomit. They could not sit up nor eat anything. They call it seasickness.

Everyone [who] goes to sea generally [has] that attack, [which] lasts three days and sometimes longer. A person [does] not feel like eating. They feel as though they could not live. I was [seasick] about a week myself before I was able to be round again (Gibson Condie, *Reminiscences and diary*, microfilm [LDS Church Archives, The Church of Jesus Christ of Latter-day Saints, Salt Lake City], 23–25).

Stephen Forsdick

(Stephen Forsdick told of his experience with seasickness. He recalled that he used to stick his head over the side of the boat, being so sick he felt he would throw up everything, right down to his boots.)

During the first week or so [on the ship], the cooks had an easy time of it, very few having much appetite and the deck was not crowded. I used to crawl up on deck and get my arms through the ratline and try to throw up my boots. My best description of seasickness is that, the first day or two you are afraid you are going to die; the rest of the time, you don't care how soon you do. All things come to an end, however, and so did seasickness to most of us and then we fell into our regular routine again (Forsdick, *Autobiography*, 12).

B. H. Roberts

(Courtesy of the Church Archives, The Church of Jesus Christ of Latter-day Saints)

ENJOYMENTS DURING THE VOYAGE

B. H. Roberts

There were frolics on deck, games and group singing. There were many beautiful voices in that list of passengers—English, Welch, [Scottish]—for they had been gathered from all the scattered branches in those countries, some of them noted for their music. There was dancing, also games for the children; among others, marbles for the boys when the ship was steady enough for the marbles to stay in the rings until shot out by the players (B. H. Roberts, *The Autobiography of B. H. Roberts*, ed. Gary James Bergera [Salt Lake City: Signature, 1990], 19).

John Chatterley

I got acquainted with a boy [the] same age as myself named Thomas Dallen [Dallin]. . . . We [played] sport every day, and many times in the night. The sailors put us to painting some of the passengers with whiskers and mustaches as they slept on deck during the time we were near the equator. It caused lots of fun, and we didn't get found out, as we were decorated with the whiskers and mustaches ourselves (John Chatterley, "Autobiography," *Utah Pioneer Biographies* [LDS Family History Library: Salt Lake City], 7:68–72, 74).

Isabelle Price Kunkel

We set sail about eight o'clock that same evening. How happy everyone was! As the ship began to move, hundreds of voices—men, women and children—began to sing: "Come, Come Ye Saints"; then "Cheer Saints, Cheer, We Are Bound for Peaceful Zion, Cheer Saints Cheer for the Free and Happy Land"; then "Oh Ye Mountains High in the Clear Blue Sky," by Charles W. Penrose. It was one of the nights that I have never forgotten (Isabelle Price Kunkel, "An Historic Letter." in *Our Pioneer Heritage*, comp. Kate B. Carter, 20 vols. [Salt Lake City: Daughters of Utah Pioneers, 1958–77], 7:260–62).

Percy Groom

The trip was quite exciting seeing whales, porpoises and other marine animals and birds. It is strange how long a flock of seagulls will follow a ship and keep up with it without resting a spell. Some thirty large icebergs were seen on the way. May is a good time to cross if one wants to see these dull, silent, gray piles of arctic glaciers as they majestically float down from Greenland and eventually melt in the Gulf Stream. One large pile of ice had as a passenger a polar bear. This [cub] was no doubt beyond his depths, [and] when the iceberg melted, which it surely would do, then the bear would be without a footing. And while very clever in water, [he would] have to come up for breathing, and eventually the poor bear would become a victim of its own thoughtlessness. It took a total of thirty days to cross the Atlantic (Percy Groom, *Biographical Sketch* [LDS Church Archives, The Church of Jesus Christ of Latter-day Saints, Salt Lake City], 3–5).

Caroline Hopkins Clark

[Today was] a beautiful fine day. We had a concert and dancing on deck. At night we went up on top deck to see the sun sinking in the west. It is the grandest sight we have ever witnessed. It is impossible to describe, but if you would like to see it, you will have to do as we have done (Caroline Hopkins Clark, "Gathering to Zion," in *Voices From the Past: Diaries, Journals, and Autobiographies,* comp. Campus Education Week Program [Provo, Utah: Brigham Young University Press, 1980], 70).

HAZARDS AND HARDSHIPS

Mary Goble Pay

When we were sailing through the banks of Newfoundland, we were in a dense fog for several days. The sailors were kept busy night and day, ringing bells and blowing foghorns. One day I was on deck with my father when I saw a mountain of ice in the sea close to the ship. I said, "Look, Father, look." He went as white as a ghost and said, "Oh, my girl." At that moment the fog parted, the sun shone brightly till the ship was out of danger, when the fog closed on us again (Mary Goble Pay, *Autobiographical Sketch,* typescript [LDS Church Archives, The Church of Jesus Christ of Latter-day Saints, Salt Lake City], 1–2).

Samuel Brannan

[The lower] quarters were ill-ventilated, unsanitary, and almost wholly devoid of light.

As the ship headed out into the Atlantic, the Saints were not long in discovering other discomforts—from which there would be no relief for months to come. Not the least of these was a lack of headroom below deck. So low were the ceilings that only a dwarf could stand erect. For a person of normal stature to move about, it was necessary to crouch monkey-fashion (Paul Bailey, "Sam Brannan and the Mormons in Early California," *Improvement Era*, November 1942, 45:725).

Alma Ash

Our food on the boat was coarse and the care and attention given steerage passengers was almost brutal, for it was only those with cast iron stomachs and digestive organs which could eat the food and drink provided. We lay on the bare boards nearly the whole of the voyage (Alma Ash, *Autobiography of Alma Ash*, typescript [LDS Church Archives, The Church of Jesus Christ of Latter-day Saints, Salt Lake City], 28).

Gibson Condie

Shortly after we left the docks, the first mate of our vessel got drunk and neglected his duties while we were in the Irish Coast or Channel. It is [a] very dangerous sea full of rocks, etc. Our ship had a narrow escape from being dashed to pieces. She ran against some rocks. The captain thought [there was] something wrong. He then saw for himself the danger of the vessel, and he took charge and changed the course of the vessel. He then took first mate into custody. He was not permitted to be on deck on daytime, only at night. His office was took from him. He was a prisoner all the way to New Orleans. The Lord was over us and preserved us from the jaws of death. [In] another circumstance, our galley (fireplace) got on fire. We were all frightened, our vessel being on fire [and] no way to escape—only to jump into the sea and be drowned. We succeeded in then checking the flames. We all felt thankful to our Heavenly Father [for] preserving us [in] the two narrow escapes we had (Condie, *Reminiscences and diary*, 23–25).

Peter Penfold

(Peter Penfold was aboard the Julia Ann, *the only ship of the 550 that sailed between 1840 and 1890, carrying Latter-day Saint immigrants to be lost at sea. The* Julia Ann *sailed from Australia, expecting to land in California. However, the ship hit a coral reef, about four hundred miles west of Tahiti. Passengers were stranded on the Scilly Isles and later traveled to Tahiti before being able to continue on to California. He wrote the following letter from Tahiti, to the Saints in Australia.)*

Tahiti February 17th, 1856

Dear Brothers and Sisters,

I now take the present opportunity of writing you a few lines hoping [to find] you all well. Since we left Australia we have passed through dangers, difficulties, hardships and trials.

We set sail as you are aware on the 7th of September [1855]. All went on pretty well until the 3rd [of] October. That evening about half past eight o-clock, when the winds were blowing free and the Julia Ann was going about 12 or 13 knots per hour, she suddenly struck on a coral reef off Scilly Island about 300 to 400 miles west of Tahiti and became a total wreck.

When she first struck, some of us were singing on the top of the midship house. We soon got down and went into the house, but finding that not very safe we went into the cabin, the sea breaking over us every moment. It was a thing impossible to stand. A rope was soon conveyed to [some nearby] rocks.

Father, mother, Stephen and most of the men went on shore by [means of] the rope while I was down in the cabin lending assistance to the women and children that was still below and to help them up on the poop [deck]. Sister Humphries and Sister Harris and infant was drowned in the cabin. Little Mary Humphries and Marion Anderson was washed off the poop [deck] and drowned. They are all that was lost.

After I had helped get them all out of the cabin and came up, I found the vessel all broken up into fragments except the cabin. Water was rushing at a furious rate [into the cabins], sweeping out all the partitions. A great many of us was still clinging to the poop [deck]. After a while I made my escape to the rocks upon the broken fragments of the vessel. . . .

We passed a dreadful night sitting on some of the broken masts, up to our [waists] in water. At daylight we were all very busily engaged [in] picking up such provisions [from the ship] as could be found.

A very small island or two was seen about six miles distant. Having one [small row]boat, with a little repairing, some were soon able to go and view the land. The islands was small, three in number, without inhabitants, barren and desolate. A few coconuts were the only things growing that was fit to eat. With these and some turtles and birds, [and] with the little we picked up from the wreck, we managed to live.

On the 20th of November, our [row]boat being repaired, the captain and crew started for Tahiti. And on the 2nd of December, to our great joy, [they returned with] a vessel for our deliverance. We embarked on the 3rd and got to the island of [Huahine] on the [11]th where we saw the grave of Sister Allen [a member who had died from childbirth on a previous voyage] who was buried on that island. We stopped there three days. We then went on to Tahiti where we landed on the 19th. When we got there the consuls would do nothing for us.

The American Consul said he had nothing to do with us because we were English subjects. The English Consul said he had nothing to do with us because we were in an American ship. So we were in a very peculiar situation with [our] friends, without [a] home, without clothes, without food, and in a strange land under the French government.

By the charity of the Free Masons Lodge we were [given] food until the 19th of Jan., when they could feed us no longer. We then went to the English Consul again and he has [given] us food ever since. But he says he shall [discontinue feeding us] at the end of this month's stay. When we shall get away from this place, I know not.

We have three orphan children stopping with us, Eliza and Francis Humphries and Maria Harris who wish to be remembered to their friends, if you should have the chance to see any of them.

There is but very little work for a man to get in this place. Mother and Father and we all are in good health though we have lost all our worldly goods. Yet, we have faith in God and trust he will deliver us soon . . . I hope to see you all before long in the land of [the] free surrounded by the Saints of the Most High God. Mother, Father, and Stephen join me in sending our love to you all, likewise remember us to all friends.

Please let Brother Farnham know of the wreck, also of our situation. Do not grieve yourself.

I remain your affectionate,

Peter Penfold

(Letter of Peter Penfold in *Diary of Augustus Farnham* [LDS

Church Archives, The Church of Jesus Christ of Latter-day Saints, Salt Lake City], 56–57).

BAD WEATHER

Annie Catherine Christensen Olsen

One day a terrible storm came up. I was standing on the middle of the deck holding to a large barrel just under the hold of the ship. I felt impressed to move under the deck and just as I did so, and had gone a short distance, a mast beam broke and fell, breaking the barrel to pieces. So you see how necessary it is to heed the promptings of the Spirit at all times (Annie Catherine Christensen Olsen, "Autobiography," *Utah Pioneer Biographies*, 22:17 [LDS Family History Library, Salt Lake City], cited in Madsen and Woods, *I Sailed to Zion*, 112).

John Chatterley

We had very rough weather the second day out of Liverpool. . . . It was quite a sight to see the passengers, those that had courage to get up. Most were in their bunks sick, some praying, some hollering, wishing they were back home (Chatterley, "Autobiography," *Utah Pioneer Biographies*, 7:68–72, 74).

Mary Larsen Ahlstrom

We had bad weather and heavy seas right from the first. On Christmas Eve the ship was struck by a hurricane and for a time it seemed that the old windjammer was doomed to be swallowed up in the sea. The storm raged so furiously that the luggage chests, which were tied to posts on the deck, broke from their moorings and were hurled about with such force as to endanger life and limbs. All passengers were therefore ordered into their bunks where we crouched in misery, listening to the shrieking of the winds and wishing we were back in our comfortable homes again.

Sometime in January our ship caught fire on the first deck and [burned] through [to] the second deck and filled it with smoke so that we nearly strangled. [Many passengers] ran up and wanted to jump overboard. Our leader, Canute Peterson said, "Stay on the ship. We will get the fire out and the ship will get to New York." And it did.

A few nights later we had a collision with another ship that almost knocked a hole in our ship. Our Captain had always been very cruel to the sailors. Now he flogged them worse than before, claiming the collision had been due to the crew's negligence (Mary Larsen Ahlstrom, *Autobiographical sketch* [LDS Church Archives, The Church of Jesus Christ of Latter-day Saints, Salt Lake City], n.p.).

Ebenezer Farnes

About the third week on the voyage there came a terrible storm which tore everything down that could be broken. So bad was the storm that the people had to stay in their beds for three days . . . When the captain was asked about the storm he said if he had known the condition of the ship he would not have sailed on her, but consoled himself [that] as he had a load of "Mormons" on board he would get through all right, as there had never been a ship lost that was carrying "Mormons." After the ship landed in New York, she was not considered fit to carry anything back but lumber; so they loaded her with that and she water-logged and was lost at sea (Ebenezer Farnes, *Reminiscences*, typescript [LDS Church Archives, The Church of Jesus Christ of Latter-day Saints, Salt Lake City], 1–3).

Isabelle Price Kunkel

On the 21st of June we had a terrific storm of wind and rain. The waves were mountain height. As one end of the ship went down, you could not see over the top of the waves, the next minute the other would be down. It was the grandest sight that I ever saw, beautiful but awful in its grandeur. But havoc in the steerage and in our quarters too. The buckets, grips, pans and all kinds of cooking utensils and trunks were skating all over the place. A great many of the women and children were frightened nearly to death. Some felt sure we would be shipwrecked. It was after this awful storm that Captain Bell told my father he always felt perfectly safe when he had our people on board (Kunkel, "An Historic Letter," in *Our Pioneer Heritage*, 7:260–62).

Caroline Hopkins Clark

The sea is very rough. None of us are able to stand on our legs. I fell down and hurt my leg badly. John has had many falls. In fact, all of us [did], more or less. The things are rolling about. The victuals are tossing about, but we cannot help laughing. . . .

[I] dare say you have heard people say they could [not] go to sleep without rocking, but we cannot go to sleep with rocking. We had plenty last night. Talk about a swinging boat, why bless your life, it is nothing compared to being rocked at sea. We can hardly keep in bed. We had to get up and turn our heads where our feet should be or we could not stay in bed at all. The tins and boxes were rolling about. The slop buckets upset. The sailors said it was as rough a night as they have ever seen, and it continued all day (Clark, "Gathering to Zion," in *Voices from the Past*, 70).

Deaths at Sea

In the twenty-two years between 1847 and 1869, almost seven hundred Saints died at sea. With no other option for burial, the bodies of the deceased had to be buried at sea.

Gibson Condie

If there were any sickness on board we would see the sharks follow the ship for days. I think we lost two children [to] death on the voyage. They sewed them up in a sheet and threw them overboard. The sharks then are ready to devour [them]. It is a very sad affair to throw the dead overboard to be devoured . . . by the sharks (Condie, *Reminiscences and diary*, 23–25).

Ebenezer Farnes

The burial at sea is a sad thing. The body is sewn in a canvas and a ball of iron placed at their feet so as to make the body sink feet first so the sharks cannot get it. A long plank is placed on the rail of the ship, part on the ship and part over the water, and the body is placed on the plank, feet to the water. After the burial ceremony the plank is lifted at one end and the body slides into the sea. You can see the body go slanting down for a long distance (Farnes, *Reminiscences*, 1–3).

ARRIVING IN AMERICA

Valborg Rasmussen Wheelwright

When the ship glided into New York harbor, a gentle breeze was blowing. Looking up, I saw the morning sun gleaming on the outstretched hand of the Goddess [Statue] of Liberty. She was wonderful to behold— so big, so glorious. I saw her as my new mother welcoming me to America, the land of my new birth. It was a sight I shall never forget. Suddenly, I felt less homesick, and tears of gratitude to God and my church dimmed my eyes (Valborg—An autobiography of Valborg Rasmussen Wheelwright, as told to his son Lorin F. Wheelwright, 20–33).

Frederick Zaugg

We saw the Brooklyn Bridge with its crown of gas lights. It had just been dedicated. It was a beautiful sight and a wonder. It was a wonderful thing to anticipate putting my feet on this wonderful and great land of America (Frederick Zaugg, *Autobiography*, typescript, 20–33, original in private possession; cited in Madsen and Woods, *I Sailed to Zion*, 137–38).

Charlotte Ann Bates

We landed on the 4th of July. It was the first time I saw firecrackers. The thing that appealed to me was the way the little girls dressed. They wore high top shoes. They looked wonderful to me. There were fruit stands there on which were the first peaches, apricots, and tomatoes I had ever seen. My brother saw the tomatoes and bought some. He took one bite and spit it out and gave me the rest. I thought it was like poison. It was many years before I learned to like tomatoes. We stayed for several days sleeping on the floor in Castle Garden [a New York immigration point]. I suppose those who had money went to hotels but we had plenty of company, all nationalities. But we didn't care. We were going to Zion to be with the people of God and mingle with the prophets of God and his people ("The Life of Charlotte Ann Bates" [LDS Church Archives, The Church of Jesus Christ of Latter-day Saints, Salt Lake City], 2–3).

Mary Powell Sabin

We did not go ashore for two days as we had to be examined first. Five hundred and twenty seven persons in all. Not one of our company was sent to either hospital. One was a general hospital and the other a mental hospital. The physicians declared that they had never seen a more healthy, cleanly company of immigrants (Sabin, *Autobiography, 1926,* 8).

Clara Durtschi Burgener

After arriving in New York, we assembled with the other passengers in a big hall, and there I found out for the first time that each passenger was required to have not less than thirty dollars in cash, or they would be sent back. All I had was fifteen cents. An officer began to read names from a paper, and as the names were called, they had to go into another room to answer questions and show the thirty dollars. I shivered and shook with fear, and I prayed like I had never prayed before. Every name was called out but mine, and I sat there alone. I didn't know how I could get away or where to go, but after a while, my cousin's baby in the other room cried so hard, the judge sent her back to the hall where I was, and as soon as I saw her I went to her, and we walked outside, and not one of the officers we met in the way asked any questions. To me that was a wonderful answer to my prayers (Clara Durtschi Burgener, "From Switzerland to Utah By the Power of Faith," in *Voices from the Past,* 126–27).

Alma Ash

(Having only enough money to travel from England to Chicago, Alma Ash received miraculous aid when it looked as though it would be impossible for him to travel on to join the Saints. His account is a testament of the faith the Saints had that God would make a way for them to obey His commandment to gather to Zion.)

We asked ourselves the question "What shall we do if left in Chicago?" for our ticket only took us that far. Instinctively we said "God help us" and then collapsed, sat motionless and awaited the verdict. We heard Brother Hunter tell Brother Hart the message of Brother Wells, but he quickly shook his head and said to us, "Boys, I should be pleased to do it if I could." He turned away and left us alone in our glory. I said to myself, "Ah, it's the same old ghost which has followed me and my father's house all our lives, namely disappointment." I bit my lips to keep back the gush of tears which were ready to come. But no, for once the specter "disappointment" was driven away by the kindly angel of "hope" which came to our rescue. Brother Hart stepped but a few paces and then as if he had received a revelation, he turned suddenly around and said, "Boys, I believe I will help you along. Come over to my office on Battle Square in two hours and we will make arrangements to send you along." These words I shall never forget and the impression made upon us at that time will endure to all eternity, for God was surely over us and had favored all we had done so far. . . .

How is it that one can ever doubt God? Surely all men have been the recipients of great and wonderful favors (Ash, *Autobiography of Alma Ash*, 28–29).

B. H. Roberts

(B. H. Roberts's mother had journeyed to America earlier, then as soon as she was able to obtain the necessary means, she sent for the rest of her children. B. H. Roberts described being reunited with his mother, amidst the crowd of Saints that had gathered to welcome the immigrant Saints into the Salt Lake Valley.)

Mary and I seemed to be so little part of this excitement and joy, because nobody seemed to come for us. Mary remained concealed under the wagon cover, and I, lonesome and heartsick, sat upon the tongue of Captain Chipman's wagon, my chin in my hands and elbows upon my knees, thinking "Zion" was not so much after all, if this was all of it. The spirit of sadness, if it was not forlornness, settled upon me.

Presently, however, approaching from the west gate, I saw a woman in a red and white plaid shawl slowly moving among the hillocks of fertilizer that had been raked from the sheds and the yard. She seemed to be daintily picking her way, and there was something in the movement of her head as she looked to the right and to the left that seemed familiar to me. The woman was moving in my direction, and the closer she came the stronger the conviction grew upon me that there was my mother. I would have known her from the dainty cleanliness of everything about her.

I stood until she came nearly parallel to where I sat; then sliding from the tongue of the wagon, I said, "Hey Mother," and she looked down upon my upturned face. Without moving she gazed upon me for some time and at last said, "Is this you, Harry? Where is Mary?" Of course Mary was in the wagon, and I led my mother to where she was hiding, and when mother and daughter met, there was a flood of tears on both sides. At last I joined them, making the trio of the united family. It seemed difficult for our mother to realize that we at last were her children after more than four years of separation, but once in a while, a smile would break through the tears and she seemed to be extremely happy (Roberts, *The Autobiography of B. H. Roberts*, 25–44).

HELP AFTER ARRIVING IN UTAH

Frederick Zaugg

(Frederick arrived in Utah in June 1884, completely alone and able to speak and understand very little English. When he arrived, he did not know how to get to the home of the family that had paid for his immigration. When a kindhearted train conductor realized Frederick's situation, he took him to the home of a family who cared for him until he was able to make his way to his new home in Park Valley. His account is an example of the faith these Saints displayed in leaving everything familiar to them and trusting in the Lord.)

After a hearty breakfast of bacon and eggs, fried potatoes, radishes and bread and butter, and a glass of milk, I took a leaf from my notebook and wrote on it in German and French, so someone could read and inform me where Park Valley is. I signed my name and indicated where I am from. This good man took the note and went into the city and found George Grael, the county clerk. This man had been on a mission in Switzerland, in the French speaking part, and could speak French. This man came back with the elder man, and when he saw me he said "Bonjour monsier, comment ça va." Well, once more, I could understand. It was like an angel's voice. Soon we were in a conversation. He took me to his home where I was treated as one of the family.

After inquiring of people who knew of Park Valley, we found it to be about 75 miles west of Box Elder (now Brigham City). In order to get there, I would have to go back to Ogden and take the train . . . to Kelton. The ticket [would] cost $6 dollars and I would still have 25 miles on a wagon trail to get to Park Valley. I drew a long breath. George Grael then said "Just be patient and time will always bring things about. You are welcome to be with us until you can get in touch with your party." This made me happy again knowing that the Lord does not forsake anyone that does his will (Frederick Zaugg, *Autobiography*, 20–33, cited in Madsen and Woods, *I Sailed to Zion*, 140).

Caroline Hopkins Clark

(Caroline Clark wrote the following sentiment in a letter to those back in her native land of England.)

I dare say you would like to know if we have regretted our journeying. As yet we do not regret the time we left England. If we had the privilege to come back we would not accept it (Clark, "Gathering to Zion," in *Voices from the Past*, 74).

~ 15 ~

THE HANDCART PIONEERS

The first winter in the valley was not an easy one. Between the drought and the damage done by insects, the Saints were in short supply of crops, and donations to the Perpetual Emigration Fund dwindled. With rising numbers of poor Saints in need of assistance to come to the Salt Lake Valley, Brigham Young devised a plan to use handcarts to gather Saints to the valley as an answer to an economic need.

The endeavor involved much preparation and planning. After coordinating travel by boat and train, Saints would ideally arrive in Iowa sometime in May or June. They would then travel across Iowa in three to four weeks, arriving in Florence, Nebraska. Companies were encouraged to leave Florence for the West no later than July. Members of each company were assigned to a handcart, each cart having four or five travelers. Each person was allowed seventeen pounds of luggage. Supplies were carried in the two or three supply wagons that accompanied each band of handcarts, bringing tools and other necessities. As the handcart companies approached the Salt Lake Valley, relief parties were sent to assist the weary travelers over the mountains.

Between 1856 and 1860, ten handcart companies crossed the planes to Utah. Although the work was hard and food supplies low, the majority of handcart companies enjoyed great success. In the eight companies that did not include the Willie and Martin companies, fewer than forty people died. Despite the many hardships, the implementation of the handcart plan allowed many to come to Zion who otherwise would not have been able to gather with the Saints.

Instigating the Handcart Program

Brigham Young

(In September 1855, President Young wrote to the president of the European Mission, Franklin D. Richards, informing him of President Young's intention to begin employing handcarts.)

I have been thinking how we should operate another year . . . We cannot afford to purchase wagons and teams as in times past. I am consequently thrown back upon my old plan—to make hand-carts, and let the emigration foot it, and draw upon them [the carts] the necessary supplies, having a cow or two for every ten. They can come just as quick, if not quicker, and much cheaper—can start earlier and escape the prevailing sickness which annually lays so many of our brethren in the dust. A great majority of them walk now, even with the teams which are provided, and have a great deal more care and perplexity than they would have if they came without them. . . .

They will only need 90 days' rations from the time of their leaving the Missouri River, and as the settlements extend up the Platte, not that much. The carts can be made without a particle of iron, with wheels hooped, made strong and light, and one, or if the family be large, two of them will bring all that they will need upon the plains. . . .

I think we might as well begin another year as any time, and save this enormous expense of purchasing wagons and teams—indeed we will be obliged to pursue this course, or suspend operations, for aught that I can see at the present. . . .

I think the emigration had better come that northern route from New York, or Philadelphia, or Boston, direct to Iowa City . . . Their passage through to Iowa City will not cost more than 8 or 9 dollars, and they will only have to be supplied with money for provisions and a few cows, which should be of the very best quality. . . . Of course you will perceive the necessity of dispensing with all wooden chests, extra freight, luggage, etc. They should only bring a change of clothing (Brigham Young, *Millennial Star* [December 22, 1855], 17:813–14).

Franklin D. Richards

(While serving as president of the European Mission, Franklin D. Richards also served as the editor of the Millennial Star. *When President Brigham Young's letter announcing the commencement of the use of handcarts for crossing the plains was published, President Richards added the following editorial.)*

Franklin D. Richards
(Courtesy of the Church Archives, The Church of Jesus Christ of Latter-day Saints)

The plan about to be adopted by the P. E. Fund Company, of substituting handcarts for ox-teams in crossing the plains, has been under consideration for several years. The plan proposed is novel, and, when we allow our imaginations to wander into the future and paint the scenes that will transpire on the prairies next summer, they partake largely of the romantic. The plan is the device of inspiration, and the Lord will own and bless it. . . .

More speedy measures must be devised for strengthening Zion . . . The system of ox-trains is too slow and expensive, and must give way to the telegraph line of handcarts and wheelbarrows. It would be much more economical both in time, labor, and expense, if, instead of spending several weeks to obtain and accustom to the yoke, a lot of wild ungovernable cattle, impairing the health of many of the brethren by excessive labor and fatigue, and bringing disease and death into the camps by long delays on the miasmatic banks of the Missouri River, on the arrival of a company of Saints on the frontier they could have the necessary handcarts ready and load them, and be 200 or 300 miles on their journey, with the same time and labor that would otherwise be expended in getting started.

It is only to those who have traveled the plains with ox-teams, that the advantages of doing without them will appear in all their force. They alone can realize what it is to get up on a sultry morning, spend an hour or two in driving up and yoking unruly cattle, and while impatiently waiting to start on the dusty, wearisome road, in order to accomplish the labors of the day in due time, hear the word passed around that some brother has an ox missing, then another hour, or perhaps half a day, is wasted and finally, when ready to start, the pleasantest time for traveling in past, during which a company with handcarts would have performed the greater part of an ordinary day's journey. There being few animals in a handcart company, there will be less to tempt the cupidity of the Indians—a large share of that most laborious and harassing duty—guarding—can be dispensed with, and the time occupied with sleep and refreshments, with songs of rejoicing and prayer.

The anxieties of mind about losing cattle by stampedes, poisonous water, and exhaustion will be avoided. It may be safely considered that the extra time and labour of a company that will be required to get started with an ox-team and take care of the cattle, aside from that spent in actual traveling, will enable that same company, with a handcart to every five persons, loaded with five or six hundred pounds, on starting, to accomplish two-thirds of the journey and besides it will reduce the cost of emigration from Britain to two-thirds of what it is at present at most, and after the first year probably to one half. This greatly decreased amount of indebtedness on the part of the emigrating Saints will be much to their pecuniary advantage after their arrival in Utah (Franklin D. Richards, *Millennial Star* [December 22, 1855], 17:813–14).

Thirteenth General Epistle of the Presidency of the Church

The P. E. Fund is designed to deliver the honest poor, the pauper, if you please, from the thralldom of ages, from localities where poverty is a crime and beggary an offense against the law, where every avenue to rise in the scale of being to any degree of respectable joyous existence is forever closed, and place them in a land where honest labor and industry meet a suitable reward, where the higher walks of life are open to the humblest and poorest. . . .

Let all things be done in order, and let all the Saints, who can, gather up for Zion and come while the way is open before them; let the poor also come, whether they receive aid or not from the Fund, let them come on foot, with hand-carts or wheelbarrows; let them gird up their loins and walk through, and nothing shall hinder or stay them. . . .

Let the Saints, therefore, who intend to immigrate the ensuing year, understand that they are expected to walk and draw their luggage across the plains, and that they will be assisted by the Fund in no other way. . . . If this project is once fairly tested, and proves as successful as we have no doubt it will, the main expense of the immigration will be avoided, consequently thousands more than heretofore can receive assistance ("Thirteenth General Epistle," *Millennial Star* [January 26, 1856], 18:52, 54).

Franklin D. Richards

When ancient Israel fled from bondage into the wilderness, they had not even the privilege of taking provisions for their journey, but had to trust to the good hand of the Lord for their daily bread. If the Saints in these lands have not seen such times, the future will reveal them.

The Lord can rain manna on the plains of America just as easily as He did on the deserts of Arabia, or as He sent quails into the camp of the Saints on the Mississippi river in 1846. Ancient Israel traveled to the promised land on foot, with their wives and little ones. The Lord calls upon modern Israel to do the same ("Editorial," *Millennial Star* [March 1, 1856], 18:138).

Millennial Star

We have a very cheering letter from Elders G. D. Grant and W. H. Kimball, who were at Iowa City, March 20. They state that the weather had been very bad, and the lakes and rivers were still a block of ice. Cattle had been offered at seventy dollars per pair, and they had purchased flour at $3.20 per hundred, and the prospect was that, as spring opened, there would be a still further decrease in the price of provisions. They had contracted for 100 handcarts of excellent quality, at about two guineas each [$10]. There were good prospects for work. Common laborers could get from three to four shillings per day, and mechanics' wages were in proportion. . . . Under the wise and judicious management of Elders Taylor and Spencer, we believe that nothing will be wanting to make the handcart operation a successful one ("Editorial," *Millennial Star* [May 3, 1856], 18:281).

DAILY LIFE IN THE HANDCART COMPANIES

Sarah Hancock Beesley

Our handcarts had handles on the front and the back too, for some must push and some must pull, you know. The wheels were high so that they could be used for wagon wheels after we got here ("Mrs. Ebenezer B. [Sarah Hancock] Beesley," in "Handcart Stories," typescript [LDS Church Archives, The Church of Jesus Christ of Latter-day Saints, Salt Lake City], 28–34).

Mary Ann Jones

On the 21st of March 1856 a company of Latter-day Saints, 534 in number left the shores of England on the ship *Enoch Train*. Arrived in Boston May 1st. Went to Iowa to wait for the hand carts to be got ready for the start across the plains. Left Iowa [City] in the 9th of June. Traveled to Florence, left Florence July 16th, went 4 miles then stopped to have hand carts fixed up they were made so flimsy they were continuly breaking down. Started again on the 20th of July and began our long march across the plains we had on leaving 274 persons in the company, had only 7 deaths on the journey which I think remarkable as we had a number of aged people and lots of children. We had 4 wagons, 3 of them drawn by oxen and one four-horse team. We traveled 1400 miles in nine weeks. We were allotted one tent to twenty persons and four hand-carts to each tent. We traveled as high as twenty-eight miles a day and always got to camp long before the wagons. We were allowed seventeen pounds of baggage each, that meant clothes, bedding, cooking utensils, etc. When the brethren came to weigh our things some wanted to take more than allowed so put on extra clothes so that some [who] were real thin soon became stout; so as soon as the weighting was over put the extra clothes in the hard cart again but that did not last long for in a few days we were called upon to have all weighed again and quite a few were found with more than allowed. One old Sister carried a teapot and calendar on her apron strings all the way to Salt Lake (*Diary of Mary Ann Jones [age 19] on her trip across the plains*, 1910, typescript copy [LDS Church Archives, The Church of Jesus Christ of Latter-day Saints, Salt Lake City], n.p.).

Mary Powell Sabin

From the Bluffs we went up the river to Florence, Nebraska. At Florence we remained two weeks fixing handcarts and wagons. There were two buildings at this place—a large store house and a mill. . . .

While we were encamped at Florence father secured work. He laid the foundation, also dressed the corner-stone for the first court-house in Omaha. He received eight dollars per day. He needed this money, for, said he, "I cannot let my children go bare-footed across the plains."

Father bought me a pair of shoes, the ugliest I've ever seen in all my life. It was the best he could get.

From Florence, Nebraska, began our real journey across the plains. All our other experiences had not been a foretaste of what lay ahead of us (Mary Powell Sabin, *Autobiography*, 1926, microfilm [LDS Church Archives, The Church of Jesus Christ of Latter-day Saints, Salt Lake City], 9–10).

Mary Powell Sabin

(Mary Sabin crossed the plains when she was "almost thirteen years old" and tells of the work she did pulling a handcart.)

We remained in Iowa six weeks. All the men were busy making handcarts. . . .

At last the handcarts were all made. There were two handcarts for our family. My brother pulled one of them all the way from Iowa City to Utah. I and father took turns pulling the other one. When I was not pulling father's handcart I was helping to pull someone else's. I walked every step of the way. I was light hearted and glad and had not self-pity (Sabin, *Autobiography*, 1926, 8–9).

Mary Powell Sabin

[In Iowa,] it became necessary for Mother to dispose of some of our things. She sold a little flat iron that I had taken care to carry with me. How I cried when it was sold. I think this was the only time I cried on the whole long journey. I felt worried and said, "Whatever will we do for something with which to smooth out our clothes when we get to Salt Lake City?" (Sabin, *Autobiography*, 1926, 8–9).

Mary Ann Jones

The Lord was with us by His spirit for all-though tired and foot sore we could sing the songs of Zion as we went along. Some stomachs may recoil at a supper cooked with the water dug in a buffalo wallow and cooked with buffalo chips but it tasted good to us (*Diary of Mary Ann Jones*, typescript copy, n.p.).

Mary Powell Sabin

Each morning at day break the bugle sounded. Up we rose and assembled for prayer. We then ate a scanty breakfast of dough cakes fried in the frying pan. Once in a while we had a few stewed apples. Then we were ready for our march. At ten o'clock we rested one half hour. Then we traveled until we came to water. At the next meal we would eat what was left over from breakfast. At night we often went to bed without supper. There was very little food to cook and we were too tired to cook it (Sabin, *Autobiography, 1926*, 10).

Mary Powell Sabin

Some days we traveled more than thirty miles to reach water. Often we would come to a place where the springs had dried down. It might be near midnight. Then little children would form a circle of eager watchers while the men dug down several feet to water. At last when they saw the chunks of wet mud they would lay it on their face and hands. Some of them would suck the water from the mud. When the water burst forth it was usually very thick. The children drank heartily, straining it through their teeth (Sabin, *Autobiography, 1926*, 11).

Mary Ann Jones

A very remarkable thing happened on the Platt river. One of the oxen died and Brother [Edmund] Ellsworth was asking the Brethren what could be done. Could they put a cow in the team so we could go on. When one of the men said look Brother Ellsworth at that steer on the hill for there stood a big fat steer looking at us. Brother Ellsworth said the Lord has sent him to help us in to the valley. Go and get him so we can move on. They did so and he worked as good as the others. When we got within two days travel of Salt Lake we met some teams sent out from the valley with provisions and to help us in the next morning. When the boys went to round up the cattle to start, that steer was gone. They hunted for hours but we never saw him again. He went as mysteriously as he came. Brother Ellsworth said the Lord lent him to us as long as we needed him (*Diary of Mary Ann Jones*, typescript copy, n.p.).

Archer Walters

Saturday [July] 5th . . . Brother Parker brings into the camp his little boy that had been lost. Great joy right through the camp. The mother's joy I cannot describe. Expect we are going to rest. Washing, etc. today (Journal of Archer Walters, "Pioneer Enroute from England to Utah, U.S.A., March 18, 1856, to September 5th, 1856" [LDS Church Archives, The Church of Jesus Christ of Latter-day Saints, Salt Lake City], n.p.).

Mary Powell Sabin

I was captivated by the place called "Deer Creek's" beauty. It was so charmingly sylvan with little groves here and there and a bright clear creek lined with timber. Said I to Father, "Let's build a little log house and stay in this place always."

"What would we do for food?" asked Father.

"Do as we're doing now," said I, "Go without" (Sabin, *Autobiography, 1926*, 12).

Mary Powell Sabin

While the company halted, I took a walk in the woods to get away from it all. There were wild grapes, persimmons, hickory nuts, black berries, walnuts and hazel nuts by the score. Here I learned to know a peach. There were many fruits new to me also. I was surprised at the variety I found there.

I went into the woods every possible chance. How I enjoyed swaying in the grapevine swings. The moss was velvety green, the wild flowers beautiful. Ah! but the time flew by so very quickly.

I was never lost in the woods. Some folks thought it remarkable how I could find my way out without the least bit of trouble. . . .

Now we halted preparing the crossing of a stream on a ferry. The dark green forest was all around us. I grabbed a bucket and ran into the woods and picked it full of black berries. I took some little girls with me. Someone in camp began worrying about us. Bro. Oakley said, "Don't worry, she'll come back, she always does."

When I came out with my blackberries they all cheered. As often as I could I ran into the woods. I loved the hills, woods, moss, and hanging grape vines and wild flowers. There were so many birds. Their joy notes swelling in the woods brought a flood of rapture into my soul (Sabin, *Autobiography, 1926*, 9–10).

Sarah Hancock Beesley

(The suffering of the trek was so traumatic for Sarah Beesley that she would refuse to talk about her experience. When a reporter questioned her about her journey, she made the following response.)

Don't ask me anything about that [her journey to Utah by handcart]. You should go and talk to Mrs. Lapish. She can tell you all about it. Oh, she is full of life and very enthusiastic about it but I am not. Those are dreadful stories and I don't see why we shouldn't try to forget them. I say "Bury them with the dead who died on the plains." My children have often tried to get me to write my handcart story but I will not. . . .

[It was only after much careful questioning that Sarah Beesley shared some of her experiences and suffering.]

We didn't have nearly enough food to begin with. There was two hundred pounds of flour to each handcart and four people to a handcart. Long before it gave out entirely we didn't have nearly enough bread. When we reached Green River, there wasn't a pound of flour in the company. When we started, we had eighteen teams of oxen and not one of them reached the Valley. They didn't seem to be able to stand the trip as well as we did. . . . Did you notice that wild rose bush in my garden near the gate? I've had it there ever since I lived here. You know there wasn't anything growing along the whole way that we could put in our mouths until we discovered these wild rose berries. When we would come to a bush we would pick just as many as we could and then eat them. Many a time they saved my life I know. . . .

Yes, Mr. Beesley carried his violin with him and we used to gather around the fire at nights and sing and listen to the music. The popular song was the handcart song. "For some must push and some must pull." Of course after a while we all got so hungry that we couldn't have good times any more. Lots of the men and women could not get out of their beds. There were about 250 or 300 people in the company and we only had eight tents. Once or twice we tried to sleep in the tents but that was dreadful. Yes, that was dreadful. Everyone was in everyone else's way. We didn't like that a bit so we used to just sleep on the ground. We would draw our handcarts up in a circle and someone would guard us all night. If it rained we would sometimes sleep under the handcarts.

Of course we didn't suffer with cold but we did with heat. The sun was so hot that sometimes it seemed as if we could stand it no longer. Or sometimes the wind would blow the sand and dirt all over us. They told us in England that everyone had to eat a peck of dirt before he died. I had more than my peck while I was crossing the plains but it didn't take the place of food. One day I remember before we got to Green River we were all literally on the verge of starvation. Some of the people could go no further and we were in the heights of despair when we met some rough mountaineers. They felt very sorry for us and told us if we would come over to their camp they would give us some breakfast. I never tasted anything better in my life ("Mrs. Ebenezer B. Beesley," in "Handcart Stories," 28–34).

HARDSHIPS

Archer Walters

Sunday [September] 7th [1856] Traveled twenty-six miles. Brother Nappriss died. Left on road (Journal of Archer Walters).

C. C. A. Christensen

Our hats, or what might once have been called hats, assumed the most grotesque shapes, seeing that the sun, wind, and rain had the superior force. The ladies' skirts and men's trousers hung in irregular trimmings, and the foot covering proportional to the rest, with or without bottoms. Our faces were gray from the dust, which sometimes prevented us from seeing the vanguard; our noses with the skin hanging in patches, especially on those who had as much nose as I have; and almost every lower lip covered with a piece of cloth or paper because of its chapped condition, which made it difficult to speak and particularly to smile or laugh ("By Handcart to Utah: The Account of C. C. A. Christensen," trans. Richard L. Jensen, *Nebraska History* [Winter 1985], 66:342).

Archer Walters

(Archer Walters's account stands as a testament to the exhausting and endless work that these handcart pioneers endured on their way to the valley.)

Thursday [June] 12th [1856] Journeyed twelve miles. Went very fast with our hand carts. Harriet still ill.

Friday 13th Journeyed seven miles. A pleasant road but journeyed so fast.

Saturday 14th Journeyed seven miles. Pleasant.

Sunday 15th Got up about four o'clock to make a coffin for my brother, John Lee's son named William Lee, aged twelve years. Meetings as usual, and at the same time had to make another coffin for Sister Prator's child. We tired with repairing hand carts the last week. Went and buried them by moonlight at Bear Creek. . . .

Saturday 21st Travelled about thirteen miles. Camped at Indian Creek. Brother Bower died about six o'clock; from Birmingham Conference. Went to buy the wood to make the coffin but the kind farmer gave me the wood and nails. It had been a very hot day and I was never more tired, but God has said as my day my strength shall be. For this I rejoice that I have good health and strength according to my day (Journal of Archer Walters).

Kersten Ericksen Benson

It was now July and August and very hot on the plains. My shoes were worn out and we had to get raw hide from the dead cattle along the road and make shoes for ourselves so as to be able to pull. Crossing the creeks and rivers would make the raw hide soft and the hot sun and roads would make them hard, and our feet were nearly all the time sore and bleeding. I being alone and having no bed clothes I had to sleep in an old shawl in the tent. Coming through the mountains the nights were cold and freezing (Anna S. D. Johnson, "The Seventh Handcart Company," *Relief Society Magazine*, July 1948, 35:451, 501).

Sarah Hancock Beesley

It may sound funny to say that it was hard to push them down the hills but it was. Often the wheels were in sand up to the hubs and it was very hard to get them down hill. We had to ford a great many rivers and sometimes some of the carts were simply washed down stream. I remember when we had to ford the Platte River for the first time. We were in water above our waists and the current was strong. We couldn't cross it single file. Ten or twelve of us had to lock arms in order to get across. As long as we had flour the men had to carry it on their shoulders. Of course our clothes had to dry on us. It was very disagreeable and of course impaired our health. . . . I think we walked about twenty-five miles a day and sometimes [more]. Oh, it was so hard ("Mrs. Ebenezer B. [Sarah Hancock] Beesley," in "Handcart Stories," 28–34).

Mary Powell Sabin

At last we reached the Platte. There was a trading post near by. Our captain asked the men at the post how much they would charge to ferry us across. The price they asked was more money than we had in camp.

The river was between two and three blocks wide. First the men took the handcarts across, then the women and girls followed wading. The water kept getting deeper and deeper. In the middle of the river it was under my chin. When we reached the opposite side we went right on in our wet clothes. We traveled thirteen miles more that day (Sabin, *Autobiography*, 1926, 12).

Kersten Ericksen Benson

About the fifth day out, I was worn out pulling over the rough roads, up hills and through the sand and was discouraged because I did not believe I could stand the journey, and I came to the conclusion that I might as well die there as suffer longer, and I was lonely for I had no relations in the company. So I purposely stayed behind while the company was traveling and laid down on the grass, expecting to die there, believing there was no one behind me and I would not be found. Soon after the captain came along and promised me that when we came to a hill or sand he would come and help me pull. And he kept his promise and helped me (Johnson, "The Seventh Handcart Company," 35:451, 501).

Archer Walters

Thursday [June] 26th [1856] Traveled about one mile. Very faint from lack of food. We are only allowed about ¾ of a pound of flour a head each day and about 3 oz. of sugar each a week. Tea good and plenty; about a ¼ of a lb. of bacon each a week; which makes those that have no money very weak. Made a child's coffin for Sister Sheen—Emma Sheen aged 2 ½ years. . . .

Tuesday July 1st [1856] Rose soon. It looked very cloudy and began to rain. Traveled about fifteen miles. Walked very fast,—nearly four miles an hour. . . . ½ lb. of flour each; two oz. of rice; which is very little and my children cry with hunger and it grieves me and makes me cross. I can live upon green herbs or anything and do go nearly all day without any and am strengthened with a morsel. Repaired handcarts. A storm came on about eleven o'clock and lasted one hour and a half. Split the tent and not a dry thread on us (Journal of Archer Walters).

Kersten Ericksen Benson

This three weeks hardships [traveling from Iowa City, Iowa, to Florence, Nebraska] had proven that my father, mother and grandmother, who was 75 years old, could not stand the journey, and it was decided that they stay in Omaha. I came to the conclusion that I could not leave my aged parents in a strange country, and so made up my mind to stay with them. The captain of the company, C. Christiansen, came to me however, and advised me to leave my parents, and promised me if I would do so that God would bless them and me, and preserve us. This was a very sore trial to me, but I put my trust in God and promises of His Priesthood, and He has brought them to pass (Johnson, "The Seventh Handcart Company," 35:451, 501).

ARRIVING IN THE VALLEY

Mary Ann Jones

We were met in Emigration Canyon by the first Presidency and a brass band and hundreds of people in carriages on horseback and on foot, it was a day never to be forgotten. We had reached the goal and on foot all the way. I never left my handcart for a day and only rode over two rivers. We waded streams, crossed high mountains and pulled through heavy sands, leaving comfortable homes, fathers, mother, brothers and sisters, and what for? To be where we could hear a prophet's voice and live with the Saints of God. I have never seen the day I regretted my trip (*Diary of Mary Ann Jones*, typescript copy, n.p.).

Mary Powell Sabin

My little sister, Annie, age four, had been promised a big piece of bread and butter when she should reach the valley. Just as we were lined up to hear a few words from Bro. Brigham Young, a lady held up a large piece of bread. Annie ran toward her. "That's my piece of bread and butter," she cried joyously. At the sight of this Pres. Young wept, "God bless the child," said he. There were tears in the eyes of the people from the valley but there were only dry eyes among us who had just arrived. Pres. Young said he could defer his remarks until a little later (Sabin, *Autobiography, 1926,* 14).

🐦 16 🐦

THE WILLIE AND MARTIN HANDCART COMPANIES

The Willie and Martin companies departed Liverpool late in the season, so that by June 1856, the two handcart companies were barely beginning their trek from Iowa City to Salt Lake City. Their departure from Iowa City was further delayed because they had to await the construction of new handcarts. Knowing that the weather would soon worsen, they left Iowa City without letting the wood for the carts season properly. When they reached Florence, Nebraska (what used to be Winter Quarters), they had to halt for significant repairs, delaying their journey yet again. The lateness of the season, inadequate supplies, and early winter storms impeded their progress and took their toll on the immigrants. Furthermore, because of the lateness of the season, Brigham Young didn't expect more Saints to be traveling to Utah. It wasn't until October that he learned of their departure and gathered the necessary assistance for the stranded Saints. Although hundreds died along the way, an even greater number survived, thanks to their faith in God and to the timely arrival of the rescue teams.

WILLIE HANDCART COMPANY

The Willie handcart company sailed from England on the *Thornton*. They reached Iowa City on June 26 but remained there until July 15. Even then it was questionable if they would be able to leave for the West. Levi Savage, who was returning from a mission to England and traveling with the company, was familiar with the trail. He discouraged the rest of the company from continuing, knowing that proceeding could prove fatal. However, such was the desire to reach Zion that more than 400 Saints in the company were willing to take that risk. They journeyed through Iowa quickly but had to remain in Florence, Nebraska, for extensive repairs on their handcarts. From there they journeyed through Independence Rock, Devil's Gate, Martin's Cove, Rocky Ridge, and Rock Creek, Wyoming, where the relief party encountered the destitute pioneers.

John Chislett

The elders seemed to be divided in their judgment as to the practicability of our reaching Utah in safety at so late a season of the year, and the idea was entertained for a day or two of making our winter quarters on the Elkhorn, Wood River, or some eligible location in Nebraska; but it did not meet the general approval. A monster meeting was called to consult the people about it.

The emigrants were entirely ignorant of the country and climate— simple, honest, eager to go to "Zion" at once . . . Under these circumstances it was natural that they should leave their destination in the hands of the elders. There were but four men in our company who had been to the valley, viz.: Willie, Atwood, Savage, and Woodward; but there were several at Florence superintending the emigration, among whom elders G. D. Grand and W. H. Kimball occupied the most prominent position. These men all talked at the meeting just mentioned, and all, with one exception, favored going on ("Mr. Chislett's Narrative," in *The Rocky Mountain Saints*, Stenhouse [New York: D. Appleton and Company, 1873], 316; as cited in LeRoy R. Hafen and Ann W. Hafen, *Handcarts to Zion* [Glendale, CA: Arthur H. Clark Co., 1960], 96–97).

Levi Savage

(Brother Savage was one of the company's leaders, and he urged the Saints to remain in Iowa City until spring, but the enthusiastic immigrants didn't want to wait.)

[We cannot] cross the mountains with a mixed company of aged people, women, and little children, so late in the season without much suffering, sickness, and death. . . . Brethren and sisters, what I have said I know to be true; but seeing you are to go forward, I will go with you, will help you all I can, will work with you, will rest with you, will suffer with you, and, if necessary I will die with you. May God in his mercy bless and preserve us ("Mr. Chislett's Narrative," in *The Rocky Mountain Saints*, Stenhouse, 316; cited in Hafen and Hafen, *Handcarts to Zion*, 96–97).

Emma James

We were called together in a meeting one evening . . . We were told that it was 300 miles to [Council Bluffs] which was the actual place for starting the trek and that was just a mile to what we had to go to reach the valley. We would have carts such as they were, but the season was late and bad weather could prove dangerous to us if we were in the mountains. Even if we had no trouble we would be late getting to Utah. There had been much talk of these dangers by experienced men in the camp, but I think that the thing which I will remember for the rest of my life and wish that we had heeded was said by a Brother Savage. With tears streaming down his cheeks he pleaded with the people, "Brothers and sisters, wait until spring to make this journey. Some strong may get through in case of bad weather, but the bones of the weak and old will strew the way." I can remember that when he finished there was a long time of silence. I was frightened. Father looked pale and sick. I turned to mother to see what she was thinking, and all I saw was her old determined look. She was ready to go on tomorrow. There were many others like her. We really didn't have much choice. There was no work here for us to keep ourselves through the winter, and our family had to live. "We must put our trust in the Lord as we have always done" said mother, and that was that (Laleta Dixon, "History of My Ancestor, William James of the Willey [*sic*] Handcart Co., 1856," typescript copy [LDS Church Archives, The Church of Jesus Christ of Latter-day Saints, Salt Lake City], n.p.).

John Chislett

(Brother Chistlett, a subcaptain of one hundred, described the organization of the company.)

To each hundred there were five round tents, with twenty persons to a tent; twenty handcarts, or one to every five persons; and one Chicago Wagon, drawn by three yoke of oxen, to haul provisions and tents.

Each person was limited to seventeen pounds of clothing and bedding.

The strength of the company was equalized as much as possible by distributing the young men among the different families to help them. Several carts were drawn by young girls exclusively; and two tents were occupied by them and such females had no male companions ("Mr. Chislett's Narrative," in *The Rocky Mountain Saints*, Stenhouse, 314–15; cited in Hafen and Hafen, *Handcarts to Zion*, 93–94).

William James

At Council Bluffs the company outfitted for the journey west. It was organized much the same as the wagon trains had been. Captains were placed over hundreds, fifties, etc. The Saints were put on a strict schedule. Each member had his chores for the company as well as for his own family. The strong were to pull the carts. Everyone over seven years of age was expected to walk. The very old and the very young could ride. The young men were expected to act as herders for the cattle. . . . The young women and girls were expected to look after the children who were walking and to gather in the fuel for the camp at night(Laleta Dixon, "History of My Ancestor, William James of the Willey [*sic*] Handcart Co., 1856," typescript copy [LDS Church Archives, The Church of Jesus Christ of Latter-day Saints, Salt Lake City], n.p.).

John Chislett

We reached [Fort] Laramie about the 1st or 2nd of September, but the provisions, etc., which we expected, were not there for us. Captain Willie called a meeting to take into consideration our circumstances, conditions, and prospects, and to see what could be done. It was ascertained that at our present rate of travel and consumption of flour the latter would be exhausted when we were about three hundred and fifty miles from our destination. It was resolved to reduce our allowance from one pound to three-quarters of a pound per day, and at the same time to make every effort in our power to travel faster. We continued this rate of rations from Laramie to Independence Rock (John Chislett, *Handcarts to Zion*, 100).

George Cunningham

(Shortly after leaving Fort Laramie, Brother Cunningham recorded the following report about the sudden and unexpected change in the weather.)

The nights now began to get very cold and feed was poor, also our provisions were running out fast. Starvation looked us in the face. We were put on rations of six ounces of flour each per day and nothing else. The old and weak began to die for want of proper food, and a great many of the young and strong ones soon followed suit. I, myself, have helped to bury ten to fifteen in a single day. We who could stand it were barely kept alive and after several weeks of this ration it was reduced to half this amount. I, however, stirred my three ounces with some water and gulped it down. To make things worse we were caught in a heavy snowstorm on the Sweetwater. It was extremely cold and the last of our flour was gone. Nothing was left but a scant supply of crackers reserved for the sick and small children. The captain ordered that every critter in the train be killed as needed but they were nearly as poor as we were. However, we used to boil the bones and drink the soup. Every particle that could be used was taken, even the hide was rationed and after scorching the hair off, we would roast it a little over the coals and cut it in small pieces and it made what we considered a delicious supper. Towards the last the weather was so cold that all but five or six men in camp had been severely frozen, and let me add right here is where the great test came—some would sacrifice by giving their food and clothing to their friends, relatives, and children while others seemed to be devoid of natural affection and would let their family members die off merely for the sake of getting their few mouthfuls of food or perhaps an old blanket that covered them (George Cunningham, "The Handcart Pioneers," in *Treasures of Pioneer History*, comp. Kate B. Carter, 6 vols. [Salt Lake City: Daughters of Utah Pioneers, 1956], 5:252–56).

Ann Jewell Rowley

William [my husband] was never to see Zion . . . he died [February 14, 1848]. I was left a widow with seven children under twelve years of age and the step children of William's first marriage. I was very grateful for the gospel of Jesus Christ and the comfort it gave me. I knew that our parting was only temporary and that viewed from the eternities, this was but a fleeting moment. I also knew that no matter how fleeting a moment it was, I had to make the best of it. I had a very real job to do. The children had to be fed and clothed, but the big task and the one I must accomplish, is to get us all to Zion. I must be among the people of my faith and I must get the Temple work done for us.

There came a time, when there seemed to be no food at all. Some of the men left to hunt buffalo. Night was coming and there was no food for the evening meal. I asked God's help as I always did. I got on my knees, remembering two hard sea biscuits that were still in my trunk. They had been left over from the sea voyage, they were not large, and were so hard, they couldn't be broken. Surely that was not enough to feed eight people, but five loaves and two fishes were not enough to feed 5,000 people either, but through a miracle, Jesus had done it. So, with God's help, nothing is impossible. I found the biscuits and put them in a dutch oven and covered them with water and asked for God's blessing, then I put the lid on the pan and set it on the coals. When I took off the lid a little later, I found the pan filled with food. I kneeled with my family and thanked God for his goodness. That night my family had sufficient. The men returned with buffalo meat, and what wasn't eaten right away by the Saints, was dried into jerky (*Autobiography of Ann Jewell Rowley*; as cited in Riverton Wyoming Stake, *Remember: The Willie and Martin Handcart Companies and Their Rescuers—Past and Present* [Salt Lake City: Publishers Press, 1997], 136).

Sarah James

We were cold all the time. It was either rain or snow or wind. Even when you wrapped up in a blanket your teeth chattered. Father told us one night that the flour was gone and that the word was that we might not get help for some time. Father was white and drawn. I knew that mother was worried about him, for he was getting weaker all the time and seemed to feel that there was no use in all the struggle. Mother had taken as much of the load off his shoulders as she could in pulling the cart. We girls and Reuben did most of the work so that father could rest a lot. Mother didn't have much to say, and I wondered if she remembered that council meeting in Camp Iowa and wished that we had taken the advice of more experienced people. I'm sure that many of us had those thoughts.

We were grateful when we heard that the captain had ordered all the animals in the company killed so that we could have fresh meat. We were so hungry that we didn't stop to think what it would do for our wagons. How good the soup tasted made from the bones of those cows although there wasn't any fat on them. The hides we used to roast after taking all the hair off of them. I even decided to cook the tatters of my shoes and make soup of them. It brought a smile to my father's sad face when I made the suggestion, but mother was a bit impatient with me and told me that I'd have to eat the muddy thing myself (Dixon, "History of My Ancestor, William James of the Willey [sic] Handcart Co., 1856," n.p.).

Robert Reeder

My father, David Reeder, would start out in the morning and pull his cart until he would drop on the road. He did this day after day until he did not arise early on October 7, 1856. He was found dead in his bed, and his fellow bedmate had not heard a thing during the night. . . .

On October 17, we awoke covered with eight inches of snow and rations about gone. We pulled our carts sixteen miles in a blinding snow storm and arrived at Rock Creek, where we sheltered against the hill as best we could to avoid the north wind and blowing snow. Weakened to such an extent and without food, thirteen died that night. All the able-bodied men dug one large grave, but not too deep. My brother-in-law, James Hurren, held out his eight-year-old girl Mary to see her little playmate lying among the dead. They were laid away in the clothes they wore, in a circle with feet to center and heads out. We covered them with willows and then earth and slid rocks down the hill to keep the wolves from disturbing them. Two of the men who helped dig the grave died and were buried in another nearby. We could go no further. The weather was severe, and we had not a morsel of food in camp. We had heard assistance was on the road, and we still had hopes (Robert Reeder, *Autobiography*, typescript; cited in Susan Arrington Madsen, *I Walked to Zion: True Stories of Young Pioneers on the Mormon Trail* [Salt Lake City: Deseret Book, 1994], 65).

James E. Faust

Two of those buried at Rock Creek Hollow were heroic children of tender years: Bodil Mortensen, age nine, from Denmark, and James Kirkwood, age eleven, from Scotland.

Bodil apparently was assigned to care for some small children as they crossed Rocky Ridge. When they arrived at camp, she must have been sent to gather firewood. She was found frozen to death leaning against the wheel of their handcart, clutching sagebrush.

Let me tell you of James Kirkwood. James was from Glasgow, Scotland. On the trip west, James was accompanied by his widowed mother and three brothers, one of them, Thomas, was nineteen and crippled and had to ride in the handcart. James' primary responsibility on the trek was to care for his four-year-old brother, Joseph, while his mother and oldest brother, Robert, pulled the cart. As they climbed Rocky Ridge, it was snowing and there was a bitter cold wind blowing. It took the whole company twenty-seven hours to travel fifteen miles. When little Joseph became too weary to talk, James, the older brother, had no choice but to carry him. Left behind the main group, James and Joseph made their way slowly to camp. When the two finally arrived at the fireside, James "having so faithfully carried out his task, collapsed and died from exposure and overexertion" (James E. Faust, "A Priceless Heritage," *Ensign*, November 1992, 84–85).

Martin Handcart Company

The Martin handcart company sailed from England on the *Horizon* and arrived at Iowa City July 8, just two weeks after the Willie Company's arrival. Since their arrival was also unexpected, they had to wait almost three weeks before they were outfitted with hastily made handcarts. On July 28, the 576 people in the company left Iowa City and continued on their journey. Since they were three weeks behind the Willie company, they too encountered starvation, severe storms, and other hardships. The W. B. Hodgett and John A. Hunt wagon trains followed closely behind the handcart companies and carried nearly 400 immigrants.

Gordon B. Hinckley

Ellen Pucell [Unthank], as she was named, was born in a beautiful area of England where the hills are soft and rolling and the grass is forever green. Her parents . . . were converts to The Church. . . . From the time of their baptism in 1837 until the spring of 1856, they had scrimped and saved to go to the Zion of their people in the valley of the Rocky Mountains of America. Now that was possible if they were willing to pull a handcart one thousand miles across a wilderness. They accepted that challenge, as did hundreds of their fellow converts. . . .

After six weeks at sea, they landed at Boston and took the steam train to Iowa City. They had expected their handcarts and wagons would be ready. They were not. There was a serious and disastrous delay. . . .

With high expectation they began their journey. Through sunlight and storm, through dust and mud, they trudged beside the Platte River through all the month of September and most of October. On October 19, they reached the last crossing of the Platte, a little west of the present city of Casper, Wyoming. The river was wide, the current strong, and chunks of ice were floating in the water. They were now traveling without sufficient food. Bravely they waded through the icy stream. A terrible storm arose with fierce winds bringing drifting sand, hail, and snow. When they climbed the far bank of the river, their wet clothing froze to their bodies. Exhausted, freezing, and without strength to go on, some quietly sat down, and while they sat, they died. . . .

They came to a stream of freezing water. The father, while crossing, slipped on a rock and fell. Struggling to his feet, he reached the shore, wet and chilled. Sometime later he sat down to rest. He quietly died, his senses numbed by the cold. His wife died five days later (Gordon B. Hinckley, "Our Mission of Saving," *Ensign*, November 1991, 52).

Elizabeth Horrocks Jackson Kingsford

The teams had become so weak that the luggage was reduced to ten pounds per head for adults, and five pounds for children under eight years. And although the weather was severe, a great deal of bedding and clothing had to be destroyed—burned—as it could not be carried along. This occurrence very much increased the suffering of the company, men, women, and children alike. . . .

About the 25th of Oct. . . . we reached camp about sundown. My husband had for several days pervious been much worse. He was still sinking, and his condition now became more serious. As soon as possible after reaching camp I prepared a little of such scant articles of food as we then had. He tried to eat but failed. He had not the strength to swallow. I put him to bed as quickly as I could. He seemed to rest easy and fell asleep. About nine o'clock I retired. Bedding had become very scarce, so I did not disrobe. I slept until, as it appeared to me, about midnight. I was extremely cold. The weather was bitter. I listened to hear if my husband breathed—he lay so still. I could not hear him. I became alarmed. I put my hand on his body, when to my horror I discovered that my worst fears were confirmed. My husband was dead. He was cold and stiff—rigid in the arms of death. It was a bitter freezing night and the elements had sealed up his mortal frame. I called for help to the other inmates of the tent. They could render me no aid; and there was no alternative but to remain alone by the side of the corpse till morning. The night was enveloped in almost Egyptian darkness. There was nothing with which to produce a light or kindle a fire. Of course I could not sleep. I could only watch, wait, and pray for the dawn. But oh, how these dreary hours drew their tedious length along. When daylight came, some of the male part of the company prepared the body for burial. And oh, such a burial and funeral service. They did not remove his clothing—he had but little. They wrapped him in a blanket and placed him in a pile with thirteen others who had died, and then covered him up in the snow. The ground was frozen so hard that they could not dig a grave. He was left there to sleep in peace until the trump of the Lord shall sound, and the dead in Christ shall awake and come forth in the morning of the first resurrection. We shall then unite our hearts and lives, and eternity will furnish us with life forever more (*Leaves from the Life of Elizabeth Horrocks Jackson Kingsford* [Ogden, Utah, 1908], Church Archives, The Church of Jesus Christ of Latter-day Saints, Salt Lake City).

Elizabeth Sermon

(November 1856)

My husband's health began to fail and his heart almost broken to see me falling in shafts. Myself and children hungry, almost naked, footsore and himself nearly done for. Many trials came after this. My oldest boy had the mountain fever, we had to haul him in the cart, there was not room in the wagon. One day we started him out before the carts in the morning to walk with the aged and sick, but we had not gone far on our journey before we found him lying by the roadside, unable to go any farther. I picked him up and put him on my back and drew my cart as well, but could not manage far, so [I] put him in the cart, which made three children and my luggage. My husband failing more each day, the Captain put a young man to help me for a short time. My other son Henry walked at 7 years old, 1300 miles with the exception of a few miles (*Elizabeth Sermon's Emigration and Journey Across the Plains*, a history written by herself to her son Henry; cited in *Journal of the Trail*, ed. Stewart E. Glazer, 2d ed. [Salt Lake City: n.p., 1996], 103–4).

Francis Webster

(Years later, while in a Sunday School class, a teacher remarked that it was unwise for the Martin handcart company to have left so late in the season. The class then began to criticize Church leaders for allowing the company to leave with scanty provisions. Francis Webster sat in the back of the classroom, barely able to tolerate the criticism. Finally, he arose and earnestly shared his experience of traveling with the Martin handcart company.)

I ask you to stop this criticism. You are discussing a matter you know nothing about. Cold historic facts mean nothing here, for they give no proper interpretation of the questions involved. Mistake to send the Handcart Company out so late in the season? Yes. But I was in that company and my wife was in it and Sister Nellie Unthank whom you have cited was there, too. We suffered beyond anything you can imagine and many died of exposure and starvation, but did you ever hear a survivor of that company utter a word of criticism? Not one of that company ever apostatized or left the Church, because everyone of us came through with the absolute knowledge that God lives for we became acquainted with him in our extremities.

I have pulled my handcart when I was so weak and weary from illness and lack of food that I could hardly put one foot ahead of the other. I have looked ahead and seen a patch of sand or a hill slope and I have said, I can go only that far and there I must give up, for I cannot pull the load through it. . . . I have gone on to that sand and when I reached it, the cart began pushing me. I have looked back many times to see who was pushing my cart, but my eyes saw no one. I knew then that the angels of God were there.

Was I sorry that I chose to come by handcart? No. Neither then nor any minute of my life since. The price we paid to become acquainted with God was a privilege to pay, and I am thankful that I was privileged to come in the Martin Handcart Company (cited in David O. McKay, "Pioneer Women," *Relief Society Magazine*, January 1948, 8).

John Jaques

A hopeful and cheerful spirit pervaded the camp, and the "Songs of Zion" were frequently heard at this time, though the company was in the very depths of privation. Though the bodies of the people were worn down, their spirits were buoyant, while at the same time they had become so accustomed to looking death in the face that they seemed to have no fear of it (John Jaques, "Some Reminiscences," *Salt Lake Daily Herald*, December 15, 1878, 1; see also *Journal History of The Church of Jesus Christ of Latter-day Saints*, November 30, 1856, 21–22).

RESCUE COMPANY

Franklin D. Richards and several other missionaries, while returning to the Salt Lake Valley from their missions to England, encountered the Willie and Martin companies. The missionaries immediately recognized the urgency of sending aid to the handcart Saints. When the missionaries reached Salt Lake, Brigham Young was shocked to learn that there were still two companies traveling so late in the season. The next day at October general conference, he pleaded with the Saints to assist their brethren in need. By Tuesday, men and supplies were en route to the impoverished Saints. The rescue Saints arrived just in time. Unfortunately, both companies still lacked hundreds of miles before reaching the valley. Suffering still continued, but at least they had food, wagons, and medicine to sustain them to the valley.

Brigham Young

(In October general conference of 1856, President Young exhorted the Saints to aid in rescuing the two handcart companies stranded on the plains of Wyoming.)

I will now give this people the subject and the text for the Elders who may speak. ... It is this, on the 5th day of October, 1856, many of our brethren and sisters are on the Plains with handcarts, and probably many are now seven hundred miles from this place, and they must be brought here, we must send assistance to them. The text will be-to get them here! . . .

That is my religion; that is the dictation of the Holy Ghost that I possess, it is to save the people. We must bring them in from the Plains, and when we get them here, we will try to keep the same spirit that we have had, and teach them the way of life and salvation; tell them how they can be saved, and how they can save their friends. This is the salvation I am now seeking for, to save our brethren that would be apt to perish, or suffer extremely, if we do not send them assistance.

I shall call upon the Bishops this day. I shall not wait until tomorrow, nor until the next day, for sixty good mule teams and twelve or fifteen wagons. I do not want to send oxen. I want good horses and mules. They are in this Territory, and we must have them. Also twelve tons of flour and forty good teamsters, besides those that drive the teams. . . .

I will tell you all that your faith, religion, and profession of religion, will never save one soul of you in the Celestial Kingdom of our God, unless you carry out just such principles as I am now teaching you. Go and bring in those people now on the plains (*Journal of Discourses*, 26 vols. [London: Latter-day Saints' Book Depot, 1854–86], 4:113–14).

Ephraim Hanks

(A few days before Brigham's plea for help, Ephraim Hanks felt impressed that the handcart pioneers were in trouble and that they needed his help. He traveled to Salt Lake City, and the day after he arrived, he heard Brigham call for volunteers. Ephraim responded to Brigham Young's call and immediately left by himself to help his destitute brothers and sisters.)

Ephraim Hanks
(Courtesy of the Church Archives, The Church of Jesus Christ of Latter-day Saints)

Early the next morning I was on my way again, and soon reached what is know[n] as the Ice Springs Bench. There I happened upon a herd of buffalo, and killed a nice cow. I was impressed to do this, although I did not know why until a few hours later, but the thought occurred to my mind that the hand of the Lord was in it, as it was a rare thing to find buffalo herds around that place at this late part of the season. I skinned and dressed the cow; then cut up part of its meat in long strips and loaded my horses with it.

Thereupon I resumed my journey, and traveled on till towards evening. I think the sun was about an hour high in the west when I spied something in the distance that looked like a black streak in the snow. As I got near to it, I perceived it moved; then I was satisfied that this was the long-looked-for handcart company, led by Captain Edward Martin.

I reached the ill-fated train just as the immigrants were camping for the night. The sight that met my gaze as I entered their camp can never be erased from my memory. The starved forms and haggard countenances of the poor sufferers, as they moved about slowly, shivering with cold, to prepare their scanty evening meal was enough to touch the stoutest heart. When they saw me coming, they hailed me with joy inexpressible, and when they further beheld the supply of fresh meat I brought into camp, their gratitude knew no bounds. Flocking around me, one would say, "Oh, please, give me a small piece of meat;" another would exclaim, "My poor children are starving, do give me a little;" and children with tears in their eyes would call out, "Give me some, give me some." At first I tried to wait on them and handed out the meat as they called for it; but finally I told them to help themselves. Five minutes later both my horses had been released of their extra burden—the meat was all gone, and the next few hours found the people in camp busily engaged in cooking and eating it, with thankful hearts.

A prophecy had been made by one of the brethren that the company should feast on buffalo meat when their provisions might run short; my arrival in their camp, loaded with meat, was the beginning of the fulfillment of that prediction; but only the beginning, for them as we journeyed along.

When I saw the terrible condition of the immigrants on first entering their camp, my heart almost melted within me. I rose up in my saddle and tried to speak cheering and comforting words to them. I told them also that they should all have the privilege to ride into Salt Lake City, as more teams were coming.

After dark, on the evening of my arrival in the handcart camp, a woman passed the camp fire where I was sitting crying aloud. Wondering what was the matter, my natural impulse led me to follow her. She went straight to Daniel Tyler's wagon, where she told the heartrending story of her husband being at the point of death, and in pleading tones she asked Elder Tyler to come and administer to him. This good brother, tired and weary as he was, after pulling hand-carts all day, had just retired for the night, and was a little reluctant in getting up; but on this earnest solicitation he soon arose, and we both followed the woman to the tent, in which we found the apparently lifeless form of her husband. On seeing him, Elder Tyler remarked, "I cannot administer to a dead man." Brother Tyler requested me to stay and lay out the supposed dead brother, while he returned to his wagon to seek that rest which he needed so much.

I immediately stepped back to the camp fire where several of the brethren were sitting and addressing myself to Elders Grant, Kimball and one or two others, I said, "Will you boys do just as I tell you?" The answer was in the affirmative. We then went to work and built a fire near the tent which I and Elder Tyler had just visited. Next we warmed some water, and washed the dying man whose name was Blair, from head to foot. I then anointed him with consecrated oil over his whole body, after which we laid hands on him and commanded him in the name of Jesus Christ to breathe and live. The effect was instantaneous. For the man who was dead to all appearances immediately began to breathe, sat up in his bed and commenced to sing a hymn. His wife unable to control her feelings of joy and thankfulness ran through the camp exclaiming: "My husband was dead but is now alive praise be the name of God. The man who brought the buffalo meat has healed him."

This circumstance caused a great general excitement in the whole camp and many of the drooping spirits began to take fresh courage from that very hour. After this the greater portion of my time was devoted to waiting on the sick. "Come to me, help me, please administer to my sick wife, or my dying child," were some of the requests that were being made of me almost hourly for sometime after I had joined the emigrants, and I spent days going from tent to tent administering to the sick . . . (Andrew Jenson, *The Contributor*, February 1893, 39:202–5).

Ruby M. F. Hall

At this time . . . the Salt Lake Conference was taking place and Brigham Young was sending a rescue party to the stranded handcart companies. James Barnet Cole, went with them. One night he dreamed he would meet his future wife with the stranded Saints. He even was shown what she looked like. She had a fur cap and a green veil tied over her cap to keep the wind off, and she was very beautiful. He told his dream to Brother [William] Kimball and he remarked, "We will see no beautiful girl with a fur cap and a green veil in these frozen Saints."

Reminiscing, James Barnet Cole said that they saw the encampment just as the sun was sinking in the west. It looked like an Eskimo village which was fully a mile away. The snow was very deep and paths had been made from tent to tent giving the camp that appearance. It was located on a plain near the river.

When the people caught sight of the train coming, they shouted, they cried, they threw off all restraint and freely embraced their deliverers. Just then, William Kimball caught sight of Lucy Ward in the green veil. He drove up to her and said, "Brother Jim, there is your dream girl." James asked her to get in the wagon and her reply was, "No, I don't know you." She got used to the idea of having him around, because on the way to Salt Lake, on November 2, 1856, they were married at Fort Bridger by William Kimball (Riverton Wyoming Stake, *Remember: The Willie and Martin Handcart Companies*, 138).

Susanna Stone Lloyd

(Willie handcart company)

You may guess the joy that was in camp the day [the relief party] arrived. We were near Fort Bridger when they met us, and we rode in the wagons the rest of the way, but we had walked over one thousand miles. When we got near the City, we tried to make ourselves as presentable as we could to meet our friends. I had sold my little looking glass to the Indians for buffalo meat, so I borrowed one and I shall never forget how I looked. Some of my old friends did not know me. We were so weather beaten and tanned (Susanna Stone Lloyd, "Information on Thomas and Susanna Lloyd" [1915], microfilm of typescript [LDS Church Archives, The Church of Jesus Christ of Latter-day Saints, Salt Lake City], n.p.).

Agnes Caldwell

(Willie handcart company)

Just before we crossed the mountains, relief wagons reached us, and it certainly was a relief. The infirm and aged were allowed to ride, all able-bodied continuing to walk. When the wagons started out, a number of us children decided to see how long we could keep up with the wagons, in hopes of being asked to ride. At least that is what my great hope was. One by one they all fell out, until I was the last one remaining, so determined was I that I should get a ride. After what seemed the longest run I ever made before or since, the driver, who was Heber [William Henry] Kimball, called to me, "Say, sissy, would you like a ride?" I answered in my very best manner, "Yes sir." At this he reached over, taking my hand, clucking to his horses to make me run, with legs that seemed to me could run no farther. On we went, to what to me seemed miles. What went through my head at that time was that he was the meanest man that ever lived or that I had ever heard of, and other things that would not be a credit nor would it look well coming from one so young. Just at what seemed the breaking point, he stopped. Taking a blanket, he wrapped me up and lay me in the bottom of the wagon, warm and comfortable. Here I had time to change my mind, as I surely did, knowing full well by doing this he saved me from freezing when taken into the wagon ("Autobiography of Agnes Caldwell," typescript of interview conducted by Veara Southworth Fife, her daughter, Daughters of Utah Pioneers Museum; as cited in Madsen, *I Walked to Zion*, 58–59).

Elizabeth Sermon

(November 1856, Martin company)

After our food had given out as I said before, we went into our tents to die. I always thought I could get through to Salt Lake City and I tried to encourage my husband, but he was starving. He had always lived good at home. There was a shout in the camp. Brother Joseph A. Young had come on packed mules with Brother Little. Brought flour, meat and onions. I got one pound of flour and some meat and two onions. I chopped the fat off the meat real fine and made some dumplings. We made a good meal and blessed Brother Little and Joseph from the bottom of our hearts. . . . We had seventy miles to get to the wagons that had been sent from Salt Lake City with food and clothing and some clothing had come for us. . . .

Well, I went again to the cart as all that could had to walk to get to the wagons. Poor Rob had to ride from this time and sometimes John, Henry and Marian (age 3) were with me. When I got into camp I would clear the snow away with a tin plate, gather my wood, get my bed clothes from the wagon. . . . I was to weak to haul much . . . get my allowance of flour and carry the children to the fire, make their beds on the ground, the tent was frozen and ground so hard we could not set it up. I think it was two weeks we were without tents. We went to bed without supper in order to get a little better breakfast. I found it some help to toast the rawhide on the coals and chew it; it helped to keep the hunger away, for I was feeling it rather keenly now. I had to take a portion of poor Robert's feet off which pierced my very soul. I had to sever the leaders with a pair of scissors. Little did I think when I bought them in old England that they would be used for such a purpose. Everyday some portion was decaying until the poor boy's feet were all gone. Then John's began to freeze; then afterwards my own. We kept meeting teams from Salt Lake City now, which rendered all the assistance they could. I remember asking one of the drivers if he could give me a cob of corn to eat. He looked so pitiful and said, "Oh, sister, I hate to refuse you but my horses haven't enough to eat now, and I do not know how we will get back to Salt Lake." I said, "I ought not to have asked you, but myself and children are so hungry." He said, "Keep up your faith sister" (Glazer, ed., *Journal of the Trail*, 76–80).

Samuel Openshaw

(Martin company)

In the midst of all this uncertainty and doubt our hopes were realized, for lo and behold, Joseph A. Young and two others with him came riding into the camp; voices from all parts of the camp, "Help for the camp." We all rushed together to hear the news. He told us that there were about ten wagons loaded with flour and sent out from the valley for our relief and was about fifty miles ahead of us at a place called Devil's Gate. After they had learned our circumstances, they started back again in order to have them come out and to meet us. In the morning, we summoned all our efforts and strength, impulsed with the prospect of deliverance, we again started on our journey. After traveling about two or three days, and they traveling towards us, we met. The last flour was all ate before we met them. We now had one pound of flour per day, which in a measure began to recruit our strength so that we were able to perform the journey before us. The brethren who came out to meet us did administer every comfort and help that was within their power to the sick and the infirm. We continued our journey until we arrived at the Devil's Gate. Here we were obliged to stop, the snow being about fourteen inches deep on the level, and not withstanding the teams that had come out to help us, there was not sufficient help to move the aged, sick and the women and children along, so that we again stopped several days.

A council was held in which it was decided that we should leave all our clothing and cooking utensils (except what was absolutely necessary, such as a blanket to wrap ourselves in and the clothing we stood in) to be left at Devil's Gate and that a number of the brethren who had come out to meet us should stay to take care of them until spring should open (when they would be sent for from the valley) and that we leave all our handcarts, except one to each tent in order to carry our cooking utensils only. Our blankets were put in the wagons that came out to meet us. Also it was decided that Joseph A. Young should go on an express to the valley in order to start out more help. We now began to gather together all the cattle that we could find, and pulled down our tents and made another start in the snow (*Diary of Samuel Openshaw* [May–November 1856], typescript copy [LDS Church Archives, The Church of Jesus Christ of Latter-day Saints, Salt Lake City], n.p.).

Elizabeth White Stewart

(Hunt wagon train)

About midnight that night all the camp had retired, and we were awakened with a noise and thought it was the yelling of Indians. We got up expecting they were upon us, but to our great surprise the noise was caused by the teamsters of a relief team, and some of the camp shouted for joy. They were loaded with all kinds of provisions: flour, bread, butter, meat of all kinds, but all frozen so hard. Everything was so good. The bread was like cake, so sweet and nice. I remember we had to cut everything with the hatchet, but oh how thankful we all were that the Lord had answered our prayers and saved us all from starvation. Through the timely action of President Brigham Young in organizing this company, we were saved ("Autobiography of Elizabeth White Stewart," typescript, in *Ancestors of Isaac Mitton Stewart and Elizabeth White*, comp. Mary Ellen B. Workman [Privately printed, 1978]; cited in Madsen, *I Walked to Zion*, 61–62).

John Bond

(After the relief team reached them, the captain asked those with sufficient strength to continue walking until more wagons arrived.)

My sister Sarah, and I had to walk a great deal of the way. Her shoes were worn out, making it necessary for her to wear a pair of English clogs. In walking in the snow, the snow stuck to them so much that the lumps would break off and skin her heals badly. We had walked some distance on ahead of the train on a bitter cold day when I noticed that my sister seemed to be very tired and the tears were rolling down her cheeks from the pain of her skinned heels. When I saw the condition of her feet, I said to her, "Sister, you sit here by the road and I will return to the captain and see if he will not let you ride. Your feet are in such a condition that I can hardly bear to see you walk." She was willing that I should try. I met the captain and said, "Captain Hodges, I left my sister on the roadside with such bleeding heels that it is exceedingly painful for her to walk and the tears are streaming down her cheeks. Can't she be allowed to ride?"

He answered in a kind hearted way, "I am willing for her to ride from now on to the valley, as she has always walked when I have asked the Saints to walk." I then returned to look for my sister, but found she had gone from where I left her. I felt alarmed at her absence as the wolves were howling all around when I left to see the captain. Was it possible that the wolves had devoured my sister in my absence? I traveled on and on in suspense. I had traveled some distance when I saw fresh blood in the snow. I then, tracked her by her bleeding heels until I finally found her lying down in the snow exhausted. When she saw me, she was so glad that the tears were falling down her care worn cheeks. She was in intense pain from the cold weather. When I told her the captain's wishes, her eyes brightened up to think that she would be allowed to ride. In a short time, the train arrived and she was helped in to ride on to the valley. My father's shoes had worn out and as he was walking constantly, some way had to be found whereby he could continue walking. He finally skinned one of the dead oxen, took a piece of its hide about two feet square, wrapped it around his feet and tied it on with some small strips of hides for strings. The worst feature of these shoes was that some one would have to get up before father and thaw the shoes out before he could wear them. When he walked in the snow, he made tracks as large as a grizzly bear and of similar shape, but he assured himself, as well as his loved ones, that he must endure everything to gain final glory in the eternal world (Riverton Wyoming Stake, *Remember: The Willie and Martin Handcart Companies*, 89–90).

Mrs. Mary S. [Higgs] Sleater

(Years after entering the valley, Mary Sleater commented on the difficulty of the trek as a seven-year-old.)

People nowadays don't know anything about traveling. . . . We arrived here [Salt Lake City] in December of 1856, after a really terrible trip . . . We came through Parley's canyon in the deep snow and, believe me, we were nearly frozen when we arrived. Our oxen had starved to death because they could find no food through the snow and we were stuck there in the canyon until teams were sent out to our aid from Salt Lake City.

They did not send enough teams from the city to take all the wagons in, so some had to stay there in the canyon for several days until the animals could make a return trip.

Those of us who stayed for the second trip were rationed a biscuit a day until the biscuits gave out, then we ceased to eat. There were one or two of the oxen left, but they were so thin there was no meat on them.

The men in the party killed them one night and we boiled the bones for soup the next day.

It was very thin soup ("Pioneer Woman, Celebrating 89th Birthday, Recalls Hardships of Trek across Prairies," *Salt Lake Telegram* [February 12, 1938], 16, Church History Library, Salt Lake City).

Gordon B. Hinckley

As the rescuers appeared on the western horizon breaking a trail through the snow, they seemed as angels of mercy. And indeed they were. The beleaguered emigrants shouted for joy, some of them. Others, too weak to shout, simply wept and wept and wept.

There was now food to eat and some warmer clothing. But the suffering was not over, nor would it ever end in mortality. Limbs had been frozen, and the gangrenous flesh sloughed off from the bones. . . . Ellen [Pucell Unthank was] among those with frozen limbs. Ellen's were the most serious. The doctor in the valley, doing the best he could, amputated her legs just below the knees. The surgical tools were crude. There was no anesthesia. The stumps never healed. She grew to womanhood, married William Unthank, and bore and reared an honorable family of six children. Moving about on those stumps, she served her family, her neighbors, and the Church with faith and good cheer and without complaint, though she was never without pain (Gordon B. Hinckley, "Our Mission of Saving," *Ensign*, November 1991, 52).

John Bond

(Hodgett wagon company)

As soon as the food was ready, the valley boys fed the weak and sick first, those who had to stay in bed. They comforted the weak as best they could, these noble hearted boys depriving themselves of many necessities, their loving mothers had prepared for them to use on this errand of mercy, giving to the needy Saints with loving hearts. Many times their eyes were filled with tears when they returned from feeding the sick. Had they been brothers in blood, they could have done no more for us.

As they handed out the food or medicine, they could invariably say, "Brother (sister or child) I have brought you something from the valley to give you strength. It is the best we have, sent by my mother and sisters to help you, as they have had to suffer the same trials you have been through while journeying to the valley. Now brethren and sisters, cheer up, all will soon be in good homes in the valleys you are longing to see." Many were helpless now, who had been in good spirits a few weeks before. The short rations and constant travel, the strain of pulling the hand carts from Fort Laramie, was enough to wear out the strongest constitution (Riverton Wyoming Stake, *Remember: The Willie and Martin Handcart Companies*, 91).

THE RESCUE AT THE SWEETWATER RIVER

Gordon B. Hinckley

I should like to tell you about three eighteen-year-old boys. In 1856 more than a thousand of our people . . . found themselves in serious trouble while crossing the plains to this valley. Because of a series of unfortunate circumstances, they were late in getting started. They ran into snow and bitter cold in the highlands of Wyoming. Their situation was desperate, with deaths occurring every day.

President Young learned of their condition as the October general conference was about to begin. He immediately called for teams, wagons, drivers, and supplies to leave to rescue the bereft Saints. When the first rescue team reached the Martin Company, there were too few wagons to carry the suffering people. The rescuers had to insist that the carts keep moving.

When they reached the Sweetwater River on November 3, chunks of ice were floating in the freezing water. After all these people had been through, and in their weakened condition, that river seemed impossible to cross. It looked like stepping into death itself to move into the freezing stream. Men who once had been strong sat on the frozen ground and wept, as did the women and children. Many simply could not face that ordeal.

And now I quote from the record: "Three eighteen-year-old boys belonging to the relief party came to the rescue, and to the astonishment of all who saw, carried nearly every member of the ill-fated handcart company across the snowbound stream. The strain was so terrible and the exposure so great, that in later years all the boys died from the effects of it. When President Brigham Young heard of this heroic act, he wept like a child, and later declared publicly, "that act alone will ensure C. Allen Huntington, George W. Grand, and David P. Kimball an everlasting salvation in the Celestial Kingdom of God, worlds without end" (Gordon B. Hinckley, "Four B's for Boys," *Ensign*, November 1981, 42).

Patience Loader

(On November 4, 1856, Patience reached the last crossing of the Sweetwater with her family.)

We traveled on for some few miles, then we came to the Sweetwater [River and] there we had to cross. We thought we would have to wade the water as the cattle had been crossing with the wagons with the tents and what little flour we had and had broken the ice, so one could not go over on the ice. But there were brave men there in the water, packing the women and children over on their backs. Those poor brethren were in the water nearly all day. We wanted to thank them but they would not listen to my dear mother who felt in her heart to bless them for their kindness. . . . They all had kind, good hearts. This poor Br. [David P.] Kimball stayed so long in the water that he had to be taken out and packed to camp and he was a long time before he recovered as he was chilled through and in after life he was always afflicted with rheumatism (Patience Loader Archer, *Autobiography, 1872* [L. Tom Perry Special Collections, Harold B. Lee Library, Brigham Young University, Provo, Utah], 182–83).

Patience Loader

After we were over the Sweet Water we had to travel some distance to a good place to camp. . . . Here we remained for nine days as we had to wait until more provisions came to us. . . . During our nine days camping on the Sweet Water many of the stout young men went out and got raw hide and anything they could get to eat. On one occasion I got a bone . . . with scarcely any meat on it. I was cooking it to make a little soup for breakfast and the brethren from the valley came and asked [us] to go to their camp and sing for them. So we left Mother to see to the cooking of the bone. The brethren had cut down logs and formed seats for us all around their camp fire but they said they had nothing to give us to eat as they themselves were short of food. Well we sang and enjoyed ourselves for two or three hours and then went to our own tent.

When [we] arrived there our fire was out and Mother was gone to bed and my ten year old brother was also in bed. Mother said [to] fetch the pot with the soup. We said, "alright. Mother we stayed longer than we ought to but the brethren did not want us to leave, but we told them we would go and sing for them another night." We were so hungry. We had nothing to eat so we went to bed but Mother says it is too bad you have nothing to eat and it makes you more hungry to sing. You had better not go to sing for the brethren again. But I must tell you that I got so hungry that I took the bone out of your soup and picked the little meat off it and put the bone back into the pot. It seemed that I could not go to sleep without telling you for I knew you would not find anything on the bone in the morning. We told her that was alright. We felt glad that our dear Mother found a little bit to eat and we all went to sleep and slept comfortable and warm until morning not withstanding it was a terrible cold freezing night (Archer, *Autobiography, 1872*, 183–85).

Mignonette Hargan

(Mignonette commemorated the crossing of the Sweetwater by writing this song.)

Chorus:
O Brigham, are you crying?
Do your tears come just for me?
Our journey's done—I'm the pioneer
You meant for me to be.
You think I'm much too little
For this heavy load you see.
Well, crossing the Sweetwater
Took the little outa me.
Don't cry for me, a prophet's tears
Are more than I can bear
You dreamed us to the promised land.
We laid down our fair share.
I lost fingers to the bite of frost
Baby sisters to the flu.
I fought my tears along the trail
Now I see the tears in you.
Winter caught us early,
Taught us Zion's price
By crossing the Sweetwater
We lost our mother's life.
I heard her voice just days ago;
We'd almost made it through.
I turned around and she was gone
Just two days short of you.
You said—
"Suffer little children to come westward with me"
Did you mean for us to suffer so
In our sojourn to be free?
You're a prophet, you're a leader.
You called us to this place.
Your welcome feels so bittersweet—
Oh, where's my mother's face?
I'm crying for my mama;
Ya need not weep along.
She's dead inside our wagon,
She's alive here in my song
A heavy load for a little girl,

> But you see I pulled it through.
> I'm all growed up, which came about
> When we chose to follow you.
> (Mignonette Hargon, "Crossing the Sweetwater,"
> *Sunstone Magazine*, September 1987, 37)

ZION AT LAST

The Willie handcart company reached Salt Lake City on November 9, 1856, and the Martin handcart company, November 30. The Hunt and Hodgett wagon trains arrived in mid-December. Due to continual urgings made by Brigham Young, these new immigrants were welcomed into the city and treated like equals. Homes were opened up, food prepared, clothing donated, and surgeries performed—all for the sake of Zion.

Brigham Young

(President Young gave the following address in the tabernacle on November 30, 1856, just prior to the Martin handcart company's arrival in the valley.)

I have a few words to say, before this meeting is brought to a close. We expect that the last hand-cart company, Bro. [Edward] Martin's, will soon be in the streets by the Council House. What preparations the Bishops have made for their comfortable reception and temporary disposal I know not, but I know what I desire and am going to tell it to the people.

When those persons arrive I do not want to see them put into houses by themselves; I want to have them distributed in this city among the families that have good and comfortable houses; and I wish the sisters now before me, and all who know how and can, to nurse and wait upon the new comers and prudently administer medicine and food to them. To speak upon these things is a part of my religion, for it pertains to taking care of the Saints. . . .

The afternoon meeting will be omitted, for I wish the sisters to go home and prepare to give those who have just arrived a mouthful of something to eat, and to wash them and nurse them up. You know that

I would give more for a dish of pudding and milk, or a baked potato and salt, were I in the situation of those persons who have just come in, than I would for all your prayers, though you were to stay here all the afternoon and pray. Prayer is good, but when baked potatoes and pudding and milk are needed, prayer will not supply their place on this occasion; give every duty its proper time and place. . . .

And I want you to understand that we desire this people to nurse them up; we want you to receive them as your own children, and to have the same feeling for them. We are their temporal saviors, for we have saved them from death (Brigham Young, "Remarks," *Deseret News* [December 10, 1856], 320).

Patience Loader

I will now conclude my hard journey across the plains by handcart and say that we that lived through this terrible journey arrived in Salt L City Sunday noon the thirtieth day of November 1856. We were met and warmly greeted by our kind brethren and sisters and taken to their homes and made comfortable and welcomed to share their home and food with them. Brother William Thorn Bishop of the Seventh Ward took home with him my mother, and my brother Robert, myself, and sisters Maria, Jane, and Sarah. My sister Tamar went with Br. Thomas Ricks to Farmington. This is the kind brother that gave us the beef at Devil's Gate and told us not to quarrel over it. The next spring he married my sister Tamar (Archer, *Autobiography*, 1872, 189).

~ 17 ~

REJOICING IN ZION

Amidst the hardships and trails, the Saints rejoiced in gratitude for their new home. They had been delivered from the mobs and hostilities in the East. Their new home would be difficult to cultivate, but it was their own. It was a place where they could worship God according to the dictates of their own conscience. It was a place where they could raise their children in the light of the gospel. It was Zion. Their journey to Zion's Hill was accomplished.

Frederick Zaugg

(Frederick Zaugg recorded his experience arriving in the valley. Although it was not what he had expected, his experience taught him about his role in establishing Zion.)

We traveled along a dusty road. It was hot and dry and I was looking for a drink of water. On the other side of Corinne by a little mountain was a little stream of water running across the road. I jumped off the wagon and dropped on my stomach, and took a swallow and almost passed out. It was terrible, salty and bitter. Surely this cannot be Zion. . . .

We passed the night some way, and [were] ready for the last lap and over the last hill, when we got a glimpse of Zion, the promised land. On and up, away from the great lake bottom, over hills and dales. Now we reached the last hill. Mr. Hirschi said, "When we get on the top of this hill you will get a view of Park Valley." I drew a long breath—"Is this Zion?" I asked. "Yes, when you make it," he answered. These words left a deep impression in my mind. "If you make it," became my motto. Things we like to live in and enjoy, we have to make. If we want a friend, we must love him. If you want a favor of the Lord, you must serve him and keep his commandments and the blessings will come by going after them

Frederick Zaugg, *Autobiography*, typescript, 20–33, original in private possession; cited in Susan Arrington Madsen and Fred E. Woods, *I Sailed to Zion* [Salt Lake City: Deseret Book, 2000], 141–42).

John Quayle

It was the promised land of peace and rest. Yes, indeed it was beautiful to us weary pioneers who had come, at the tiring pace of the oxen, that slow dreary thousand miles from Winter Quarters. . . . To me it was not the desert that so many have called it. ("God and Gold—1847," in *Our Pioneer Heritage*, comp. Kate B. Carter, 20 vols. [Salt Lake City: Daughters of Utah Pioneers, 1958–77], 16:494.)

Carter E. Grant

Oh, children, you do not know how happy we were, even during these severe days of hardest trials! As young as I was, I knew the gospel had been restored. More than once I had heard Joseph Smith declare that our Heavenly Father and his Son Jesus, the resurrected Savior, had come and talked with him. To this day this testimony has never left me. And when I am gone, I want you to tell this to your children and grandchildren (Cater E. Grant, "Robbed by Wolves, a True Story," *Relief Society Magazine*, July 1928, 15:355–64).

B. H. Roberts

(As young children, B. H. Roberts and his sister traveled across the plains without their parents. He recorded his feelings upon arriving in Zion and being reunited with his mother.)

There was one thing remembered in this reunion [with my mother], and that was on my part. I felt that I had arrived, that I belonged to somebody, that somebody had an interest in me, and these were the thoughts that were in my mind as I sat in the wagon on the drive home to Bountiful (B. H. Roberts, *The Autobiography of B. H. Roberts*, ed. Gary James Bergera [Salt Lake City: Signature Books, 1990], 25–44).

Tamma Durfee Miner

I have passed through all the hardships and drivings and burnings and mobbings and threatenings and have been with the saints in all their persecutions from Huron County to Kirtland and from Kirtland to Missouri back to Illinois and then across the desert. I write this that my children may have a little idea of what their parents passed through. For want to time I have passed over some things of importance. I hope my children will appreciate these few lines, for I do feel highly honored to be numbered with the Latter-day Saints, and I pray that our children will all prove faithful, that they may receive a great reward (Tamma Durfee Miner, "A Memorial," in *Voices From the Past: Diaries, Journals, and Autobiographies,* comp. Campus Education Week Program [Provo, Utah: Brigham Young University Press, 1980], 82–83).

The Harvest Song

(On the morning of August 10, 1848, the Saints in the valley gathered on the temple block to celebrate the first harvest gathered in their new home. At this occasion, they sang a song composed by Parley P. Pratt, to the tune of "How Firm a Foundation.")

> Let us join in the dance, let us join in the song,
> To the Jehovah the praises belong;
> All honor, all glory we render to thee
> Thy cause is triumphant, thy people are free.
> The gentiles oppressed us. The heathens with rage,
> Combined all their forces and hosts to engage;
> They plundered and scattered and drove us away,
> They killed their shepherd, the sheep went astray
> Full long in the desert and mountains to roam,
> Without any harvest without any home;
> They're hungry and thirsty and weary and worn,
> They seemed quite forsaken and left for to roam.
> But lo, in the mountains new sheep folds appear,
> And a harvest of plenty our spirits to cheer;
> This beautiful vale is a refuge from woe,
> A retreat for the Saints when the scourges o'erflow.
> The States of Columbia to pieces may rend,
> And mobs all triumphant bring peace to an end;
> The star spangled banner forever be furled,
> And the chains of a tyrant encircle the world.
> The storms of commotion distress every realm,
> The dire revolutions the nations o'erwhelm;

Tho Babylon trembles and thrones cast down be,
Yet here in the mountains the righteous are free.
(Levi Jackman, *Journal of Levi Jackman*, August 10,
1848 [LDS Church Archives, The Church of Jesus
Christ of Latter-day Saints, Salt Lake City], n.p.)

"HERE WE SHALL BUILD
A TEMPLE TO OUR GOD"

Only four days after arriving in the valley, Brigham Young set apart a forty-acre plot of land for the temple site. The plot was later reduced to ten acres. One day, while walking through the land set aside for Temple Square, Brigham Young thrust his cane into the ground and declared, "Here we shall build a temple to our God" (James H. Anderson, "The Salt Lake Temple," *Contributor* [April 1893], 14:243). Wilford Woodruff then drove a stake into the spot, marking the future location of the Salt Lake Temple.

Brigham Young

This afternoon, accompanied by Elders Heber C. Kimball, Willard Richards, Orson Pratt, Wilford Woodruff, George A. Smith, Amasa Lyman, Ezra T. Benson, and Thomas Bullock, I designated the site for the Temple block between the forks of City Creek, and on motion of Orson Pratt it was unanimously voted that the Temple be built on the site designated (*Manuscript History of Brigham Young 1846–1847*, ed. Elden J. Watson [Salt Lake City: Elden J. Watson, 1971], 567).

Brigham Young

(After laying the temple cornerstones on April 6, 1853, Brigham Young made the following remarks, speaking of a vision in which he saw the completed temple. He also foretold the building of the Conference Center.)

Brethren, we have accomplished the design of our hearts, that we listed to accomplish. And really, this thought inadvertently rushes upon my mind—Wherein have we not accomplished all we have listed to do? Not only in excavating the earth, and laying down the Corner Stones in the centre of the main body of the building we shall rear for the Temple, but wherein have we contemplated doing one thing we have not done, to build up the Kingdom of God? If there has been a failure, it does not occur to my mind at present. I cannot now recall to my mind one circumstance of that kind, with all the mobbing, driving, and afflictions that this people have passed through. . . .

From the day that [Joseph Smith] fell, until this day, if there is one item of business, if there is one thing that should have been done by this people, that has not been done, I cannot call it to mind. . . .

I am not a visionary man, neither am I given much to prophesying. When I want any of that done I call on brother Heber— he is my Prophet, he loves to prophesy, and I love to hear him. I scarcely ever say much about revelations, or visions, but suffice it to say, five years ago last July I was here, and say in the Spirit the Temple not ten feet from where we have laid the Chief Corner Stone. I have not inquired what kind of a Temple we should build. Why? Because it was represented before me. I have never looked upon that ground, but the vision of it was there. I see it as plainly as if it was in reality before me. Wait until it is done. I will say, however, that it will have six towers, to begin with, instead of one. Now do not any of you apostatize because it will have six towers, and Joseph only built one. It is easier for us to build sixteen, than it was for him to build one. The time will come when there will be one in the centre of Temples we shall build, and, on the top, groves and fish ponds. But we shall not see them here, at present (*Journal of Discourses*, 26 vols. [London: Latter-day Saints' Book Depot, 1854–86], 1:131–33).

Brigham Young

Will [the Lord] dwell in it [the Temple]? He may do just as he pleases; it is not my prerogative to dictate to the Lord. But we will build him a house, that, if he pleases to pay us a visit, he may have a place to dwell in, or if he should send any of his servants, we may have suitable accommodations for them (*Journal of Discourses*, 1:376).

Wilford Woodruff

(Thirty-nine years after the cornerstone ceremony, Wilford Woodruff placed the capstone on the nearly completed temple on April 6, 1892. Speaking in the tabernacle, with forty thousand Saints crowded onto Temple Square, and thousands more on the roof tops of nearby buildings, Wilford Woodruff made the following statement.)

If there is any scene on the face of this earth that will attract the attention of the God of heaven and the heavenly host, it is the one before us today—the assembling of this people, the shout of "Hosanna!" the laying of the topstone of this Temple in honor to our God (James H. Anderson, "The Salt Lake Temple," *Contributor* [The Young Men's Mutual Improvement Associations of Zion], April 1893, 14:270).

Alma Ash

(Alma Ash described the reverence and awe he and his company felt at entering the Salt Lake Valley and seeing the temple.)

Never shall I forget how our hearts throbbed with emotion as we peered all around us to catch a glimpse of the place and people, as silently our little company trudged along South Temple Street towards the tithing yard where we expected to stay until morning. Oh, how reverently we regarded everything and everybody, and so sacred did everything appear to us that we wondered almost how people could be rude or light-minded in such a sanctified city. We gazed up at the temple which was at that time about up to the roof with the towers just commenced and silently in our hearts we resolved to begin a new life with new ambitions. We felt that we were quite an important addition to them both. We spoke in a quiet manner, I may say in a whisper, for fear of appearing boisterous or in any manner unbecoming. . . . It seemed as if we were in paradise (Alma Ash, *Autobiography of Alma Ash*, typescript [LDS Church Archives, The Church of Jesus Christ of Latter-day Saints, Salt Lake City], 30–31).

INDEX

A

Adams, Catherine, 146
Adams, William, 13, 17
Ahlstrom, Mary Larsen, 232–33
Alexander, Sara, 130–31
Allen, James, 73–75, 79
Anderson, Edward H., 80
Angels, 51, 53, 55, 166, 199, 215, 219, 267, 277
Appleby, William I., 169
Ash, Alma, 157–58, 183–84, 219, 229, 236–37, 291
Ashby, Benjamin, 14

B

Babbit, Alman W., 9, 38
Backenstos, Jacob B., 7–8
Ballantyne, Richard, 161
Barnes, Emily Stewart, 195
Barney, Lewis, 44–46, 102

Bartlet, S. M., 7, 29
Bates, Charlotte Ann, 235–36
Battle of Nauvoo, the, 67–73
Beesley, Sarah Hancock, 245, 250–54
Benson, Ezra T., 127–28, 204, 209, 288
Benson, Kersten Ericksen, 252–53, 254
Bigler, Henry W., 89
Blackburn, Abner, 169, 173
Bolton, Curtis Edwin, 170, 218
Bond, John, 276, 278
Brannon, Samuel, 39, 173, 228
Brown, James, 79, 87, 89
Bryant, James, 130
Buckwalter, Henry S., 71
Bullock, Thomas, 68, 71, 100, 179, 182, 292
Burbank, Sarah, 69, 115, 130, 135, 155
Burgener, Clara Durtschi, 209–10, 236

J

K

L

M

Morris, George, 20
Mousley, Sarah, 130
Murray, Fanny Young, 119

N

Nauvoo Brass Band, 51
Nauvoo Charter, 8–9
Nauvoo temple, 23, 27–28,
    45, 52, 70
Nebeker, Maria, 192
Neilson, Peter, Sr., 127
Neville, Ann L., 225
Nielson, Andrew Christian,
    144
Noall, Claire, 106–7

O

Olsen, Annie, 232
Openshaw, Samuel, 274–75

P

Pace, William B., 9–10, 46
Palmer, Louisa, 127
Pay, Mary Goble, 228
Penfold, Peter, 230–33
Perpetual Emigration Fund,
    the, 211–13, 215, 240

Persecution: from Illinois
    mobs, 4, 29–31, 39;
    against the Church, 164,
    218, 287
Phelps, Paulina, 5
Phelps, William W., 15–16
Polk, President James K., 73,
    95–97
Pomeroy, Irene, 36
Pratt, Ann Agatha Walker:
    on life in the wilderness,
    125–26, 137–38; ascend-
    ing the mountains, 174: on
    arriving in the Salt Lake
    valley, 181
Pratt, Louisa Barnes, 38, 146,
    148
Pratt, Orson: on sacrifice, 33;
    on crossing the Chariton
    River, 56; arrival in the
    Salt Lake Valley, 177–76;
    sustaining a new prophet,
    203–4; on the gathering
    of the Saints, 206
Pratt, Parley P.: on sacrifice,
    33; on Garden Grove,
    60–62; arrival at Coun-
    cil Bluffs, Iowa, 67; on
    Devil's Gate, 171–72; on
    thanksgiving, 200

Q

Quayle, John, 286

Sutter, John, 87
Sutton, John Allen, 217–18

T

Talmage, James E., 197
Tanner, Mary Jane, 143
Taylor, Jane B., 50–51
Taylor, John, 8, 40, 119, 193,
201, 215
Taylor, Robert Burton, 19
Thompson, M. J., 120–21
Tracy, Nancy, 135–36, 143–
44, 147, 153–54, 156–57
Tyler, Daniel, 82–83

V

Vanguard Company, the, 62,
117–18, 177, 179, 201

W

Warburton, Richard, 133
Walters, Archer, 248, 251–
52, 254
Webster, Francis, 267–68
Wells, Emmeline B., 103, 105
Wheelwright, Valborg,
210–11, 223, 235

Whipple, Nelson W., 172
Whitaker, George: on the
Nauvoo temple, 23, 25; on
mobs, 32, 39: on general
conference, 35–36; on the
Camp of Israel, 47–48;
journey to Winter Quar-
ters, 55–57, 63–64; on
Garden Grove 60; illness
at Winter Quarters, 101;
preparation for the jour-
ney west, 107–8; Emi-
gration Camp, 118–19;
crossing streams, 124; on
the Sabbath, 128; on life
in the wilderness, 133,
150; on faith, 157, 209
White, Elizabeth, 149, 275–
76
Whitney, Helen, 51, 98–99,
114, 148
Whitney, Horace K., 54,
167–68, 173
Wight, Lyman, 5
Willie Handcart Company,
the, 257–58, 272–73, 282
Winters, Mary Ann, 18
Woodruff, Wilford: on
the transfiguration of
Brigham Young, 22; on
the completion of the
Nauvoo temple, 26–27;
missionary service of, 45;
on the Saints' tribula-
tions, 103; on the building
of Zion, 162; on the trek